John Huston

JOHN HUSTON

Essays on a Restless Director

Edited by TONY TRACY
and RODDY FLYNN

McFarland & Company, Inc., Publishers
Jefferson, North Carolina, and London

Frontispiece: John Huston at home in St. Clerans, County Galway, Ireland, in 1970 (photograph by Joe Dillon)

Acknowledgments: The editors gratefully acknowledge the support of Rod Stoneman (Director, Huston School of Film & Digital Media, JUI Galway) in the realization of this project (and the conference from which it grew) and the kindness of Maura Dillon in providing previously unpublished photographs of John Huston taken by her late husband Joe. We are also grateful for the generosity of the contributors and interviewees.

LIBRARY OF CONGRESS CATALOGUING-IN-PUBLICATION DATA

John Huston : essays on a restless director / edited by Tony Tracy and Roddy Flynn.
    p.   cm.
    Includes bibliographical references and index.

    ISBN 978-0-7864-5853-0
    softcover : 50# alkaline paper ∞

    1. Huston, John, 1906–1987 — Criticism and interpretation.
I. Tracy, Tony. II. Flynn, Roddy.
PN1998.3.H87J655   2010
791.4302'33092 — dc22   2010010357

British Library cataloguing data are available

©2010 Tony Tracy and Roddy Flynn. All rights reserved

No part of this book may be reproduced or transmitted in any form or by any means, electronic or mechanical, including photocopying or recording, or by any information storage and retrieval system, without permission in writing from the publisher.

Front cover: John Huston, 1964 (MGM/Photofest); background ©2010 Shutterstock

Manufactured in the United States of America

McFarland & Company, Inc., Publishers
  Box 611, Jefferson, North Carolina 28640
    www.mcfarlandpub.com

Table of Contents

Introduction
    TONY TRACY *and* RODDY FLYNN 1

"Let's Just See If It Matters": An Interview with Anjelica Huston
    TONY TRACY 9

Strange but Close Partners: Huston, Romantic Comedy
and *The African Queen*
    PABLO ECHART 22

The Ideological Adventure of *The Man Who Would Be King*
    JULIE F. CODELL 33

The Way We Were and *White Hunter, Black Heart*: Huston in
Fiction and Reel Life
    PATRICK MCGILLIGAN 47

Huston's Mexico
    RICHARD VELA 56

The Discreet Charm of Huston and Buñuel: Notes on a
Cinematic Odd Couple
    NEIL SINYARD 73

Huston and the American South: *The Night of the Iguana*
and *Wise Blood*
    GARY D. RHODES 83

Re-Visioning the Western: Landscape and Gender in *The Misfits*
    GEORGIANA BANITA 94

Ethical Commitment and Political Dissidence: Huston, HUAC,
Hollywood and *Key Largo*
    REYNOLD HUMPHRIES. 111

King Adapter: Huston's Famous and Infamous Adaptations
of Literary Classics
    PAGE LAWS 123

The Melodramatic Conscience of *In This Our Life*
    VICTORIA AMADOR 136
The Irish Accent of *The Dead*
    MICHAEL PATRICK GILLESPIE 147
A Walk with Love and Death: From the Jacquerie of 1358 to the Turbulence of 1968
    PETER G. CHRISTENSEN 160
The Western, *The Westerner*, The Westernest: William Wyler, Menippean Satire and John Huston's *The Life and Times of Judge Roy Bean*
    LESLEY BRILL 173
John Huston and an Irish Film Industry
    RODDY FLYNN *and* DIOG O'CONNELL 185
Recollections of Huston: A Conversation with Wieland Schulz-Keil
    TONY TRACY 199

Bibliography 207
About the Contributors 215
Index 219

Introduction
TONY TRACY *and* RODDY FLYNN

> "A picture is made. You put a frame around it
> and move on. And one day you die. That is all there is to it."

When John Marcellus Huston died in August 1987 at the age of 81, the obituaries focused as much on the man as on his films. His Hemingway-esque existence offered plenty of colourful material for journalists: he had been a noted boxer, trained as a painter and received a commission in the Mexican cavalry. He had married five times, enjoyed numerous liaisons, raised four children and adopted a fifth. Several of those children followed him into a career in cinema, as Huston himself had followed his own father.

Yet if, more than 100 years after his birth and 20 years after his death, John Huston remains an enigmatic and compelling figure, it is primarily because of his cinematic legacy, first as a writer, occasionally as an actor but, in the main, as a director. His output in this last role offers students of cinema endless scope for exploration not least because his career spanned virtually every conceivable genre: his early *noirs*, gangster films and melodramas were followed not just by westerns, spy thrillers, screwball comedies and period films but also musicals, epics, horror films and even one (perhaps best forgotten) sports film. This diversity was possible because Huston was too restless to fully commit to the studio game — famously describing Hollywood as "a cage" — and his lengthy self-imposed exiles in Ireland and Mexico were strategies for maintaining a deliberate distance from the orthodoxies of mind and action in a company town. This distance probably harmed him professionally and perhaps critically in the short term but it also ensured a longer career than many of his peers and left us with a number of late-career gems in films like *Fat City* (1972), *Prizzi's Honor* (1985) and *The Dead* (1987). However, this widely noted variety — from his early work as a contract writer for Warners through his genre films for the studios to his late "small" films — also presents an audacious challenge to those who, in thrall to *auteurism* and its privileging of personal patterns, seek to identify thematic or stylistic consistencies over nearly half a century of filmmaking. Huston himself repeatedly repudiated such intertextual inclinations. Elsewhere he commented:

> It's a curious thing that so many people ascribe to me a distinct style. Believe me I am not conscious of any such thing ... I do not think any filmmaker should — though many do — consciously strive to maintain a permanent style in all his films [Laurot 1956: 17].

Indeed, at the moment when *auteurism* began to circulate as a critical concept in the mid–1950s, he dismissed the idea of a "personal, permanent style" as too limiting: "This could only be possible if [a director] made the same picture over and over again" (17). Thirty years after that comment he was still breaking new artistic ground.

Nevertheless there persists a strong urge to understand Huston's films collectively; to interpret them as an *oeuvre*. Andrew Sarris' famously caustic description of him as "coasting on his reputation as a wronged individualist with an alibi for every bad movie" was surely less a dismissal of his talents than frustration that such a talented figure had not produced a more sustained, coherent body of work from which an auteurist critic could map a larger underlying purpose. Arguably this desire owed as much to the personality of the man as his films. By the time of his death Huston's public persona and reputation was, among filmmakers of his generation, rivaled only by Orson Welles (they died within two years of one another). Like Welles, this knowledge about him, from frequent TV appearances and intermittent film roles, was mostly gleaned from Huston's status as a public figure; a dimension obliquely referred to in Daniel Day Lewis' performance in *There Will Be Blood* (2008) which, in its blending of a Hustonesque caricature and the Rosebud theme of corrupted innocence, interpolated these near-mystical figures of American cinema. (They were linked professionally, too, through Huston's role in Welles' *film maudit*, *The Other Side of the Wind,* and inversely by Welles' role in *Moby Dick.*) Unsurprisingly, critics have been drawn to speculate whether such largeness of personality gave rise to an equal largeness of purpose.

Geoff Andrews has suggested that because Huston "favoured working from literary sources, [he] seldom made films that seemed at all personal ... often he seemed content to shoot character actors in exotic locations, unsure as to the thematic substance, weight or tone of his material" (Andrews 1999: 99). At face value it's a criticism worthy of reflection and its attention to Huston's reliance on adaptations seems to have merit. It may be true that Huston does not have as distinctive an auteurial voice as, say Hitchcock or Ford (who described him in less polite terms as a "phony"), but what fundamentally fascinated Huston was not movies *per se* — that is, form — but the human condition; a subject as quixotic, unpredictable and varied as his films. And literature offered a road map for exploring that condition. When he encountered James Joyce's *Ulysses* at the age of 21 he later said: "After reading it, doors fell open" (Grobel 1989: 121). While his filmography includes such pulp adaptations as *The Mackintosh Man* (1973), he frequently took on canonical texts which undertook profoundly complex explorations of the nature of the human species: *Moby Dick* (1956), *Wise Blood* (1979), *The Dead* and even, most audaciously, *The Bible* (1966). Contrary to Andrews' assertion, he worked towards an exploration of the human predicament from an intensely personal, if nonetheless multifaceted, perspective.

It is never less than remarkable to reflect on the longevity of Huston's career, to remember that he directed films which stand with the best of them in each decade from the 1940s to the 1980s. But the length of his working life also reminds us that he was a resolutely twentieth-century figure and his films reflect the philosophical and intellectual currents of that extraordinary period of transformation. What ties the best of his disparate oeuvre as director together — from *Asphalt Jungle* (1950), *The Treasure of the Sierra Madre* (1948), *The Misfits* (1961), *Freud* (1962), *The Man Who Would be King* (1975), *Fat City*, *The Dead* — is not simply genre or Hollywood history or particular actors or styles — although all are important tools of analysis. His films stretch the limits of definition because they almost always — in ways obvious and opaque — engage with the big themes of that fractious century: faith, meaning, truth, freedom, psychology, colonialism, war and capitalism. This interest in the grand narratives of his era relates back to his attempt to understand the human condition via the persistent respect for, and interest in, the individual which his films evince; a theme which links his unassailable and essential American-ness with his interest in older cultures. (He was a noted collector of pre–Columbian art, for example.) It is the dialectic of the modern individual and human nature that engages Huston, centering on a wry and inherently existential view of freedom and its limitations. If there is an emblematic Huston film, it might not be the better-known Bogart films or *Asphalt Jungle* but *Freud: The Secret Passion*. Co-written — at least initially — with the existentialist philosopher Jean-Paul Sartre, *Freud* concerns the early expeditions of the Viennese adventurer of the mind who sought to explain the human condition as a dark and barely understood tension between forces known and repressed. For Freud, as for Huston, the dictate of the ancients to know thyself was as imperative as it was foolhardy. Analysis is not a matter of resolving the conscious and unconscious but bringing them more clearly into the light. Huston revelled in that contradiction but was never dismayed by it.

In the essays that follow we find critical analysis which points up this concern not merely with humanity's ongoing struggles but also with the pressures and changes visited upon it by modernity. Huston was repeatedly drawn to tales revolving around extreme and larger than life characters. Or, as Pablo Echart argues in his discussion of *The African Queen*, to characters who are enlarged by their experiences. His characters frequently survive on the margins of society. Indeed, as Julie F. Codell's discussion of Peachy and Danny in *The Man Who Would Be King* suggests, they are often entirely beyond the conventions of western society or in the case of Judge Roy Bean, as Lesley Brill observes, characters who are literally laws unto themselves. Such characters were intrinsically compelling but, in addition, by focusing on those who exist *in extremis*, Huston fashioned opportunities to dissect the ontology of the species. Of course, Huston himself was a larger than life presence and his work as a writer, director and later actor seems to blend and fuse with his restless and powerful intellect. His embodiment of such character traits presented an irresistible opportunity for other writers to produce thinly veiled portraits of the man in fictional form. Two of these representations — *The Way We Were* (1973) and *White Hunter, Black Heart* (1990) are discussed at length in Patrick McGilligan's essay, which explores the distinction between Huston the man and Huston the director.

In his personal life, Huston was fascinated with the exotic, living almost half his life outside the United States, first in Ireland and subsequently in Mexico. St. Clerans, his Georgian mansion in rural Galway where he lived from the mid–1950s to the mid–1970s, was incongruously filled with *objets d'art* collected from around the world. As a young man he regularly absconded to Mexico, where he acquired an interest in pre–Columbian art and briefly, an honorary commission in the Mexican cavalry. (He even adopted a Mexican child — Pablo — during the filming of *The Treasure of the Sierra Madre*.) This offered him a southern perspective on the Yanqui north that would inform his work on four films set south of the U.S. border. Richard Vela's "Huston's Mexico" offers an overview of these films with particular emphasis on *The Treasure of the Sierra Madre*, *Under the Volcano* (1984) and *Night of the Iguana* (1964). While Vela sees in these films a continuation of the long cinematic tradition of imagining Mexico as Other he cites Huston's deep personal interest in the country and its people as informing an unusual subtlety and even a subversive preference for the native against the foreigner. Indeed, in these films, it is not clear who the Other is. For Western audiences, the Mexican natives may initially appear to occupy that status in *Sierra Madre*, but as the film progresses we are increasingly invited to regard Fred Dobbs and his associates from a native perspective: the Americans have become the "Other." In a linked study, Neil Sinyard's wide-ranging essay finds unexpected shared stylistic stamp. While some of Huston's films are unquestionably characterized by self-conscious cinematic flourishes, it is difficult to identify continuity in their application across his oeuvre because, for Huston, form followed content. There was no requirement to make the work cinematic for the sake of it, though it invariably was. This is acknowledged in Victoria Amador's examination of the overlooked *In This Our Life* (1942), Huston's follow-up to *The Maltese Falcon,* from which it differed in almost every respect. Adapted from Ellen Glasgow's Pulitzer prize-wining novel of the same name, Amador examines the film's groundbreaking treatment of African American characters and the recurrent Hustonian theme of the destructive effects of greed. Huston was never daunted by the challenge inherent in bringing well-known writing to the screen but even he waited until his ninth decade before commencing James Joyce's short story *The Dead*, discussed by Michael Patrick Gillespie (as well as in the interviews with Anjelica Huston and Wieland Schultz-Keil), who foregrounds the pressures of familiarity Huston faced in adapting the "the most critically acclaimed and widely anthologized English language short story of the twentieth century." Gillespie's close reading of the film combines both a deep knowledge of the source story and an attentiveness to *mise-en-scène* and performance in Huston's cinematic rendering that sidesteps questions of fidelity through an original investigation of Irishness as a critical tool. Likewise, Peter G. Christensen's analysis of the almost entirely overlooked *A Walk with Love and Death* (1969) (notable amongst other things for being the screen debut of Anjelica Huston), is enriched by a scholarly knowledge of the medieval period setting of the film and the 1961 source novel by Hans Koningsberger which accepts the fable-like qualities of the tale — and thereby its attractiveness to the director — without surrendering the historical specificities of the story. Finally, Lesley Brill brings his wide knowledge of Huston to bear on a film unique in the director's catalogue of adaptations, the under-regarded *The Life and Times of Judge Roy Bean* (1972). In a sophisticated reading, Brill considers the film as a reworking of William Wyler's *The Westerner* in *carnivalesque* mode or as Menippean satire — an exuberant, often incoherent form that seeks to send-up not only the objects of the writer's scorn but the whole human condition, himself included.

It is tempting to suggest that Huston's move to Europe in the early 1950s following his disgust at the HUAC hearings was somehow a contributory factor to the longevity of his career and in his ongoing ability to turn out work of a superior quality late into his life. However to do so would be to ignore the fact that regardless of his domicile, the vast majority of Huston's work even after 1951 was funded from the United States. As the essay by Roddy Flynn and Diog O'Connell argues, Huston's engagement with an Irish film industry, despite appearances, was by and large superficial and perhaps even self-serving. He never became nearly as integrated into the European industry as, say, Joseph Losey, another Hollywood émigré who famously sought refuge from HUAC in Europe.

Balancing the discussion of the man with the work, this volume is bookended by two interviews by Tony Tracy with people who knew Huston personally and professionally: Anjelica Huston and Wieland Schultz-Keil. Anjelica made three films with her father, including her Oscar-winning performance in *Prizzi's Honor*. She also starred in *The Dead*—produced by Schultz-Keil—and alongside the scholarly essays in this book, their recollections of the man add depth to our overall understanding of Huston as a director and artist. Particularly touching in their memoirs is their recollection of Huston working right to the very end; an exemplary artist endlessly curious about humanity even as his own grip on life weakened.

This collection represents a snapshot of Huston scholarship as it stands in the twenty-first century. Growing out of a conference at the Huston School of Film and Digital Media, National University of Ireland, Galway, it offers a montage of perspectives on an American artist who continues to compel and intrigue over a century since his birth.

"Let's Just See If It Matters"
An Interview with Anjelica Huston
TONY TRACY

Anjelica Huston, John Huston's first daughter, was born in 1951 and spent her childhood years living in Ireland, first in Courtown County Kildare, then in Craughwell County Galway. Her upbringing in such a remote and rural setting was in stark contrast to her later domicile in Venice, California, but it lent her a unique perspective on how her father worked as a director, one subsequently augmented by her direct collaboration with him on a number of projects over the course of three decades. Her first lead role came at the tender age of seventeen on *A Walk with Love and Death* [1969], an experience which she found so bruising that she effectively retired from acting for a period, working instead as a fashion model in New York. While it was Elia Kazan who lured her back to the big screen when he cast her in *The Last Tycoon* [1976], two of her most memorable subsequent roles would come in films she made with her father. In 1985 she was nominated for and won her first Oscar [in the best supporting actress category] for the role of Mae-Rose in *Prizzi's Honor*. And two years later she demonstrated her extraordinary range when she appeared as Gretta Conroy in John Huston's final film, the appropriately titled *The Dead* [1987]. In this interview Anjelica offers a personal and professional insight into how John Huston worked, thought and lived.

You grew up far from where your father, grandfather and you would make your names — in Hollywood. What was your experience of cinema as a child?

Well, it's funny; my very first memories are actually to do with the cinema — of *Moby Dick* [1956] being made. I remember seeing Gregory Peck dressed as Captain Ahab in Fishguard [Wales], he was in a big top hat and rather imposing. So there was always a consciousness of my father doing what he did, and what he did was quite otherworldly to a small child. And of course as we grew older, we saw more of his films and this consciousness grew. I mean I must have seen *The African Queen* [1951] one hundred and fifty times as a small girl. We had a home projector at St. Clerans [the family home in Galway] and the main movies we watched were the war documentaries, *Let There Be Light* [1946], and *Battle of Saint Pietro* [1945]. We watched *Moulin Rouge* [1952] a lot! And other than that we watched *The Devil and Daniel Webster* [1941] — my grandfather was in that movie — and *The Treasure of the Sierra Madre* [1948]. My father had pretty good prints of those movies. I remember one particular incident where my father was watching Kubrick's *Lolita* [1962] — we were not allowed to watch *Lolita* — and it was my first realization that other people were doing the same thing and there were other movies. I belonged to the pony club and we would occasionally have Disney movies shown at the Great Southern Hotel in Galway, but my father's movies were pretty much the only movies that we saw!

Did you often go on the set of his films?

I remember when my father was shooting *The List of Adrian Messenger* [1963] and I was going to a riding school in Stillorgan [Dublin], my brother was cast in that film and I remember feeling very jealous, because he got to wear riding britches and high boots and he got to ride a horse that wasn't a pony. And also I went to visit my father on the set of *Freud* [1962]. But really for the most part he kept my brother and I away from prolonged visits to his sets, we'd go for a couple of weeks and then we'd come back home.

Did people come and see films at the house?

No, I don't remember it being a big social thing — Dad never watched the movies with us. It was very intimate, just us — Tony and I — and whoever was in the house at the time. Betty O'Kelly, who ran the estate, always had a big problem putting the film into the projector because there were various knobs and shutters that you had to lock the film into and this generally took at least an hour and a half to set up, but that was always part of the anticipation of watching the film. We never tired of it. And we were always triumphant when we got the projector to work.

Did he talk about films, about making them, to you?

He told stories about what would happen on sets, but he wouldn't really talk about movies, as such.

Someone once said to me that he was really a writer manqué, that he really wanted to write. Did you ever have that sense, or was he just very committed to the cinema?

No, no, he was a writer first, he wrote on all his screenplays. One of my earliest memories was of being on top of the stairs in Courtown house in County Kildare, I must have been no more than three years old, and watching my father work, I think it must have been with Dalton Trumbo, and when my father worked he would stride up and down and up and down from the living room into the hall and back again, and I remember that being part of my father's process and that being mysterious to me because I didn't know exactly what he was doing, and it was called writing, but I didn't necessarily see a pen go to paper. But I always associate the walking with my father at work on a script. I remember this as being a time when my father was not to be disturbed ... a rather sacred time.

I think as you started visiting the sets, and as you started getting a little bit older, you started getting non-credited roles.
    Yes, he did a movie called *Sinful Davey* [1969] here, and I mean there was absolutely no need for me to be credited, I simply rode side-saddle in the movie.

So A Walk with Love and Death *[1969] was your first credit?*
    Yes, *A Walk with Love and Death* was my first movie really. Years before, I remember there was some discussion with my brother, because Jack Clayton was making a movie called *The Innocents* [1961] and he wanted to maybe cast my brother and me. He had asked my father if he would consider it and my father would not consider it.

So this was a big leap when it happened. How did it happen, what was the lead up, were you nervous? Was he nervous?
    He had a three-picture deal with Fox and this was the second picture. And since I had expressed a big interest in being an actress, I think he felt he was doing something very good for me and for my future career. Of course, when it came to it I didn't really like the script. I was 15 at the time and living with my mother in England. My parents had separated by that point and I was into a bit of avoidance from my father who had become rather critical of my looks, my habits, my developing sense of myself and I felt that he wanted to drag me back to childhood. And I wanted independence, so he found himself with a very reluctant individual on his hands, and I had no idea of the responsibility of what was going on, I really didn't. I didn't associate time with money in those days and I think I wasted a good deal of his time. I wasn't clear on my lines; he was very dismayed by our relationship at the time. I remember being at school in London and being summoned to Paris for fittings with Alexandre [de Paris] who was Liz Taylor's hairdresser, and also to have costume fittings with Leonor Fini who was a very highly esteemed painter working in Paris also at the time. I recall getting on a plane in a yellow wool suit which my mother felt my father would think appropriate — my father didn't like the way I dressed at the time either, he was very critical —

and of going to Paris and doing these fittings and coming back to his hotel. I think he was staying in the Bristol hotel in Paris. I had my own room off his suite and I hadn't brought so much as a hairbrush. Then the French revolution broke out [it was summer 1968] and there was no way of leaving Paris, and I was in that room for three days and I remember not asking for so much as a hairbrush and the suit was a mess and the last thing I wanted to do was work with my father. Then it was decided that the film would be shot in Vienna, because the atmosphere was very volatile in Paris. So then we started shooting and I hated every moment of it. I was not allowed to wear make-up, I was a maiden in fifteenth century France, and at the time I was highly insecure, my nose was growing faster than anything else and I was extremely unhappy not being able to wear make-up which was my biggest crutch and of my father being extremely difficult. There was one day when he just let me have it in front of the whole crew and from that moment I just shut down. It was sort of a miracle that we got through that movie. I remember Gladys Hill, his assistant at that time — it was before they started writing together — I remember her saying, "Your dad was wrong to do that." Basil Fenton Smith was Dad's soundman — he'd been Dad's soundman since *The African Queen*. My father liked to surround himself with familiar faces and people he could have shorthand with. So there was Ted Scafe, his cameraman, and Russ Lloyd, his editor. I remember Basil being very kind to me and being very solicitous and understanding. But for the most part my father treated me quite harshly and I think really he was probably very hurt by the fact I was so non-compliant and at the same time, he didn't go about it gently either.

Were you very close to him when you were young?
　　Oh yes, very close. I was Daddy's little girl.

How did you feel about acting after that?
　　I knew in my heart somewhere that I was right. And I knew in my heart that I did not care for the script. I thought it was corny and Americanized. It was about a girl in fifteenth century France. I felt I was more of a classicist having been raised in the British Isles; I had seen various productions by then — my mother was always very diligent about taking me to plays — and I had a rather good repertoire of things to draw on. I had opinions! And somehow my opinions weren't being taken into consideration and I thought my opinions were valid. That was one of the big problems. The other was a school search that was launched by Franco Zeffirelli for *Romeo and Juliet* and I wanted very much to be Juliet and work with Zeffirelli in Italy. My father wrote him a letter and asked him to please desist; that I would be working with him. I really resented that because I felt it was a chance to do something on my own

and to make my first steps in something I really wanted to do. But that wasn't to be, and that was a bit of an issue.

Looking at the subsequent development of your career, how important was that experience; you didn't take a lead in a film for some time after that.

Well, after we'd finished *A Walk with Love and Death*, I came back to London swearing I'd never work with my dad again. My mother was friends with Tony Richardson and he interviewed me for Ophelia for his new stage production of *Hamlet*. I didn't get the part but he asked if I would like to understudy. So I found myself understudying Marianne Faithful to Nicol Williamson's [celebrated] Hamlet. We were in rehearsals when my mother was killed in a car accident. After that that I decided I didn't want to live in London. I didn't want to be under my father's auspices. I thought he might send me off to a convent or something, I didn't know what he would do with me, so I took off to America. It was a confused time, I remember my father taking the train from Rome because he was too ill to fly to my mother's funeral in London, so there was also the question of would my father live, would he survive, because we knew at that point that his lungs were very bad; my brother and I having met him at London's Victoria station. This was a few days after my mother's death, and I, not having a thing to say to him and he not having a thing to say to me. I remember his being very cold and unsympathetic and we didn't communicate much. I then left the country as part of the cast of *Hamlet*. I flew to New York and understudied Francesca Annis, who had taken over the part. I had hoped that Tony Richardson would cast me but that wasn't to be. It was more fun understudying Marianne as she was off a lot and I think already battling some demons, so I had been on quite a lot in London, maybe four or five times, but when Francesca took over, of course she was so professional and a perfectionist, and I never got to go on again. But being in New York was a new horizon. I was also on a publicity tour for *Walk with Love and Death*, which I despised — this was almost worse than making the movie because you had to talk about it. I remember not being comfortable at all and at a certain point actually confessing on the David Frost show how I had loathed every second of the making of the film. I remember my father's publicist, Ernie Anderson [who had represented some of the great jazz musicians of the time like Louis Armstrong] saying, "Well if that doesn't sell seats then nothing will!"

I was then offered to do some photographs for *Vogue* magazine by Richard Avedon who had been a very good friend of my mother's; a friend of both my parents. So we came back to Ireland and did quite a famous portfolio of pictures for American *Vogue*; lots of pages, really wonderful. We did these sort of tinker caravan pictures of myself and a very handsome blonde guy called Harvey. While we were there, man landed on the moon for the first time, and I remember being out in Connemara in the middle of nowhere and being conscious that men were landing on the moon and of being furious about that! Then later, I remember thinking, "Well this is a good thing, I'm having a good time, I'm working with a photographer and I love his direction."

So you thought you'd become a model?

Absolutely, I thought what a good idea! I don't get criticized! Also at that time I had some rotten reviews of *A Walk with Love and Death*—John Simon in particular was very mean.

So The Last Tycoon *[1976]—almost a decade later—was your step back to acting? What was Elia Kazan like compared to your father?*

He was fantastic, I loved it. I auditioned for *The Last Tycoon* with another actor and I remember very clearly coming out of the audition and Kazan saying "I'll walk you downstairs." I wasn't driving at that time and he walked me down and we sat on a bench at this bus stop at Beverly Drive and there was this woman sitting there. He turned to the woman and said, pointing to me, "Do you think she's beautiful?" and the woman said "No, I wouldn't say she was beautiful, she's interesting maybe, but she's not beautiful," so I knew then I hadn't got the part. And then I went home. I think he'd really only seen me because of Sam Spiegel. Sam was producing this film and at that point I was seeing Jack Nicholson and we'd been to Cannes together and he'd won the best actor award at the festival and we'd sailed on Sam's yacht so I think it was mostly as a favor to Jack.

He was an old friend to your dad, too, was he not?

Well, friend ... not really. I think they'd had some problems! But, you know Sam was prone to helping me along at that point probably because he wanted Jack to play in *The Last Tycoon*. But I got a call offering for me to play "the wrong girl" in the movie, not the "right girl"; she was to be played by Ingrid Boulting. Of course I accepted. I remember going to Paramount, there was this huge head bobbing in this tank—this was the head of the goddess—and Kazan coming to my dressing room before my first scene. He was riding around the lot on a bicycle. He came in and he said, "OK here's how it goes"—this was to be an improvisation. He said, "There's a house on the lot that's two streets from here and two over, this girl is new in town, you don't really know her, you've seen her around a few times, but you've got a hot date tonight and you're going to wear a see-through blouse and you need a slip to wear underneath it. You don't really have the money to afford that for yourself so do you think she might have something for you to wear under that blouse? Give us about 10 minutes and come down to the house." I said, "OK" and sat there for a while then went down the street and knocked on the door and finally it opened and there was Ingrid Boulting with tears streaming down her face and it was one of the greatest lessons in acting I've ever had. I was going to this house anticipating one thing, only to be totally surprised and knocked off my guard. It made me realize what drama was.

Given your earlier experience working with your father how did you come to make Prizzi's Honor *[1985]?*

Well then I did more small parts in films. I did a small part in *The Postman Always Rings Twice* [1981], I did some episodes of *Laverne & Shirley*, which were very kindly offered to me by Penny Marshall, who was great. I didn't want big handouts, I was always very reluctant to accept that kind of thing, but at the time, my father was about to be honored by AFI [American Film Institute] and they asked me if I would MC the evening. Of course I was so nervous, but in my speech that night I asked Dad if he would ever consider working with me again, and I said basically that I was sorry for being such a difficult actress the first time around and I hoped that he would give me another chance. Shortly after that, his producer from *The Man Who Would Be King* [1975], John Foreman, called me up and asked me to audition for a part as the best swordswoman in the universe, in a movie he was going to do called *The Ice Pirates* [1984]. So I went ahead and auditioned and got the part and I loved it. I had a great time: it was a fairly sizable part and it was tough and I got to stride around in body armor with a lot of monkey skulls hanging off my hair and I really liked it — I was completely my own person. While we were shooting that, like in the last week or so, John came to me with a book by Richard Condon called *Prizzi's Honor* and said, "Why don't you read this and look at the part of Maerose?" So I took it home and read it and was enchanted with the whole thing, so I went back to him and said that I loved it. Then he said, "What do you think about Jack Nicholson to play Charlie Partanna and your father to direct?" and I wasn't so sure about that. My father was living in Mexico at the time, in the jungle, and you couldn't get to him by phone — it was all CB radio. John Foreman wanted very much for him and me to fly to Puerto Vallarta and for me to get Jack to go there to see Dad and I said "I'm not going to do that, they are just going to tell me what they don't like and I don't want to be in the middle of this." John was furious with me. He actually showed up at my house at 6 A.M. to take me out there, but I told him I wasn't going. So he left without me and when he got there he found Jack in town buying huaraches and he said, "Jack what are you doing here?" And Jack said, "It's fine, I'm doing the movie, don't worry." Jack had gone out to the jungle and he and my Dad had watched the female gymnasts in the Olympics on satellite it was the 1984 games — and I guess they had decided almost instantaneously that they were going to work together and all was great. My father had explained to Jack that the movie was a comedy, which Jack had been hitherto unaware of. We all assembled and we went off to New York. I remember my father being a little restive in those first days. We had a table reading and everything seemed to be going OK but there was something not quite satisfying to him. It didn't seem to be my fault which I was grateful for. He had already started casting and a lot of the actors were Irish, Bill Hickey, John Randolph. Anyway, my father was also determined to cast his ex-secretary, Annie Selepegno, in the part of my Aunt Amalia, and this appeared to the rest of us to be a disastrous choice. Meanwhile there was this quite extraordinary, very talented actress who was clamoring for the part, her name was Julie Bovasso. But Dad had this very clear idea that Anne was it, she was the part. Jack and I were in Jack's suite in the Carlyle Hotel. Dad called and came over. He said, "I have found it! The voice of the movie." And the voice of the movie was Julie Bovasso and, you have to understand, this was a good two years or so before *Moonstruck* [1987], before *The Sopranos*, and he had actually fixated on the accent and that was the "voice of the film."[1] Poor Julie, I don't think she ever made it to screen but she was the voice of the film, she'd come in with her accent and after that we were all talking with her accent the entire time. I think we all stayed in character the entire time — Jack certainly did. He had this tissue paper under his lip, and I would go to Catholic mass with the Italian women in Brooklyn and he would go down to the gaming parlors with the boys and it was a fantastic moment for us. We all got on really really well. My father and Jack were in love with each other, and I remember a lot of laughs. I remember doing this one scene when I say, "You should have seen him Papa, he was this big!" and my father saying "Make him a little smaller" and the entire crew just cracking up! And being on location in Brooklyn and walking into a bar one day for lunch with my Dad and there was an elderly man at the bar ... and he narrows his eyes ... and he says to my Dad: "Walter's kid!" And from then on we all called my dad "Walter's kid."

So your experience working with him this time was completely different from the first time around?

It was fantastic! Don Feld [costume designer for the movie] came with a bunch of dresses for me to try on. There was one in particular that was a black wool dress and it had a black taffeta swath from the shoulder to the hem. I remember saying, "Maybe this dress would be great if the swath was Schiaparelli pink or a strong green"—I had worked in fashion so I knew my stuff. Don was unconvinced and said "Well let's show what we've got to your father first," and I put it on for Dad and I remember him looking me up and down and saying, "Perhaps if that swath was Schiaparelli pink." So we were totally in sync.

There was another great moment when we had to go to California for some of the shooting at the end of the movie. Kathleen Turner was in her trailer at one point and she looked out the window and she saw these period cars, and she'd worn Adidas shoes in one of the scenes, and so she said to the second assistant director "Is this a period movie?" He says, "Why don't you ask John Huston?" So she goes across the street to the car where my father is sitting with John Foreman and she leans in and says, "John, excuse me for asking this so near to the end, but is this a period movie?" And my father leans back and says, "Well, honey, let's just see if it matters."

He must have been very proud when you won the Oscar for your performance.

I think so. We were nominated for seven Academy Awards, and we were all packed in at the ceremony. John Randolph's wife had a heart attack early in the evening and he had to leave immediately and that was really distressing. Then suddenly Best Supporting Actress came up and I was sitting right behind John Foreman, next to Jack and across the aisle from my Dad. And, when they called out my name I don't know how I got up to the stage; it was a rush like I'd never had before. I remember Richard Dreyfuss and Marsha Mason were standing on the stage and there were motes of dust and light and they seemed very tiny in the distance and finally I reached them, they congratulated me. I've no idea what I said, but I forgot to thank John Foreman or Jack. I made my speech, I was quivering and then I ran down the stairs back into the audience. You're supposed to be taken back stage to the press room, but I'll always be grateful for that, because when I came back up the aisle, I looked to Dad and there were tears pouring down his face and I thought, "What's he crying about?" and then I looked over to John Foreman, and he was crying, and then I looked to Jack and he was crying too. And I was dry as a bone!

That's when the true impact of the thing came home to me. We were in the car on the way to Spagos, where Swifty Lazar had his Oscar party, but Dad was on oxygen at the time, so he was pretty tired out. So we went up to his hotel room with him and I felt really bad because I had wanted them all to win too and I was the only one who had won, but I could tell how proud he was that evening. Tremendous!

What about The Dead *[1987]? Was that around for a long time, and were you set to act in it?*

I had no idea about *The Dead*. My father was in the Jules Stein Eye Clinic having an operation on his cataracts, and I went in to see him. He was bandaged up and he said, "There's a script on the bedside table, honey, could you read it to me." I sat by his bed and read the script of *The Dead* to him. At that point it went sort of without saying that I was going to play Gretta Conroy. I don't think he even asked me, I think that was his understanding.

My brother and he had been working on the script, but I wasn't aware of it at the time. I think they went back then and wrote some more on it. Tony was working on it all the way through and he actually used a piece that was really nice that I'd shown to him some years before. On *A Walk with Love and Death*, I had a book of Irish poetry and there was an anonymous poem that had been translated by Lady Gregory that I fell in love with called "Broken Vows." I thought it was so beautiful and he used it in the script. I remember when my father got out of hospital he rented a house up in Laurel Canyon somewhere and I remember Donal McCann and Fionnula Flanagan and all these wonderful Irish actors that Wieland Schulz-Keil had found, coming in.

What was the shooting process like?

We went up to Magic Mountain, of all places, which is an amusement park about forty-five minutes out of Los Angeles and we went to work. It was in a warehouse there, and every time a plane went over, we had to stop. It wasn't insulated, it was one of the first warehouses in Valencia, which is now a sea of dotcom warehouses and model homes. But, we were all there, everyone stayed at The Black Angus which we called The Black Anguish and all the Irish actors were two-stepping every Wednesday night. And Tommy Shaw, my father's first assistant director, was in control of the purse strings, so I don't even know if the poor actors ever even made it to Hollywood during the making of the movie. They were penned into The Black Anguish!

We started with some round table readings and I remember early on, we got through one of these readings and my father would listen with his eyes closed and I was thinking he'd gone to sleep. But then he would give the most succinct commentary. I remember him saying to Donal Donnelly, "Now Donal remember, Freddy Malins is an alcoholic, he's not on cocaine." And then he said to me, "Don't bog it down, don't try to out–Irish the Irish." But everything he said was spot on — he had a great ear.

How did he direct, did he do much rehearsal?

Just those round table rehearsals and then the camera turned on. All of the props were downstairs and all the action was upstairs in this warehouse.

So while we were working we had the smell of goose, fish scale-fed goose — it stank! It permeated that studio for weeks. On the first day the plum pudding was appealing, but by week three it wasn't quite so delightful at the dinner table, but at the same time it was like a life, it wasn't even like a play, it was like living it. And each day we shot very much in sequence, so each day followed the next day and it felt like a piece. At the end of the film, of course, there is this big scene in the hotel room and I'd felt this thing was looming and up until then there wasn't very much for me to do. There was the entrance basically, then there was the dinner, then there was the dancing and everything was leading up to this scene, and I had this fearsome sense of anticipation about the scene and I remember being very primed, being very nervous about it and coming in to work that day in a high state of anticipation. We did a rehearsal on the scene and I did it full on like it had just happened, like the entire thing had just happened. And he said, "Great honey ... now just put it in the past," and I think we did it in just two takes. One on Donal McCann, one on me.

So his notes as a director were always succinct.

Succinct, sharp and absolutely on the money. No mystery to them — absolutely clear.

What do you think was the key to his skill as a director?

Well, the thing about my father was that he had an amazing sense of humor, an amazing sense of irony and I think one of the reasons was that he really loved the Irish character. Even today there is still an essence of innocence in the Irish character. If there's a deviation, there's still a sense of innocence and I think that was really important for him to preserve that idea, and I think that was part of what he really loved about the Irish character. I think that that is what *Treasure of Sierra Madre* is about for instance; you know the Tim Holt character is basically the innocent. The old man is wise but he's kept his innocence. I think my father was quite cynical, but it was something that he saw and appreciated and isolated. You can see it exemplified in *Fat City* [1972] too.

One aspect of his films is his enduring interest in men and masculinity.

What he loved most was character, he had no snobbery in his character whatsoever. My father would be as happy sitting with a bunch of workmen on a building site as he would with lords and ladies and he was as good with both. He could travel anywhere and I think that was part of his extraordinary attraction to Ireland is he had absolutely no class rules whatsoever. I was talking with Paddy Lynch who used to look after my father's horses. He's 85 now and living in Craughwell, County Galway. Paddy said with perfect clarity that my father was the best friend he ever had. In those days the Anglo-Irish were the ruling class really, but when they were out and around looking at horses, my father would always insist that Paddy eat with him. My father had no snobbery at a time when that class distinction was part of life.

And was he like that with everyone?
Yes, everyone. He had no definition of who was above anyone else. And so it allowed him a great passport into any society. He flew a lot obviously, and he would deplore when some American businessman would reach for his passport or wallet and bring out a picture of his wife and kids for approval or appraisal. My father having been in the Belgian Congo on *African Queen* contrived to have himself photographed with a native naked woman and her seven children, and so when the businessman would produce his own picture my father would then reach to his wallet and produce this picture! That would really close that conversation very fast. He had this great sense of fun and that was what he loved and what he shared.

Is that why he didn't live in Hollywood?
He despised Hollywood, he especially despised Beverly Hills. I remember him being absolutely incredulous at me wanting to live there. I think he thought it was just fake from the ground up. He didn't like any of that; he was not at all intrigued or attracted by it. He liked to be in the wild places, he liked animals as much as he liked people. Living around my father was also living with a menagerie of animals. In Ireland he had his wolfhound Seamus and various other dogs that would come and go, and he had his horse Frisco. I remember my father's great pleasure in Ireland — my brother and I used to get embarrassed because he was an American. He took a proprietary pleasure in this country and we'd go out to Connemara and Clare and he'd have visitors in the back of the car and they'd say, "Oh it's beautiful, John" and he'd go, "Isn't it, isn't it," like he owned the place and my brother and I would just cringe. "Our Dad thinks he owns Ireland." But he got on with everyone, if he saw a horse or a countryman across the field, he'd go over and meet them and share a drink with them in their cottage.

When he went to make a film, there was his great feeling for character, but how aware of the visual element was he, did he sketch storyboards?
Yes, he did constantly. But it was a form of study, and my father was a painter, a very good one. I think he admired painting as much as anything and he had a really fine eye. There was an extremely developed sensory quality about my father, he didn't miss a trick, which made him a difficult father when I was young. Most parents, you run upstairs and wash off the makeup, or take a bath to get the smell of smoke out of your hair, but not my father, actually both of my parents were like that. They were very acute and

critical, they used to watch very closely and I remember that was a big problem with me at one point. It was how to get by that and I remember at one point talking to a therapist about it when my father was in hospital in the 1980s after he'd had his aneurism. We were dreadfully worried that he wouldn't make it at the time and I remember saying to her that when I went in to visit he had this expectation of me and I had to provide him with stories and this and that and that I was nervous and always scared of his disapproval and she said, "why don't the next time you go in to see him don't feel as though you have to bring all that baggage and consciously don't say anything, go and sit down by his bed and see what happens?" So that's what I did the next day, and instead of coming in and providing him with scattered information about this and that I just sat there and he started to talk that day and he talked and talked and talked and we had the most fantastic time. So this day was a real breakthrough — our relationship changed tremendously and we became much more relaxed together. I think my father was just basically worried about me a lot of the time and as soon as I allowed him to stop worrying he relaxed.

He was in ill health for a long time.

It was touch and go there many times. It was a miracle he lived so long, but you know if I missed a day, he would deteriorate and that was a big responsibility, I started to realize how much he loved me. But in the end there was nothing we could do to save him.

We were making *Mr. North* [1988, directed by Danny Huston] in Rhode Island, and he became very sick, he wanted to play the part of the old man but he had called Bob Mitchum before we went to Rhode Island and asked him to stand by in case anything happened to him and Mitchum had agreed. My father became very very sick the week before the principal photography and we had to send him to hospital in Fall River which was about an hour from where we were located and Mitchum came in like a Prince on the red-eye and did a perfect reading the next day. We went down to Fall River after Bob had shot his first day and Dad was lying in the bed and Bob went to the door and called a nurse into the room and Bob said, "John I hear you haven't been eating," and my Dad ignored that, so Bob said to the young and pretty nurse, "Would you roll your skirt up a little?" She happily complied and then at Bob's request she rolled it even a little higher, and my Dad was lying there literally dying — he died two days later — and, finally he said, "You're right, Bob, I haven't being eating enough!"

Note

1. Julie Bovasso was later credited as dialect coach on *Moonstruck*.

Strange but Close Partners
Huston, Romantic Comedy *and* The African Queen
PABLO ECHART

If John Huston seems an awkward and elusive director for cinema auteurists (Brill 1997: 1),[1] *The African Queen* (1951) is, at least at a first glance, a *rara avis* in a filmography defined by its multiple registers and genres. There are several reasons why this masterpiece deserves consideration, among them the fact that it was Huston's first colour film and his first comedy, as well as his greatest box-office success. However, despite its originality, *The African Queen* has solid bonds with the "Hustonian" universe. The first part of this text explores the particularity of *The African Queen* in Huston's work, to illuminate the second objective of this chapter: to demonstrate the links between *The African Queen* and the best tradition of the Hollywood romantic comedy in its defining era from the mid-thirties to the early forties. In fact this film, and the earlier *Adam's Rib* (1949) — which also featured Katharine Hepburn — are probably the best examples of the extension of the cycle into the late forties and fifties.

Anatomy of a Film

In *The Secular Scripture* (1976: 24, 26), Northrop Frye points out that the key elements of the romance are, on the one hand, the exciting adventure, and on the other, the love story. This statement can also be applied to *The African Queen*, where remarkably, the love story plot is developed through comic conventions. Thus, it may be stated that Huston and his screenwriters (James Agee, Peter Viertel and John Collier) succeeded in the craft of fusing the traditional conventions of comedy and romance. Following Frye, Brill demonstrates in detail why the film fits the realm of the latter, understanding by "romance":

> not these films that are focused on a courtship — though a love story is often at the center of such movies — but adventurous narratives full of hairbreadth escapes, terrifying descents and ascents, and clearly differentiated good and evil characters who tend to be larger than life [1995: 6].

Taking into account these basic elements, it can be claimed that *The African Queen* focuses its narrative — what screenwriters would call "main plot" or "plot A" — on the adventure of a couple who sails down a river. However, developing the love relationship — plot B or the subplot — is a task that the characters themselves have to tackle. There is no escape from facing each other — literally. Rosie and Charlie start the trip through the river to avoid being captured by the Germans. In the same vein, they cannot escape the diverse dangers that the river hides, such as rapids, crocodiles and the labyrinth of the undergrowth, among others. Their physical descent of the river implies a terrifying approach towards death, as represented by the rope tied around Rosie and Charlie's necks at the climax. However, that threat suddenly vanishes and gives path to life; notably, a life that is not mediocre, but one blessed by the love they declare in their last minute marriage. In this sense, they are — as Brill suggests — characters "bigger than life," since the vices that stigmatise them at the beginning of the film are reversed by their mutual care and understanding. Indeed, to borrow from Brill's description of Thornhill and Eve in *North by Northwest* (1959) — they are at least "slightly greater than human in their virtue" (1988: 12). Instead, the Germans are one note characters from the beginning to the end, a representation of the Leviathan common in romance.

Beyond these outstanding characteristics, the film shares other features of the romantic narrative form. A brief consideration of them helps illuminate *The African Queen* in relation to its conventions. A first influence of romance is the idealistic nature of the film. It cannot be understood from a realistic perspective because romance departs from reality and comes close to the realm of fantasy. This is why *The African Queen* takes place in a quasi-mythical territory, somewhere distanced from daily life, an amazing adventure seasoned with extraordinary and unlikely events. The aim is not to reinforce the causality of the action, but to fascinate the audience with the overcoming of consecutive obstacles. The almost miraculous events perfectly fit an ascendant structure that highlights the world of innocence and fulfilment within which the characters achieve their new and complete identities. This is a rebirth that cannot happen without tenacity and audacity. Huston's characters, in common with those of Hitchcock's comic romances, "hardly admit the possibility of defeat and seem congenitally incapable of despondency" (Brill 1988: 149). Although at various stages in the narrative both characters express scepticism about their chances, they encourage each other not to fall into despair.

Nonetheless, in spite of the many aspects that *The African Queen* shares with the conventional romance, it is, to some extent, *sui generis*: Charlie does not possess, at least not to start with, the exquisite manners or virtues of a great gentleman. He is — reluctantly — involved in the heroic struggle because of his female companion who pushes him into action. As in other Huston films, it is not the finding of the Grail that counts; rather stress is laid on the journey undertaken in pursuit of that goal. What matters is the process by which a character changes while dealing with a conflict, and how, on this occasion, it changes thanks to love. Besides, the love story does not play a supporting role in the adventure but is essential to the plot: one is essential for the other, completing each other in a perfect symbiosis. The beloved is not an absent and subjectively idealized being, but someone to share a close — even inevitable — relationship with, not to mention an extra-marital bed, an aspect that notably breaks the rules of the classic romance.

The hero's initially low profile, the equality of the woman in the adventure, the mutual metamorphosis brought about by love, the evolution of the characters from contrast to harmony, and the outstanding role of love in the story, are features that bring the romance closer to the field of comedy and, in particular, of romantic comedy. In his study, Brill claims that because of its simple nature romance was not the suitable formula for the complexity Huston tended to bring to his stories (1984: 4). Such a claim could also be made for comedy. That said, *The African Queen* is probably Huston's most vital and sensual adventure, and "the most tender and least cynical" of his comedies (Heredero 1984: 150). The happy ending, the most universal convention of comedy, does not leave room for doubt: like David facing Goliath, Rosie and Charlie manage to defeat the German enemy and they are rewarded with a love which ends in marriage at the last moment. This end is totally positive, and it moves away from those other more open, bittersweet, often clearly disheartening conclusions which earned Huston his reputation for making movies about losers.

The knowledge that generic conventions demand a happy ending[2] allows the audience to distance themselves from the tribulations the characters have to bear, although some of them are as physical as the pain and disgust caused by mosquitoes and leeches. As usual, the seeds for the comedy are shown in the first few scenes in different ways: by contrasting the characters (the civilized missionaries face-to-face with untutored Charlie), by showing how serious the former are about their futile scheme, and in the characterization of the Rev. Samuel Sayer as priggish and feeble (which ultimately makes his death less shocking: he embodies a way of life that is not healthy for Rose).

The dichotomy between the virtuous (Rose and Charlie) and the bad (the Germans) deserves further consideration. This clear bifurcation is accompanied by a psychologizing of the lead characters which is potentially limited to the archetypes they represent: the boozy rogue and the old maid. Such stereotyping is frequent in romantic comedy but less common in Huston's films given his preference for more complex characters (see for example, *The Misfits* [1961], *The Night of the Iguana* [1964], or *The Dead* [1987]). However, this is not necessarily a negative, but rather a standard of the genre that the movie respects. In fact, *The African Queen* is outstanding for the subtlety of its characterization and its nuanced development of the relationship between the leads. The playing of Bogart and Hepburn meshes effectively with the skilfully constructed script, allowing a notional adventure narrative to simultaneously operate as a comedy.

Playing the likeable Charlie, the role for which he was awarded his only Academy Award, Bogart broke away from the hard-boiled image forged in his earlier work with Huston. It is, for example, a complete turnaround from the greed and perversity of his role as Fred Dobbs in *The Treasure of the Sierra Madre* (1948). And the effervescent female role of Rose forces us to reconsider the cliché of Huston as a filmmaker limited to the macho world.

This happy comedy, however, is not as atypical of Huston's work as has sometimes been suggested. This impression has been largely fostered by the legend — authored by Hepburn along with Peter Viertel, Clint Eastwood and Lawrence Grobel among others — that Huston merely regarded the film as an excuse to go elephant-hunting in Africa. Its distinctiveness within the Huston canon makes it difficult to appreciate its Hustonian features, which go far beyond the mere fact of its being another literary adaptation.

In a dossier on Huston published by the Spanish cinema journal *Dirigido por*, Àngel Quintana argues that Huston's films are more about willpower than about failure: "The secret is in the adventure, not in the outcome, and to have an adventure, you must have great willpower" (2005: 71). Brill says something similar about *The Misfits*:

> Gay, like Roslyn, has the resiliency to look hopefully ahead, to trust that things can get better. Such resiliency characterizes Huston's most sympathetic — though not always triumphant — characters from Miss Roy (Olivia de Havilland) of *In This Our Life*, through Rosie (Katharine Hepburn) in *The African Queen*, Billy Tully (Stacy Keach) in *Fat City*, and the title character (Aileen Quinn) of *Annie* [Brill 1997:81].

As the denouement of *The Treasure of the Sierra Madre* categorically shows, for Huston the objective of the search is not of great importance: what is decisive is the adventure itself. Huston shared Hemingway's credo, which held that victory belongs to those who resist, struggle and persevere. This is followed to the letter in *The African Queen*, where the protagonists secure not only a moral victory by keeping faith with their own credo but subsequently an actual victory over the Germans. As Gabriel Insausti maintains (2004: 235), in Huston's universe a fulfilled life is a life of adventure, because simply clinging to life is a terrible waste. The inevitability of death becomes the lens through which we see life, encouraging us to live the present moment as a chapter of the adventure (for example, in *The Man Who Would Be King* [1975]), or a chapter of love (in *A Walk with Love and Death* [1969]). *The African Queen* is no exception: with the protagonists facing constant danger — whether it be crocodiles, rafts or the German gallows — we are constantly encouraged to celebrate adventure and love. With the valiant tenacity of the protagonists and their victory over death, *The African Queen* sits comfortably among the second of the two groupings delineated by Stuart Kaminsky in his categorization of Huston's work: not a story of those who are doomed to failure (Kaminsky's first category), but of those potentially romantic couples who survive or end up together (*The African Queen*, *Heaven Knows, Mr. Allison* [1957], *The Unforgiven* [1960]).

If *The African Queen*'s stress on the leitmotif of adventure and its focus on tenacious protagonists is characteristic of the Hustonian universe, so too is exotic setting. The shooting of *The African Queen* in the Belgian Congo marked the beginning of a 10-year period when Huston filmed away from Hollywood, and is further evidence of his interest in foreign countries and cultures demonstrated in *The Treasure of the Sierra Madre* (México), *Beat the Devil* (1953, Italy), *We Were Strangers* (1949, Cuba), and *The Barbarian and the Geisha* (1958, Japan).

Apart from the elephant hunting, this exotic setting allows Huston to present other features that are typical of his work: the contrast of cultures and ethnic groups, and a criticism of institutional religion. Rose and Samuel's failure to convince the natives to sing a religious hymn — the classic image of exasperated teacher — suggests that cultural identity is innate and cannot be "re-conditioned." Their failure also demonstrates the missionaries' lack of sensitivity towards others, and therefore, their inability to understand and lay a basis for comprehension. Over and above confirming practically insurmountable cultural barriers, it must be conceded that in contrast to films such as *The Man Who Would Be King*, *The Unforgiven*, *The Barbarian and the Geisha* or *The Treasure of the Sierra Madre*, the caricatured portrayal of the natives is less than respectful, although it does fit in with the humour of the story. They appear twice, and on both occasions they come off badly: in the first instance when Charlie throws away his cigar, the natives dive headlong to grab it like children squabbling over sweets. In the second, as recruits to the German army, they shoot at Rosie and Charlie unskilfully, as if they were shooting ducks in a fairground. In short, they are portrayed as childish, primitive and scarcely rational.

Nor is the image of the British missionaries particularly positive. Their good intentions are neutralized by their inability to understand and communicate with the natives. The mendacity of the Reverend Samuel has already been mentioned: he is portrayed as envious, selfish and mean, and responsible for, or even guilty of, Rose's spinster status. However Samuel is merely the physical embodiment of how an impoverished Puritanism has submerged Rose, limiting her personal fulfilment and her enjoyment of this earthly life. The prayers she says on the boat when about to die points to a shift in her thinking, however, which fits in with Hustonian ideology: a fulfilled life implies risk, danger, even if it means making mistakes, showing weakness, committing sins. This is always better than trying to have an immaculate life in a glass cage. There are echoes of Rilke's prayer: "If my devils are to leave me, I am afraid my angels will take flight as well." Thus, Rose's religion does not disappear; it simply takes on a new shape; more spontaneous, immediate and intimate, released from the public mediation of the Church.

Rose's allegorical rebirth comes hand-in-hand with close communion with Mother Nature. Like her namesake, Rose blossoms, and the splendor of the landscape approves. Charlie and Rose adapt themselves to the rhythm of Nature to which their destiny becomes linked. In this poetic sympathy, all four elements play a role, but that of water is exceptional. Rose's immersion into real life is expressed symbolically by her contact with the liquid element. Frye (1965: 122) links romantic comedy (in its Shakespearian version) to the myth of Christianity (where what is not natural is death), whose rite of initiation is precisely baptism in water (an element previously associated with Hepburn in *The Philadelphia Story* [1940] as the catalyzer of her figurative "death and resurrection"). Apart from a detailed exploration of the association of water with a "revival and rescue," which is also clear in the torrential, divine, saving rain, Brill also stresses the link between water and fire, which can be found in several of Huston's films, although not always with the positive significance of *The African Queen*. All these are Hustonian traits, but also a fertile fusion of opposites, a communion with Nature, a renaissance in life, a window on the extraordinary character of romantic comedy.

The African Queen *and Romantic Comedy Tradition*

The African Queen is relevant not only from the perspective of its position in Huston's work, but also because of its relationship with the romantic comedy genre in 1951. In the previous decade romantic comedy had lost not merely its importance within the panorama of genres, but had also abandoned its formerly daring and progressive nature, as gender relations were realigned during the U.S. involvement in the Second World War. This can be clearly seen in its image of women: the "women on top" gave way to the "girls next door," and their independence became a "taming of the shrew." After the war, there were relatively few movies which, like *Adam's Rib* (1949) or *The African Queen* itself, deviated from the dominant tendency and showed their affiliation to the older tradition: this tradition was not of great importance in the '50s, when romantic comedy followed gentle, and sometimes patronizing paths (see Audrey Hepburn's comedies), or entered the arena of the emerging sex comedy (Marilyn Monroe first, then Doris Day).

Among the great female stars of the 1930s — Barbara Stanwyck, Ginger Rogers, Jean Arthur, Irene Dunne — only Katharine Hepburn maintained the essence of a certain conception of American femininity into the late '40s and early '50s, in films like *Adam's Rib*, *The African Queen* and *Pat & Mike* (1952). After Cukor's *Holiday* (1938) Hepburn's characters in romantic comedy became increasingly open to the idea of developing a closer relationship with the world, with their male partners, and with themselves. This "apprenticeship" seen in films like *The Philadelphia Story*, *Woman of the Year* (1942) or *Adam's Rib* did not exclude the possibility of intelligence, professional qualities, a sense of humor and tenderness even if these characters are often characterized by a certain stiffness which must be eliminated over the course of the narrative so as to show them in all their glory.

The African Queen exhibits the quality that Stanley Cavell called "the creation of woman" (1981: 48). In screwball comedies like *Topper* (1937) or *Fifth Avenue Girl* (1939), characters are "educated" to allow them to abandon those values — excessive attachment to routines, work or money — which had been an obstacle to enjoyment of life's true pleasures. In the best screwball romantic comedies, many of which Cavell dealt with in his study of the remarriage comedies, moral growth goes beyond the elimination of certain negative characteristics, and becomes instead the discovery of one's true identity, a development of unknown potential, a "becoming who you really are."

This is the case of *The African Queen*, where Rose and Charlie, through romantic love, reach fulfillment beyond their wildest dreams. In a character arc similar to the Tracy Lord role played by Hepburn in *The Philadelphia Story* (although its problems are not comparable) Rose will discover that she is human, descend from her ivory tower, and embrace her corporality. And she will do so because of the excitement of the voyage and her relationship with Charlie. He will have to go beyond his physical nature and find rewards that are more important than the satisfaction of his instincts. (Comically, the story implies a parallel between Charlie and the jungle animals: first when he imitates their gestures and sounds, and second, when his argument with Rose provokes a resounding reaction from the animals.) As individuals, their relationship allows them to find a life that is more fitting to their human condition, under God and above the animals. As a couple they develop mutual caring based on consideration, attention and gratitude.

Such virtues allow them to overcome their opposing characterizations of old maid and boozer, the Puritan and the sinner. As is often the case in classic romantic comedy, these contrasts are demonstrated through dichotomies, the clearest of which is Rose's link with tea, and Charlie's with gin. (At the end of the film, she regrets having thrown all the alcohol overboard and he forgives her by offering her a cup of tea.) But there are also contrasts between nature and civilization, wandering and settling, spontaneity and convention, dirt and cleanliness, and a sense of duty and laziness. This last aspect is particularly obvious when Charlie says: "Never do today what you can put off for tomorrow."

In spite of the fact that it is his manifesto — Charlie is at the beginning the image of a *bon vivant*—the reality is that once Rose and he accept the mission, they desperately work to complete it. But, as often happens in Hawk's comedies, the duty becomes an exciting and playful task. *His Girl Friday* (1940), for example, shows that the greatest danger for a lead man is to get involved in a neat, conventional, domestic life without surprises. The "other man" (Ralph Bellamy) is comically punished for his dreary desire for security, which is radically opposed to the vitality of Walter (Cary Grant) who is used to walking a tightrope. This search for security — translated into worries about loans and other materialistic concerns — may also be another reason why middle-class post-war Hollywood comedies lose their vitality in comparison to the great comedies made before the Second World War (Brouwers and Paulus 2006: 21–34). In any case, this spirit of security went against Huston's values.

The Hustonian adventure in *The African Queen* shares the old ideals that praise fun and playfulness. It doesn't take long for the audience to agree with them, as we can see in the scene where Charlie and Rose recall their past in England: like Charlie, one may miss the hustle and bustle of the pubs on Saturday nights, but cannot share Rosie's nostalgia for the calm of Sunday afternoons. A year before he collaborated on the script, James Agee, in his famous article on Huston, remarked on how the director's characters expressed a romantic leaning towards danger. For them, risk, adventure, and the fact of tackling overwhelming obstacles are like a game. Talking about remarriage comedies, Stanley Cavell emphasizes that love is experienced by the romantic couple as an adventure and, as a result, ordinary life becomes extraordinary. As we have seen, this is what Huston's films are about, although they are the result of a primarily existentialist vision of life that seems to advise making the most of the present. In the credo of romantic comedy, and probably in Huston's too, the worst sin is boredom, and travel is the best way to beat it. In *The African Queen*, moreover, this travel is down a river, which emphasizes the idea of movement, in contrast with the quiet land Rose is uprooted from. Once again, this is not far from Hawks' view: comedies such as *Bringing Up Baby* (1938) (Hepburn again) or *His Girl Friday* both use contrasting rhythms and images of movement to typify on the one hand the vitality of the vigorous characters and on the other, the deathly dullness of the dreary ones (Mast, 1982).

The African Queen also uses some of the recurrent strategies of the best romantic comedies of the '30s to wear down the differences between the central characters, and in doing so, to build on a growing complicity and intimacy. Logically, the first step is forcing them to live together, and with this in mind a road movie that isolates them is the best option (as in *It Happened One Night* [1934]) or better still a *river movie*, like this. Like a latter-day Adam and Eve, as Charlie and Rose move down the river they are in perfect harmony with their surroundings, privileged to discover what is for them a new world (as happens with those beautiful flowers whose name they do not know). They may also bring to mind Noah and his wife, surrounded by incalculable fauna and witnesses of a redeeming divine flood.

Other renowned romantic comedies use the Book of Genesis, and in particular the story of Adam and Eve, to tackle problems that typified the genre, such as temptation (*The Lady Eve* [1941]) or the issue of the difference/equality of both genders (*Adam's Rib*). All the possible variations on these themes have one thing in common: companionship between man and woman. Woman was created, the Bible tells us, because God saw that it was not good for man to be alone. The union of a man and a woman, signified by the usual denouement of romantic comedies — marriage — is conceived in the first place to overcome loneliness.

Even *It Happened One Night*, usually considered the first screwball romantic comedy, focuses on this idea. In this film — Cavell reminds us — the couple's coming together is the result of a feeling of familiarity between Peter and Ellie, partly because they behave in front of people as if they were married. This and other remarriage comedies (*Adam's Rib*, for example) emphasize the importance of the home, something we also find in Huston's filmography. According to Brill: "Quests for homes of one kind or another are nearly as pervasive in Huston's films as quests for identity and love, and they are often portrayed as practically equivalent" (1997: 8).

This is what happens in *The African Queen*, in which the boat is represented as home. Here everyday domestic routine takes place: acts such as removing a splinter from a foot emphasize the intimacy of the couple. As in Capra's movie, there is a breakfast-in-bed scene in *The African Queen*, a very humble version of the walls of Jericho (the canvas sheet that momentarily separates the characters' beds), and the inevitable but necessary marital arguments (Rose gives a clear example of this convention when they argue over who should bomb the Louisa).[3] The arguments, like the shared songs,[4] laughter (for Rosie, a new facet of her corporality) or sexual intimacy are part of that "meet and happy conversation," which Cavell, like Milton, sees as "the chiefest and noblest end of marriage" (1981: 87). Thus, just as Amanda cannot stand Adam's silence in *Adam's Rib*, Charlie despairs when Rosie does not answer him the morning after he got drunk. Is it any wonder that Charlie agrees to sail downriver precisely at this moment?

This kind of conversation has a lot in common with what Gilles Lipovetsky calls "post-romantic seduction," which can be summarized, in short, as a rejection of the asymmetric distance corresponding to courtly love, but also as an acceptance of a relation between equals. That is to say, of closeness and complicity between a man and a woman (Echart 2005: 267–274). As both *Adam's Rib* and *The African Queen* suggest, it no longer makes sense to venerate the beloved, but there remains the possibility of demonstrating mutual esteem. Consider how Charlie tells Rose that she is "a living picture of the heroine," or the way she in turn praises his incredible bravery (is there a better way to describe an adventurer?). Although such words may express love, post-romantic seduction clearly prefers to free itself from the pompous rhetoric of courtship, and express love through action: Charlie's descent into the leech-infested river is probably the most visual and eloquent declaration of his devotion.

As has been suggested, '30s and '40s romantic comedy posits the couple in terms of equality and symmetry, terms which are presented in the screenplay and the movie of *The African Queen*, but not in C. S. Forester's novel from which it was adapted (Fultz 1982: 21). Besides, Joseph Kupfer (1999: 61–89) points out how the couple find love and stability basically through their physical work. Rose's failure in her spiritual labor contrasts with her success in manual labor, whether it is mending the propeller, sailing downriver handling the tiller, or destroying the Louisa. These tasks allow Rose to experience her corporality, but also emphasize the aforementioned mutual respect and equality between the two characters: neither is superior to the other.

In *The African Queen*, love does not threaten the adventure, but strengthens it. Only a couple can triumph over situations as crazy and apparently impossible as those that Rose and Charlie take on. Together they make the present extraordinary and memorable. If a noteworthy life is one worth telling, then Charlie and Rose's lives are noteworthy. As Charlie concludes, "we will never lack for stories to tell our grandchildren."

Notes

1. I am grateful to Professor Lesley Brill by his useful comments to improve this text.
2. Although the memories of the people who were involved are contradictory, it seems that the ending of the movie was not clear while the shooting of the film advanced. To start with, Huston rejected the two different endings from Forester's novel (the first for the American audience, and the second for the English one). He hesitated between a more realistic ending where Charlie and Rose were hanged after getting married, or a more optimistic and unlikely end. Finally, he decided to shoot the second one (Grobel 2003: 389).
3. *The African Queen* shares with *It Happened One Night* another visual convention: the suggestion of the female naked body (Rosie undresses to have a bath in the river). Cavell, on remarriage comedies, relates this trope to the "creation" of the woman.
4. The songs point out the change in Rosie. The first time we see her, she sings a religious hymn; however, at the denouement, she sings an absurd sea chanty with Charlie, exactly the same Charlie sang when drunk. This fact shows a profound change in Rosie, but also a new basis for the relationship. Other funny songs play an important narrative role in screwball comedies like *It Happened One Night* or *Adam's Rib*. Cavell's comments on the subject are again of a great interest.

The Ideological Adventure of *The Man Who Would Be King*

JULIE F. CODELL

Long dismissed as a mere adventure story, *The Man Who Would Be King* (1975) contains more serious ideological content than meets the eye. The film's advertising posters and trailers endorsed the "adventure" content, as did most of its critical reviews. Directed by John Huston, the film's contributors and cast included cinematographer Oswald Morris, actors Michael Caine, Sean Connery, and Saeed Jaffrey, and Richard "Dicky" Drew-Smythe, an ex–British Indian Army and Gurkha Battalion military expert who supervised the battle scenes. This understudied film is as rich in historical, cultural and political subtexts as other Huston films (Sklar 1993: 65), as it glances backward to the Victorians and forward into the film's own historical moment.

Of course, the adventure story is ideological and naturalizing; boys' adventure stories were a major venue for Victorian imperial propaganda.[1] But Huston's film takes on new significance in the context of the rise in 1970s Britain of the National Front, police violence,[2] immigration and its backlash, and aggressive speculation in banking and real estate. In these contexts Huston's film exemplifies the manner in which films of the 1970s represented individualism, racial hostility, class divisions, national identity and doomed heroes. Alexander Walker described the decade as one of gritty realism and sensationalistic "unrestrained ambition," of real estate speculation, banking boom and merger mania in "a breathtakingly cynical view of an entrepreneur acting out his imperatives in response to the tribal law of the fittest man's survival" (e.g., *The Reckoning* [1969] and *Get Carter* [1971], in which Caine played the protagonist [Walker 2005: 26–27]). These same themes are subliminally played out in *The Man Who Would Be King*'s epic visuality, Victorian imperialist narrative, its anti-hero protagonists and representation of ethnic "Others." Like corporate aggression, empire was constituted by amoral ruthlessness and raw power.

Yet, Huston's film is about implausible adventure in a decade of realism and imagined kingship in a world of realpolitik. Huston recalls 1930s imperial adventure films so well that the *New York Times* critic Vincent Canby in 1975 was able to forgive its imperial ideologies by assuring readers that the film apolitically echoed 1930s films in which

> cities teem with unruly humanity, with beggars, blind men, snake charmers, demented holy men, starving children. In the upland territories British soldiers guard the frontiers to places of which someone will say, quite seriously, "No white man has ever gone in there and come out alive.
> ... like "Lives of the Bengal Lancers" and "Gunga Din," this world is very far removed and terribly romantic, as it still is in John Huston's highly entertaining new film [McCarty 1987: 194].

Canby defended the movie as serious because of its fidelity to Kipling's views, but then cavalierly discarded the criterion of fidelity or literary quality: "It's a tall tale, a legend, of steadfastness, courage, camaraderie, gallantry and greed, though not necessarily in that order," with "enough romantic nonsense in it to enchant the child in each of us" (Canby 1975: 62). Roger Ebert also insisted the film was "unabashed and thrilling and fun" reminiscent of 1930s empire films and Huston's other "straightforward action" films. He concluded that "when it's over we haven't learned a single thing worth knowing and there's not even a moral, to speak of, but we've had fun" and feel "exhilarated" (Ebert 1975: 56). Some reviewers were more critical. Danny and Peachy, in Charles Champlin's view, represented "an exploitative society invading" another culture "only to grab and split" (McCarty 1987: 195; see also Fussell 1958: 198). Roguish, charismatic and imaginative protagonists Peachy Carnehan and Danny Dravot simultaneously replicate, inflate and satirize the imperial enterprise. Scott Hammen described this film as both modern in its "documentary-like" representation of the exotic and old-fashioned in its "absolute loyalty" to Kipling and to 1930s empire films (Hammen 1985: 130). I agree that this film is modern and old-fashioned but for entirely different reasons: it alludes to both social changes in 1970s Britain and to 1930s empire films, but is neither as loyal to Kipling as Huston and Hammen claim nor as documentary as Hammen claims. The film's construction as an ideological adventure can be understood as influenced by a variety of contexts: diegetic elements within the film (setting, music, character and landscape); the film's relation to British social history and the film industry (e.g., transnationalism in film production) in the 1970s; Huston's additions to Kipling and much of Huston's *oeuvre*. The merger of modern and old-fashioned emerges from the film's imperial ambiguities, especially in those scenes invented by Huston.

As Jaikumar (2006) and Chowdhry (2000) point out, classic empire films which reached their zenith in the 1930s — *The Lives of a Bengal Lancer*

(1935), *Gunga Din* (1939), *The Four Feathers* (1939), among others — share many features: risky adventure, danger, male bonding, women as intruders, "Others" as uncivilized or cruel or childlike, and a dream of empire as civilizing and orderly. Most have at least one war and vast landscapes that draw on the Western, itself a kind of empire film. Shaped by big budgets, lavish costumes, exotic sites, and droves of supernumeraries, these films mix a *faux* documentary approach (depictions of everyday life in the army, battles and artillery) with heroic self-sacrifice, loyalty, honor and obedience to the state and its institutions. Men are good-hearted, boyish and playful pranksters, taking their imperial roles lightly.

But Huston's film, despite its budgets, settings, battles and supernumeraries, differs from these — there is no salvation, no army arriving at the last minute, and no crisis from which our protagonists save civilization at the boundaries of empire. Instead, they cross boundaries to escape the imperial bureaucrats who put them in jail for their misdeeds and thought them unfit to serve. Instead, Peachy feminizes bureaucrats as "narrow-chested" teetotalers. Peachy and Danny admire privateer James Brooke, Raja of Sarawak, whose anarchic oppression lacked even the requisite imperial civilizing rhetoric, despite the later historical cleansing of his reputation. The film distinguishes imperialism from Danny and Peachy's fantasy, which, although rooted in imperial hubris and megalomania, rejects the empire's rule of law (itself historically used to disguise military force). Sarah Kozloff maps similarities between the film and a book Huston read as a child, William Bolitho's *Twelve Against the Gods: The Story of Adventure* which contained a story of Alexander the Great and a belief in adventure as beyond laws or social order (Kozloff 1994: 194).

In 1952 Huston discussed the idea of the film with Peter Viertel, and he considered Humphrey Bogart and Clark Gable for the leads. Huston went to India to a tiger hunt in 1955 with a friend of the Maharaja of Cooch Behar, descendent of historically pro–British maharajas. By 1973 Huston had three scripts for the film and approached Paul Newman who turned it down and suggested Caine and Connery. Huston rewrote a new script with Gladys Hill, "a little closer to the story by Kipling," adding "a lot of invention ... supportive of tone, feeling and spirit underlying the original short story" (Huston 1980: 352). It became Huston's favorite screenplay. The budget was initially estimated at $5 million, but when no studio would take on the film, Huston combined Columbia Pictures for European distribution rights and Allied Artists for North and South America; Allied added Canadian-tax-shelter money (*ibid*.: 352) while Caine and Connery worked for a flat fee plus a percentage of the gross. Huston himself worked for a share of the new take. The final budget was $8.5 million.

Huston's autobiographical account of the film's long gestation from a Hollywood film in the 1950s to a British film by 1975 is a conscious self-fashioning of his imperial identity in a parallel autobiographical "adventure" story. In his autobiography Huston (1980: 350) describes hunting, travels in India, mosquitoes, crowded processions, jolts to his senses, poverty, streets "teeming with people," and temples "where women anoint Shiva's lingam with butter." He also cites Afghanistan as having the "highest homicide rate in the world." Huston details problems finding a country to film in — Kafiristan was closed to outsiders, Turkey was interested (Ephesus was preferred), but the United States and Turkey had a falling out. Eventually Morocco was chosen and "made to look sufficiently Indian" (*ibid.*: 355). Costumes by Edith Head were based on reproductions of Greek jewelry, weapons, armor, coins and "Greek Tanagra figurines" (*ibid.*: 357). Huston describes life in Marrakech and trouble with customs officials and bribery. He hired Berbers — "a bizarre, wonderful, wild people." His emphases on corruption, bribery, violence, the "Other's" sexual oddities and wildness, and uncooperative natives were also standard topics of Victorian travel narratives. For Huston making the film recapitulated Victorian adventurers in exotic places full of corrupt, poor, "savage" and lascivious natives.

Critics praise Kipling's ironic story as a "satirical tour-de-force" that presents imperialism "at its most horrific and absurd" (McCarty 1987: 217). As Meyers (1968) argues, Kipling at 23 was not yet jingoistic but saw the ironies and cruelties of imperial lower-class adventurers with positions (usually in the military) they could never have enjoyed in Britain's class-ridden society (as Peachy says, "Go home to what?"). Their dreams echo historical cases of individuals (e.g., Raja Brooke of Sarawak, Cecil Rhodes) who struck out on their own and were later supported by official Britain, the violent beginnings of their white rule cleansed by heroic biographies, knighthoods, and wealth. Kipling's model for the story was Josiah Harlan (1799–1871), an adventurer from Pennsylvania, who traveled to Afghanistan and Punjab hoping to be made king. He won the title Prince of Ghor in perpetuity for himself and his descendants in exchange for military aid to Shah Shujah al-Moolk who attacked Dost Mohammed Khan in Afghanistan.[3]

Huston adored and memorized Kipling as a child (Huston 1980: 345). Noting that Kipling was renounced as "an unmitigated imperialist," Huston nonetheless argued that:

> Kipling's version of imperialism was by no means without redeeming values, especially in a country such as India, where, before the advent of the English, most of the population were slaves to a handful of warring rulers. India is today a democracy — shaky perhaps, but a democracy nonetheless — with an

increasingly vocal and literate middle class," the result of "imperialism's ugly head" [Huston 1980: 345].

As Kozloff notes, the film reaffirms imperial adventure by bifurcating its implications. Carnehan and Dravot are rogues, but as played by the charismatic Caine and Connery, are also lovable, independent, and inventive. In absorbing what Huston called the "tone, feeling and spirit" of Kipling's story, Huston eliminated its rogues' most vicious racist murders, while sustaining imperial racism (see Hammen 1985: 130; and Kozloff 1994:190).

There are many characteristics of Huston's style here. The film expresses ambiguities about failed masculinity, especially in its rhetoric of soldiering, to destabilize Hollywoodian heroism. There is the adaptation of literary sources Huston's departures from which often introduce visual symbols and allegorical meanings. There are striking camera angles: here Huston uses the view from behind a listener, often in the dark, facing the speaker, so that the camera claustrophobically suggests the viewer as a fly on the wall, present and absent. The film deploys national ideals, in this case British and Victorian, through marginalized, eccentric, adventurous, Hustonian protagonists.

Huston added scenes to the story, claiming that they increased its proximity to Kipling in text, meaning and feeling. It is important to examine these not because fidelity to Kipling measures anything, but because Huston claimed these scenes increased the Kiplingesque content. But these scenes are problematic, even racist and ethnocentric beyond Kipling's story. Among Huston's expanded topics is the theme of Freemasonry with its ritualistic verbal phrases, ancient sources (whose antiquity legitimates Danny's claims to kingship), clubby loyalty, and the mystical symbols left by Alexander the Great which so entrance the story's priests. Kipling was a Freemason, a largely British-dominated institution from the early eighteenth century with interest in kingship, especially the Hebrew kings (Fussell 1958: 226–227). Freemasonry represents both the difference and the similarity between British adventurers and Kafiris.

Huston invents several scenes that focus on imperial and existential encounters to expose differences and similarities simultaneously. He invents a celebration conducted by the Kafiri chief Ootah, characterized as greedy, foolish, macho and cowardly, who offers Peachy and Danny his daughters and sons for sexual pleasure. Peachy is horrified, but Danny tells him to respect different customs. Then Peachy and Danny excitedly watch tribe members play polo, a game both similar to and different from their own version (the "ball" is much larger). The tribe's ball is the head of an enemy; what seemed at first a technical difference becomes a cultural one. Polo-loving Danny is outraged, but Peachy gives him back his own advice. In Kipling's story these tribes are white descendents of Aryan Greeks (Almond 2002: 275–287). In Huston's film, this ancestry is eliminated to keep the natives as Othered as possible. The film's score by Maurice Jarre endorses Huston's intentions with orientalizing sounds, European military music, and ethnographic snatches, some geographically misplaced and grouped without ethnic distinction (Tibetan instruments in the "Hindu Kush," Berber dancing in "Kafiristan") to distinguish differenced/distanced Kafiris from British adventure motifs. Generalized ethnographic music contrasts with Peachy and Danny's "Minstrel Boy" motif used diegetically and non-diegetically with Jarre's marching music.[4]

Another Huston scene in a train car emphasizes this harsh othering. It incorporates and modifies Kipling's narrator's opening paragraphs on his disgust over traveling with Eurasians and Indians in "intermediate" class and his romanticizing of Peachy:

> There had been a Deficit in the Budget, which necessitated traveling, not Second-class, which is only half as dear as First-class, but by Intermediate, which is very awful indeed. There are no cushions in the Intermediate class, and the population are either Intermediate, which is Eurasian, or native, which for a long night journey is nasty, or Loafer, which is amusing though intoxicated. Intermediates do not buy from refreshment room. They carry their food in bundles and pots, and buy sweets from the native sweetmeat-sellers, and drink the road-side water. That is why in the hot weather Intermediates are taken out of the carriages dead, and in all weathers are most properly looked down upon. ... a big black-browed gentleman in shirt-sleeves entered.... He was a wanderer and a vagabond like myself, but with an educated taste for whiskey. He told tales of things he had seen and done, of out-of-the-way corners of the Empire ... and of adventures in which he risked his life [Kipling 1994: 113].

But in the film Kipling, a thoroughly cautious, properly employed bourgeois foil for Danny and Peachy, travels in a first-class car which Peachy enters without a ticket. In a scene which Brill (1997: 45) sees as intentionally comic (despite its racism), Peachy has just stolen Kipling's watch but, seeing the Masonic emblem on its chain, surreptiously attempts to return it, treating the theft as an opportunity to enlist Kipling's help on a different matter. A respectable Indian "babu,"[5] an educated middle-class professional, enters the car with a watermelon. He introduces himself to which Peachy replies "shut up." He offers the Englishmen melon, which they refuse, and then proceeds to eat it, spitting seeds on the train car floor. Disgusted, Peachy angrily tells him to spit seeds out the window. When he complies, Peachy opens the door and tosses him off the train. Kipling (Christopher Plummer) shouts, "you could have killed him," whereupon Peachy replies that the train was only going five miles an hour (it seems faster in the film). The danger, humiliation and injustice of this act are mind-boggling. The babu had a ticket, was living in his own country and travelling according to his own customs, which was unlikely to include spitting seeds in a train car. He met his fate trying to comply with an Englishman's request.

Was this scene, at which audiences invariably laugh, meant to deride the Indian or meant to show us Peachy's darker side? The camera view is almost Peachy's — the Indian introduces himself looking into the camera — though the camera is behind Peachy's back. We see Peachy's disgust in a shot/counter shot. We see all three figures together when they are grouped at the train car door, as Peachy pushes the Indian out and the sleeping Kipling wakes shocked. The intended humor of the Indian's appearance — large turban, face into the camera — ends abruptly and cruelly, but this is not the end of this sequence. Kipling and Peachy now converse, treating what happened as unimportant, even legitimizing it. Certainly for British imperialists, the "natives" hindered "progress," resulting in violent oppression by the Raj. The film does not appear to condemn Peachy for his colonial violence, but aligns him by the sequence's end with Kipling, the film's sympathetic framing narrator.

Claustrophobic opening scenes of vermin-like masses of people in excessive close-ups — stereotypical snake charmers, blind beggars, working children and bazaar merchants — posit an othered Orient of weirdness, poverty and danger, recalling images in previous empire films (and presaging films like *Raiders of the Lost Ark* [1981]). These scenes precede the credits which are accompanied by the "Minstrel Boy," the film's British musical motif, sharply distinguishing the "Other" world from the British one from the outset. Brill (1997: 35) considers the opening a sign of the collision of cultures,[6] but I see it as a string of stereotypes, as did the Afghanis who banned the film.[7] Writing on 1930s empire films, Richard Slotkin describes filmic myth's transgenerational "ways of telling or transmitting stories, making symbols, structuring systems of representation" through which bits of history are transformed "into fictive resolutions of real ideological dilemmas," in genres that "shape the formal structures of our cultural productions, suggesting that such forms have a life and logic of their own" (Slotkin 1990: 1). Viewers learn to recognize "a visible landscape, whose topography is readily understood." This reality is "a densely imagined pseudoculture, with ... its systems of hegemony and legitimacy" (Slotkin: 3). Huston deploys this pseudoculture's disparaging views of "Others."

The disdain for the Other is tied in a complicated fashion to issues of masculinity. The Other is not necessarily feminized. The kafiri chief Ootah appears cowardly; he's afraid to meet Peachy and Danny and sits under an umbrella during battle. Since cowardice and bravado are usually the obverse of each other, he is also full of bravado. Despite his failure to fight, he claims victory and draws his sword to behead his enemies. Danny stops him and pledges no more violence or retribution, joining two tribes in brotherhood as the British way of doing things, despite the Raj's historic violent reprisals for resistance.

Masculinity is tied to an ambivalent militarism which dominates their relationships to each other and Others. Military rules and rituals heighten Huston's troubled and unresolved fascination with "masculine behavioral norms," to use Gaylyn Studlar's phrase (Studlar 1993: 182). Peachy and Danny march like soldiers into the bureaucrat's office (another scene invented by Huston), an excessive, out-of-place ritual that contrasts "the world's noblest profession" with a bureaucrat who threatens to deport them until they blackmail him. They obsessively train Kafiris in picky military postures. Life in the military has brought out their talents for sharp shooting, protocol, and order, while undergirding their excesses and overconfidence. It has given their lives structure, purpose, drama, even melodrama, and escape from women ("let's go find safety in battle," says Peachy after a Kafiri woman tries to seduce him). But, although Peachy and Danny are excellent soldiers, they sometimes prefer not to fight and treat fighting like a boyhood, not a deadly, game. They recognize that military training turns men into robots who unthinkingly fight and die.

Above all, it is official language that defines them. Huston said of Kipling, "I love the doggerel," and it is doggerel the protagonists speak (Long 2001: 86). In their mouths these words lose their signification and point to an empty meaning (Peachy: "It's got a ring to it"). The imperial language that seems to speak them (rather then they speaking it) cleanses, legitimates *and* satirizes their actions. Approaching large fake mountain figures, Peachy says, "I'll reconnoiter," as if on a military mission. Their initial speech to Ootah is filled with commercial, inflated, ornate and calculated promises and flattery. Both protagonists are constructed by a pompous, self-righteous imperial language through which the film presents subtle ironies. Their parodic long, Biblical phrases ring with ritual Masonic authority ("we come from the East" or "brother to a Prince and fellow to a beggar") (Fussell: 225). They combine high and low language: "You have our permission to bugger off," King Danny tells Peachy. Peachy's "urgent business" is blackmailing a maharaja. Their misapplied institutional language ritualizes their asocial, illegal and anarchic adventure and measures the distance between official rhetoric and their use of it to undergird their greed. Nonetheless their deployment of official rhetoric inevitably calls into question what lies behind official language and institutions. Kozloff (190) notes that Huston endorses and expands Victorian imperial ideologies and racial othering. I would also suggest that he introduces troubling ambiguities in invented scenes full of such language to offset the protagonists' charisma. The contract which refers to them as "you and me" is somewhere between a legal document and boys' tree house pledges. When Kipling calls them lunatics, Peachy asks rhetorically, "Would lunatics draw up a contract like this," as if the fact of the document guaranteed their sanity. But when read aloud, it *is* the contract of lunatics. Just being British defines them; when grabbed by the priests, Danny asks how dare they harm a British citizen in a language and with a set of assumptions the Kafiris cannot understand.

Other institutions and myths construct them and their fantasy. Peachy and Danny entering *terra incognita* recapitulate the mythic origin of empire: explorations into the "unknown." Recapitulation of the originary myth of empire as exploring the "unknown" without self-interest and the myth's existential frailty are foregrounded in the mountain trek following their caravan journey through the Khyber Pass (another scene Huston invented). The French Alps at Chamonix are shown in a series of jump cuts of uninhabited high snow-covered mountains. Geographically the range is supposed to be the Hindu Kush, a very high mountain range between the Pass and Kafiristan (now Nuristan). The cuts represent discontinuity, the endless intractability of this journey between one world (Indian empire) and another (Kafiristan), and the passing of time. The range is gigantic on the screen and in sharp contrast to urban sites full of Indians crowded like insects on trains, stations, and streets, or with Kipling's disheveled office. It is both a barrier and a path, a road to glory and to death.

In Kipling's story the mountains are filled with tribes of people with whom Danny and Peachy entangle. In the film the high, snow-covered mountains are uninhabited and uninhabitable. Shown in very long shots, Peachy and Danny, who goes snow blind (another Huston addition), appear tiny, almost invisible, against a harsh yet sublime setting: in contrast to their success in manipulating people, the natural environment is something they cannot control. These long shots, echoed later when Danny is condemned to his death on the bridge, remind us how nature is grander than even the grandest ambitions.

The mountains appropriate the spectacle, reducing Peachy and Danny, hitherto seen in close-ups and middle shots, to insignificant figures. For Studlar (1993: 189) Huston despecularizes them to open an authentic existential moment in their conversation by the fire, thinking they are about to die, as a crevasse prevents them from continuing their journey.[8] Here they assess the meaning or meaninglessness of their "uncertain and provisional" lives and their "continually defined and redefined" heroism, as Martin Rubin (1993: 154) describes other Huston protagonists. They acknowledge they have not made the world better and no one will weep for them. On the credit side, they saw and travelled further than anyone in their class could imagine. They recall an incident in which a fellow soldier, who lost his moneybag in battle, went back to retrieve it followed by his troops who thought he was charging. That soldier was awarded the Victoria Cross, the final absurdity of heroic masculinity. They laugh hysterically and loudly, causing an avalanche to fill the crevasse, permitting them to continue.

The mountain sequence constructs a third space, described by Homi Bhabha as a place in which fluid identities can be constructed, re-constructed and de-constructed by "enunciation, which makes the structure of meaning and reference an ambivalent process" that threatens to dissolve "this mirror of representation in which cultural knowledge is customarily revealed as an integrated, open, expanding code." One function of third space is to challenge "our sense of the historical identity of culture as a homogenizing, unifying force, authenticated by the originary Past, kept alive in the national tradition of the People," i.e., to undercut "homogeneous, serial time" (Bhabha 1994: 37). Bhabha considers such spaces to be "discursive sites or conditions that ensure that the meaning and symbols of culture have no primordial unity or fixity; that even the same signs can be appropriated, translated, and rehistoricized anew" (*ibid.*), as Peachy and Danny do with official institutional language. A parallel notion is Gilles Deleuze's notion of filmic transitional spaces, the point between two established spaces that permits the emergence of new or unique identities. Such spaces undermine presuppositions of the identity of character, placing our presuppositions into crisis and opening identity up to questioning. The transitional space permits characters to redefine themselves in spaces in which they have no pre-ordained role or are among strangers (see Bell 1997).

Third space is where life is recognized as ambiguous, capricious, discontinuous and complex. The mountain dangers and thoughts of death open up a third space for Peachy and Danny in which they see the absurdity of their lives and laugh in the face of death at a turning point; before the mountain trek they are rogues, ex-cons, soldiers, and adventurers, conditioned by their classed imperial identities. Saved by the avalanche, they proceed to fit their dreams to new readings in which they will diverge from each other while seemingly enacting their imperial dreams. Peachy remains a realist and an existentialist, acknowledging the capricious universe, but in Kafiristan Danny weaves a narrative of his life by misreading caprice as destiny, and thinking he can tame the Kafiris who, in the film, are aligned with nature — dangerous, unpredictable, and unconquerable. Peachy, too, is within the film's existential critique. During the final chase, Peachy's wealth, loaded on a besieged mule, spills out of the bags onto the dirt, echoing the spilled gold in *The Treasure of Sierra Madre* (1948).

Death also offers a third space. Danny and Peachy die well, vowing loyalty to each other. Danny apologizes and Peachy forgives him, re-enacting Christian forgiveness and martyrdom and re-mythologizes them into Christian symbols (Peachy is crucified but survives to "rise" again at Kipling's office at the film's end), however imperfect the fit. The underlying theme of martyrdom is further endorsed by the Christian words of "The Minstrel Boy." The original secular lyrics of the song allude to a failed Irish rebellion, but Huston's film uses later, religious lyrics by Reginald Heber.[9] Peachy and Danny's final duet is thus part of their ambiguous redemption. Facing death, Danny sings the third verse on Christ's death. Combining the tune's association with failed Irish rebellions with later religious lyrics, Huston economically layers the characters' class, rebelliousness and fate, with a Christianizing overlay.

Huston's additions emphasize metaphorical meanings: Danny's snow blindness foreshadows his later, fatal exclamation when he suddenly realizes his destiny as king, "as if the bandages were removed from my eyes," while still blind to the realities of his limited power. In the caravan Peachy and Danny disguised as a magician and his servant fit into the world of blind beggars, snake charmers and haggling merchants, and in the novel Danny acts even crazier by taking off his clothes and shaving part of his head. But appearing to themselves larger than life in Kafiristan, they mismeasure themselves. Danny, taking caprice for destiny, says "It all adds up"; but since throughout he is depicted as literally unable to do addition, his metaphorical addition is suspect (Peachy is excellent at math).

Peachy and Danny misrecognize empire, while mirroring it. Like other Huston characters, they are "consistently misprisioning the world" (Cooper 1993: 108). Punished for their arrogance, they die in a kind of redemption, though not sacrificed for any cause, nation or other people. Yet, Danny insists on justice and peace, not revenge, to settle disputes at the durbar, recalling a Christian attitude, as does Peachy's forgiving Danny. Their final reaffirmation of mutual loyalty has a cleansing function that raises them above their mortal fate, while simultaneously contrasting with and emphasizing the barbarism of the Kaffiris. But when Danny dies, it is like a tree falling in the woods without anyone to hear him. If Peachy had not survived to tell the story, however mad he became, Danny would not have been remembered, a final example of chance or destiny which brings the story back not to Kipling the journalist but to Kipling the poet who is writing a poem on a Burmese king in the opening scene.

Lesley Brill (1997: 33) argues that this film, like many Huston films, is about finding the self. I suggest that the film is less about finding the self than about how language defines the self, leaving a gap between rhetoric and authenticity, and about returning to an infantile self of unimpeded wish fulfillment. Without engaging the Kafiris emotionally or psychologically, Danny and Peachy cannot change. They remain completely within the loyalties and hierarchies that propelled them from the start. Peachy's retelling of the story that frames the film (but which appears in Kipling's novella only half-way through) helps distance the story's political and moral implications. Peachy and Danny are interpellated by the imperial world they served as soldiers, but they can only fulfill their dreams by receding from that empire. Their ambitions resonate with Huston's other films, but these protagonists remain impenetrable to the outside world except as a venue for their desires. Even the existential moment in the mountains recedes, so Danny may rule.

Danny's decision to stay in Kafiristan by domesticating himself and ruling justly permits him to enter the symbolic patriarchy as father of his people and his lineage. But Danny's entry is ironically into the institutions he despises. His wish for knighthood and honors from the Queen represent recognition from an official empire that threw him out. Here Danny writes himself into history with a capital H that, as Slotkin (1990: 6) puts it, "must always feel and look larger and more important than the history that is documented by journalism, which comes to us as fragments of a story, its symbolism half-formed or unresolved."

Rubin (1993: 139), drawing on Roland Barthes, sees the hero's construction as "an accessible and stable platform for viewer identification." Heroes in film are marked by speech, prominence on the screen, control of narrative and actions, and cinematic cues, like shot/counter shot and point-of-view. But for Rubin (141), heroism does not exist solely in codified "adjectival qualities ... that cluster around the name (and, in cinema, the bodily presence) of a fictional character." These traits also mark the antihero, "a variant on the heroic norm rather than a true alternative to it ... an anticonventional hero — heroic precisely for the way he transgressed reigning (and often declining) conventional notions of heroism." Identifying an anti-hero depends on reception more than on conventional, coded cinematic techniques: "Yesterday's villain can, through revisionism, become today's antihero and then, through familiarity, tomorrow's conventional hero" (Rubin 1993: 141). Such anti-heroism by 1975 was an emerging convention in *Butch Cassidy and the Sundance Kid* (1969), clearly on Huston's mind when he invited Newman to be in the film.

Huston's invented scenes create nexus of simultaneous difference and similarity (polo, Masonic symbols) to create third spaces, cultural ambiguities and unifying symbolisms necessary for History. Still, ambiguities intervene and undermine the hero-rogues. The camera stays in the shadows listening without comment much of the time. The "objective" camera distances itself and viewers from these connivers and liars (Brill 1997: 34). Pauline Kael mentions Huston's limiting, passive camerawork as part of the economy of heroism, while also avoiding homoeroticism as Studlar (1993: 188) notes.

The camera-work functions in several ways in this film: aligned with but not identical to Peachy's view of the Indian on the train, very long shots of tiny Danny and Peachy in the mountains, viewing scenes from behind listeners often sitting in the dark, and multiple views of Kafiristan from below as they approach and from above as they look from their fortress window. These variations endorse their discussions about cultural relativism and their lives' meanings in the carnivalesque empire they created. Their gestures and speech are grand but empty, echoing rituals and official language that have neither any real bearing on their situation nor the power to sustain them. Huston captured Kipling's "seriocomic underpainting" (Fussell 1958: 217) by simultaneously aggrandizing and distancing his characters.

Huston's narrative framing through Peachy asks how art can redeem misspent lives without simple-minded didacticism through both our identification and our critical distance. This film implicates the viewer in the erotics of imperial fantasy and its dark side lacking concern for those forced to submit to this fantasy, such as the self-sacrificing Billy Fish. The film's themes of male bonding, friendship and loyalty plus the charismatic cast seem to whitewash the racism of Huston's train scene. But his existential moments suggest moral judgment alternately suspended and applied. Lawless adventure legitimates itself both by representing as heroic the escape from social norms and by punishing such free spirits, permitting viewers to access both infinite freedom and the satisfaction of not suffering the adventurer's deserved fate, as Kozloff (1994: 195) notes. Huston distances and engages the protagonists, exposing and submerging racism,[10] as did Victorian boys' stories of fictional and real adventurers in which readers' suspension of disbelief endowed imperial knavery with legitimacy, righteousness, truth, and, worst of all, fun.

Notes

1. Saeed Jaffrey (1998: 201), describes the film's U.K. ads as like a *"Boys' Own* yarn," making the film appear a mindless adventure.
2. For example, Kevin Gately's 1974 death by a policeman's truncheon. The National Front, founded 1967, opposed immigration and compulsory repatriation of immigrants

who as Commonwealth citizens could enter Britain as equal citizens. The NF grew to 20,000 members by 1974, mostly blue-collar workers, the self-employed and some Conservatives.

3. The background for Kipling's story is George Scott Robertson's 1896 book, *Kafirs of the Hindu Kush*. See Macintyre (2004).

4. I thank my colleague, ethnomusicologist Ted Solis, for his insights on the score.

5. The English-educated Indian babu was satirized by both nineteenth-century Britons and Indians.

6. Brill (36) also argues that the film "embodies" humorous comments on cultural relativism by displaying an anti-idyllic Other. But this only justifies the protagonists' trickery.

7. Kaminsky (1978: 202) describes this representation of indigenous people as typical of Huston and as why Afghanistan banned the film.

8. The mountain crossing is briefly described in Kipling's story, though some of Danny's comments are in the film.

9. The original song by Thomas Moore (1779–1852) was an Irish partisan tune; religious lyrics came from "The Son of God Goes Forth to War" (1812) by Reginald Heber (Bishop of Calcutta, 1823–26).

10. Jaffrey (197) mentions staff racism on the set.

The Way We Were and *White Hunter, Black Heart*
Huston in Fiction and Reel Life
Patrick McGilligan

"The liberals were the worst."[1]

Few of us knew or ever even met John Huston, perhaps one reason why we long to know him better. We know him primarily through his films. How relevant is his life story to understanding and appreciating his films? This is a question biographers always struggle with.

There are not that many good American novels with film directors as central figures, but there are two that revolve around Huston and they both depict him during the same crucial phase in his career, in Hollywood, just after World War II and before his emigration to Ireland (which would inspire a third Huston-centric novel by Ray Bradbury).[2] These years, 1947 to 1952 roughly, were a high mark of creativity that includes *The Treasure of the Sierra Madre* (1948), *Key Largo* (1948), *We Were Strangers* (1949), *The Asphalt Jungle* (1950), *The Red Badge of Courage* (1951), *Moulin Rouge* (1952), and *The African Queen* (1951).

These were also the early years of the Hollywood blacklist, with, for me, one of the mysterious episodes in Huston's life: his co-leadership of the Committee for the First Amendment, a coalition of screen liberals and progressives formed to oppose the first subpoenas of the so-called Hollywood 19 by the congressional House Committee on Un-American Activities, known as HUAC. This was in 1947. The Committee for the First Amendment made a big show of traveling to Washington, D.C., along with the accused Reds, publicizing their opposition to HUAC's investigation of the motion picture industry. However, the Committee for the First Amendment buckled and evaporated after the first witnesses, the Hollywood Ten, angrily denounced HUAC and refused to cooperate with the inquiry. Huston was one of the bucklers.

Arthur Laurents's *The Way We Were* and Peter Viertel's *White Hunter, Black Heart* are the two novels that attempt to probe the complexities of Huston's character, roughly corresponding with this time. Both became well-known films, although it is more accurate in the case of *The Way We Were* to say that Laurents wrote his novel as a corrective to the film after his script had been tinkered with. And there are interesting differences between Laurents's novel and the 1973 film, which stars Barbra Streisand and Robert Redford; differences which elaborate on the author's feelings about the ambiguities of Huston's role in the blacklist.

White Hunter, Black Heart was written contemporaneously, in 1953, but let us start with *The Way We Were*, which is fixed in time, chronologically, earlier in Huston's life story. Huston is a pivotal character in both the book and film versions of Laurents's story: a director named "Bissinger," who is the doyen of a vaguely left-liberal circle in Hollywood to which the fiery radical Katie Morosky (Streisand) and her writer-husband Hubbell (Redford) are attached. Hubbell is "Bissinger's" latest protégé co-writer—"his Midas touch"—and they are collaborating on a project just as HUAC sends out its subpoenas in the fall of 1947. In the film "Bissinger" is played by Patrick O'Neal. O'Neal was a Huston actor himself, an alumnus of the cast of the Cold War thriller *The Kremlin Letter*, and thus O'Neal's slyly negative imitation might be interpreted as a subtle payback to a man not always gentle on his actors.

In most ways Laurents's novel is harder on Huston than the film. "Bissinger" is Huston to a "T": he is "a long skinny cat with a sudden crest of pure-white hair which he cultivated like a rare plant" (1973: 100); he has "a courtly Edwardian manner abetted by Edwardian rancher clothes" (100); he speaks "very, very gently" (100) but is a "complete cynic" (121). A macho dandy, "Bissinger" takes boxing and tennis lessons and likes to swim nude in the swimming pool of his "big old Tudor mansion" (99) in Beverly Hills, which has a giant Italian marble fountain and a private theater with a Matisse that can be electronically lowered from the wall for screenings. ("Bissinger enjoyed the symbolism of lowering it" [100].) He has several ex-wives and a child he treats roughly. He smokes an omnipresent cigar. People he doesn't like (he doesn't like that many) are "fools" (130) or "assholes" (120).

Huston wrote about his own politics in the late 1940s in his own autobiography, the deceptively titled "An Open Book." He admits knowing some of the Hollywood Communists, even some of those first subpoenaed, personally. (For one, he had collaborated on scripts with Howard Koch, one of the first 19 called to Washington, and one of the few among the 19 who definitely was *not* a Communist Party member.) They were "liberals and idealists," he wrote, "and would have been appalled at the idea of trying to overthrow the United States government. At that time no one knew about the Gulag Archipelago and Stalin's mass murders" (1980: 145). Huston even confessed to attending Marxist reading groups in private homes in Hollywood "two or three times," purely "out of curiosity" (147). Sometimes he attended Communist or front group fund-raising events where people like Paul Robeson were headliners. "I wasn't revolted" by the Communist activities of the Hollywood personalities, Huston wrote. "On the contrary, I found it all very childish" (148).

The Way We Were, book and film, sticks to generally agreed-upon history after HUAC's subpoenas rained on Hollywood. Huston, William Wyler and Philip Dunne were having lunch at a studio when their conversation led to formation of the Committee for the First Amendment. Huston donated his house for a fund-raising party and chartered a plane from, of all people, the right-wing Howard Hughes, which would take him, Humphrey Bogart, Lauren Bacall, Gene Kelly, Danny Kaye, and other "righteously angry" (Huston's words) Hollywood citizens to Washington, D.C., in October 1947. In D.C., Huston and Dunne met privately with the accused Communists, who refused, partly on the advice of their lawyers, to accept their (Huston's and Dunne's) advice to publicly declare their Party membership on the steps of the Capitol before the hearings began. Huston and Dunne left the meeting "feeling uneasy," Huston wrote in his memoirs. "Not that my idea had been all that good; it was rather that the response to it had been weak and shifty" (160).

The hearings ensued. The Hollywood Ten, the first ten called as witnesses, refused any pretenses, engaging in shouting matches with the HUAC members; they were eventually cited for contempt of Congress. "One after another, they were knocked down," Huston wrote. "It was a sorry performance. You felt your skin crawl and your stomach turn. I disapproved of what was being done to the Ten, but I also disapproved of their response. They had lost a chance to defend a most important principle. It struck me as a case of thoroughly bad generalship" (163).[3]

What followed is glimpsed in *The Way We Were* and briefly chronicled by Huston in his book. The first public statements of retreat by people like Bogart on the way home to Hollywood. The turning of the press. The drumbeating by right-wing columnists and the public as well as the secret circulation of lists of names of Hollywood Reds and their sympathizers—including Huston and Dunne. The firing of the Ten. The institution of the blacklist.

"The thing that was most disappointing to me," wrote Huston in his memoir, "was the submissiveness of the American people" (171). But wasn't he also, ultimately, submissive?

The film of *The Way We Were* shows "Bissinger" returning from Hollywood after the debacle, already washing his hands of former friends who refused to accept his generalship of their tragedy. The Ten should have denied everything and confused everyone, "Bissinger" tells a reporter — curious advice, and not at all what Huston himself advised. The Ten had adopted a terrible strategy, "Bissinger" adds, that looked like they were running toward martyrdom (1973: 37). "Boring masochistic assholes!" (129) is "Bissinger's" review of the Ten's performance in Laurents's nuanced novel, which is at once disapproving and magnanimous towards Huston.

It is important to note that Huston was a vice-president of the Directors Guild in 1947, and later on, in 1950, he played a significant role in leading the charge against the "loyalty oath" that Cecil B. DeMille and other conservatives tried to impose on the directors' organization. This might be seen as self-preservation, however: a fight on his terms, his own turf. Jules Dassin told me the Directors Guild was not a hotbed of Communists: it was a "tepid bed" and most blacklisting was aimed at writers, actors, and militants in the craft unions of the industry.

* * *

We will come back to *The Way We Were* but for the moment let us turn to *White Hunter, Black Heart*, Peter Viertel's engrossing *roman a clef* about the filming of *The African Queen*, which Clint Eastwood made into a film forty years after it was written.

The novel's portrait of John Wilson, the Huston stand-in, is, if anything, more virulent than Laurents's, who after all was himself a victim of the blacklist. Viertel sketches the same physical profile of "Wilson": his "gaunt shoulders," "fine, graying hair" (1990: 12) and "long, thin legs" (14) But it is the biographical detail and psychological portrait that is brutal. Viertel mentions that "Wilson" once ran over and killed someone in an automobile accident, which was true of Huston. "Wilson" is vain about himself and contemptuous of most others. "He publicly abused all the women he was involved with" (2). "Wilson" is "a monstre sacré," as Viertel put it in a letter to me, "but sacré as well as monstrous." "Wilson's" success as a filmmaker is based on a "deep-seated sadism" that is evidenced, in various ways, in the story. Viertel proves an astute analyst of Huston's oeuvre, describing him as a "screw-you-all filmmaker" (2) whose greatest films are devoted to the theme of "romantic futility"—that is, "stories of great endeavors that finished in futility" (42).

I won't go into the main thrust of Viertel's story which has "Wilson" less interested in the flawed ending of the script he's supposed to be writing, than in the great adventure he plans of stalking big game in Africa while on-location. The Hollywood macho has "a secret desire to risk his life" (17) and is so careless about others' that tragedy befalls one of his retinue.

White Hunter, Black Heart takes place four years after the first HUAC hearings, with the Hollywood blacklist really revving up. There are only brief allusions to the witchhunt in America in the novel (none in the rosier film), with, at one point, "Wilson"—the Huston figure—declaiming, "We are all potential outcasts from society.... Every one of us, and everyone we know has really only one personal loyalty, and that loyalty is to himself, his own survival. That's why the loyalty hearings are so ridiculous. Our society makes life so perilous that it is almost like feudal times. We're all little fish struggling to keep from being eaten. We're loyal when it helps us. And we're potential criminals when our safety is threatened" (72).

The novel touches on Huston's politics. It's one of the things Viertel admires about "Wilson." "He supported doubtful political causes on the basis of integrity and not because of a romantic, adolescent political conviction," (14) Viertel writes. And key scenes in the novel are meant to illustrate "Wilson's "loyalty to the underdog" (35). In one scene he tells off an anti–Semitic socialite for her remarks sympathetic to Hitler and in another he fistfights an East African hotel manager who abuses his black workers. Both villains are cheap targets, however, and "Wilson" is a complicated man. In the novel he also makes disparaging remarks about "fags," in private calls Kivu, the native guide who is the sacrificial victim of the story, "this little jig," and refers to his producer as a "Balkan rug peddler"—which might be construed as veiled anti–Semitism.

I am an admirer of the Clint Eastwood movie, and Eastwood's imitation of Huston, partly because Eastwood rarely steps so boldly outside his own persona. But the film version is something of a gloss on the tougher-minded novel, as Viertel himself admitted to me when I interviewed him for the book I was writing about Eastwood, dating back about some years now.

The script was filmed as it existed, after being rescued from dormancy, a studio draft that had been written years earlier by Viertel, with rewrites by James Bridges and Burt Kennedy. Political correctness had erased from the script the word "nigger"—conspicuous in the book—and there would also be none of Wilson's private, offensive talk about "fags" or "jigs." Alternatively, there'd be a key line of dialogue in which "Verrill" (the Viertel character, who narrates the story) tells "Wilson," the filmmaker devoted to romantic futility that "Somewhere deep inside of you is a tiny spark of hope" (73), of decency. That character assessment would lead to a payoff unique to the film.

Viertel, who then lived in Marbella, Spain, with his wife, actress Deborah Kerr, was invited to Africa for the filming in 1993, and he developed some qualms about the shooting script. He didn't warm to the scene at the beginning of the film with "Wilson" galloping on a horse across the English countryside, reminding audiences of Clint's cowboy image, or the white-water river scene reminding audiences of *The African Queen*. But he liked least the radical change that was Eastwood's own prescribed ending, and here I am quoting from my biography, *Clint: The Life and Legend*.

The novel "was predicated on the narrator's disgust with John Wilson's obsessive desire to stalk and kill an elephant, which is carried through to a sorry conclusion. In Africa, Clint began to rethink the ending, discussing it with author Viertel. Huston himself had changed his mind by the time he wrote his autobiography, *An Open Book*, declaring, "I've never killed an elephant, although I surely tried. I never got a shot at one whose trophies are worth the crime. No, not crime—sin. I wouldn't dream of shooting an elephant today—in fact, I've given up all shooting."

"To Viertel, Clint confided his hesitation about shooting one of Africa's tuskers, even for pretend purposes" (331).

So this became the Hollywood ending. "After several disappointing hunting trips, Wilson finally has managed to track and corner a small herd. When one of the largest of the elephants charges Wilson, he lifts his gun and aims to fire. The beast slows to a halt, trumpeting his challenge from just a few yards away. Wilson finds himself mesmerized, deeply touched despite himself, and gradually he lowers his gun. Then (as happens in the book) the small herd is spooked, and Wilson's native guide, Kivu (played by Boy Mathias Chuma), dashes forward to save Wilson, only to be trampled by the elephants" (333). Wilson/Clint fights back ashamed tears.

This is followed by a coda with "Wilson" returning to the set, where the camera and crew waits for the cameras to be turned on for the first time. Grief spreads among the villages, as news of Kivu's death is spread by drums and whispered reproaches: "White hunter, black heart!" As Wilson slumps in his chair and calls action, there is one last change from the harsher portrait of the book: "You were right, Pete," Clint/Wilson mutters. "The ending is all wrong." Not in the book: so Eastwood's portrait of Huston is softened, finally, by an acknowledgment of mistake and contrition; an apologia—confirming, indeed, the tiny spark of humanity in Wilson, or Huston.

Viertel agreed with me when I first broached the subject with him, that Clint had somewhat romanticized "Wilson," which was perhaps inevitable with the passage of time. Later, he felt more strongly about endorsing the film. "Of course like any novelist whose work is adapted to the screen, there are many omissions that I regret, as well as a lack of the mood and the full verbal high-jinks of the novel," he wrote to me in 2006. "But by and large, Eastwood tried to bring my story to the silver screen. That he lacked the biting sarcasm of John Wilson ... well, that might have been an inborn shortcoming. But as a filmmaker, I admire him, perhaps more now than in 1990."

* * *

But back to 1952, with Huston finished with the filming of *The African Queen*: "Angered by the HUAC investigations and the Hollywood blacklisting," Ephraim Katz (2006: 213) wrote in his definitive one-volume *Film Encyclopedia*, Huston "moved" with his wife and children to Ireland in 1952. This is part of the commonly accepted wisdom about Huston.

The book of *The Way We Were*— not the film — has a different explanation. The film pretty much leaves "Bissinger" behind after HUAC, in favor of the tear-jerking love story between Streisand and Redford. But in the novel, "Bissinger" suffers political fallout because of his leadership of the failed Committee for the First Amendment. All along he has been stalked by Red squads, at one point finding a microphone "bug" behind his screening-room Matisse (a Picasso in the film). Now he too is subpoenaed, and must go to Washington, D.C., and commune with HUAC. What he tells the witchhunting committee is left vague and mysterious, and upon his return "Bissinger" vows, "This is the last film I make in this asshole town" (1973: 178).

"What will you do, George?" asks Katie, the Streisand character.

"Leave this pismire of a country," "Bissinger" replies (179).

In reality Huston made four or five more movies before leaving Hollywood and heading for Ireland — leaving America, I'd venture to say, as much for personal as political reasons.

Yet he did have his political reasons, and Laurents is close to the mark. John Sbardelatti, a professor at the University of California in Santa Barbara, who is writing a thesis taking a fresh look at the blacklist, tells me he has located numerous documents indicating that the FBI and Red Squads had indeed tracked Huston's movements. In Joseph McBride's biography of John Ford he quotes the screenwriter Nunnally Johnson as saying that Ward Bond and his ilk made Johnson "ashamed of the whole industry.... Think of John Huston, having to go out and debase himself to an oaf like Ward Bond and promise he'd never be a bad boy again, and Ward Bond would say, 'All right, then, we clear you, but we've got out eye on you'" (2001: 451). McBride also quotes a 1953 cable from John Ford to an Irish relative: "Your letter received with the discouraging news that the Reds — one John Huston — are seeking refuge in our lovely Ireland. This aint [sic] good" (456).

So even John Ford thought of Huston as a Pinko, and it is likely that Huston was caught in the HUAC dragnet in some way — if not in the dramatic fashion invented for Laurents's novel, then secretly, in private. He would have had to "clear" himself somehow, even if working in Europe, if his films were to be distributed in the U.S. For example, at the height of the anti–Red hysteria, Huston made films for Warner Bros. (*Moby Dick* [1956]) and Twentieth Century–Fox (*Heaven Knows Mr. Allison* [1957]; *Roots of Heaven* [1958]; *The Barbarian and the Geisha* [1958]), while pure blacklistees like Charles Chaplin, Joseph Losey, John Berry, and Jules Dassin could not get their films financed by American companies or expect to have them shown in the United States.

According to Nunnally Johnson, he apparently met with the right-wing Motion Picture Alliance in order to wash his skirts of any Red taint. He may have had to write a secret Bogie-style retraction of his political activities to the studios as well. Perhaps, like so many people caught up in the widespread fear, he also made a financial payoff to the inquisitors, one of those brown bags of cash that went to the California Republican Party.

I met Huston once, at a Directors Guild of America event on board a ship docked in Southern California, where his films were being screened and he answered questions from the audience. Not knowing what I know now, I raised my hand and asked him if his emigration to Ireland had anything to do with the blacklist. It was intended as a perfectly innocent question, as I knew of many liberals — Comden and Green, Garson Kanin and Ruth Gordon, for example — who left Hollywood out of disgust, not fear, during this period. I didn't write down Huston's answer, partly because I was mortified by the anger and dismissiveness of his reply, something on the order of. "No! The Hollywood Communists were fools who got what they deserved!" I had pushed a button. Childish fools! Assholes! The very people he denounced were those whose civil liberties he had once defended.

The opposite side of a sadist is usually a coward. Who did Huston cooperate with during the blacklisting era, and to what extent? Did he talk about those Marxist reading groups and try to recall the names of others in the room? What did he say? Who did he pay? That part of the story is left out of Huston's *An Open Book* and it isn't covered in Lawrence Grobel's otherwise fascinating biography of the Huston clan, *The Hustons*.

Remember: "We're loyal when it helps us," as Wilson/Huston declaims in the book of *White Hunter, Black Heart*, "And we're potential criminals when our safety is threatened."

I enjoy the films *The Way We Were* and *White Hunter, Black Heart*, but prefer the novels for their fine points and their toughness on the character of Huston. In the end, Laurents, the "fellow traveler," goes easier on Huston than Viertel, perhaps because he so admires his films. In a scene missing from the film, "Bissinger," in Laurents's novel, shows up at the hospital to hold Katie's hand after she gives birth to her baby; her husband is divorcing her for being a known subversive. That was the spark of decency in "Bissinger." And then, more surprising, in the novel "Bissinger" goes out of his way, in spite of his own problems with HUAC, to offer a job to the "graylisted" Paula — the ex–European actress, dialogue coach and screenwriter for foreign leading ladies — who is obviously intended to be Salka Viertel, the mother of a writer named Peter. That's a clear and intriguing link to *White Hunter, Black Heart*.

"I would see Huston now and then, here and there," Laurents said in a recent email, when I told him I was writing this piece. "I thought he was a man of exaggeration. And sadistic if given the chance. Politically? All I know he was on that plane which has been given an aura comparable to the Spirit of St. Louis. But all they did was fly loudly East to stand up once and, with one or two exceptions, to crawl back silently to disappear."

Then Laurents added something generous and, especially for a biographer, I think, arguable, "His films were made by a very different man."

Notes

1. Black-listed writer-director Abraham "Abe" Polonsky in an interview with Joseph McBride.

2. Interestingly, Huston appears in a barely fictionalised form in at least two other novels: Ray Bradbury's *Green Shadows, White Whale* (1992), a semi-autobiographical account of collaborating with Huston on the script for *Moby Dick*, and the little-known *The Crazy Kill* (1956) by Charles Hamblett, which offers a fictionalized account of the filming of *Moby Dick*.

3. Bertolt Brecht was also called and testified — he was the "11th" — but parried the committee ingenuously and shortly thereafter left the U.S.

Huston's Mexico
RICHARD VELA

John Huston's extended involvement with Mexico began in late 1925, when Huston, then nineteen years old, wanted to escape the cold New York winter and spend time in a warmer climate while he recovered from mastoid surgery. With five hundred dollars from his father, he traveled by boat to Vera Cruz, which still "had a blasted, pitted look" from the Mexican Revolution (Huston 1980: 42), and then took a train to Mexico City. He ended up staying a year and a half and studied dressage under Colonel José Olimbrada, who, when Huston's money was running out, offered him "an honorary commission in the Mexican army that included free meals, a free bunk in the barracks, a temporary rank of lieutenant, and a choice of horses" (Huston 1980: 42–46; Grobel 2000: 115–116). His second trip came only a few months after he had returned to California, when he took a steamship to Acapulco, and then traveled to Mexico City by mule train, a seventeen day trip. About ten years later, while working as a writer for Warner Bros., he was assigned the script for *Juarez* (1939), one of a string of prestigious film biographies starring award-winning actor Paul Muni.[1] Given the opportunity to write about the native Mexican leader, Benito Juarez, who defeated the European-supported Emperor Maximilian, Huston notes, "I couldn't have asked for a more attractive assignment. It seemed almost providential, tying in with my knowledge of Mexico and my love for that country" (Huston 1980: 73).

This combination of knowledge and love outlines Huston's long involvement with Mexico, both in his life and in his films. Although he never loses his youthful and perhaps romantic enthusiasm, his films become complex dissections of the interactions between the Mexican people and the variety of foreigners, both Americans and others, who come to Mexico seeking refuge and rewards. Huston would make three other films about Mexico, *The Treasure of the Sierra Madre* (1948) from B. Traven's novel, *The Night of the Iguana* (1964) from the Tennessee Williams play, and *Under the Volcano* (1984) based on Malcolm Lowry's novel. Over the years, he often traveled to Mexico. In a 1964 documentary on the making of *The Night of the Iguana*, Huston says

"I've been in Mexico for a long time now, not consecutively, but I always return to Mexico. It's one of the countries that I like best in the world" (*On the Trail of the Iguana*). In 1978, entering the last decade of his life, Huston moved to Puerto Vallarta, Mexico, near the Mismaloya peninsula where he had shot *The Night of the Iguana*.[2] He spent Christmas there in 1986, just before adapting James Joyce's "The Dead," which was to be his last film. According to Lawrence Grobel, "The film, to be shot in early 1987, was something to look forward to, but before they got started, John wanted to spend the Christmas holidays in Puerto Vallarta and Las Caletas. He had been away from Mexico for too long." Even though "his doctors advised against it" (2000: 777) writes Grobel, "once Huston had made up his mind to see Mexico for possibly the last time, no one was going to talk him out of it" (1).

Huston began writing about Mexico during the era of Franklin Delano Roosevelt's Good Neighbor Policy, when the Office of the Coordinator for Inter-American Affairs, headed by Nelson Rockefeller, shaped the way that Latin America appeared in American films by promoting positive images of Latin America and encouraging films ranging from Disney's *Saludos Amigos* (1942) and *Tres Caballeros* (1945) to Orson Welles's *It's All True* (1942).[3] What the Good Neighbor Policy meant for Latin America's image, according to Ana Lopez, was that "After decades of portraying Latin Americans lackadaisically and sporadically as lazy peasants and wily señoritas who inhabited an undifferentiated backward land, Hollywood films between 1939 and 1947 featuring Latin American stars, music, locations and stories flooded U.S. and international markets." Lopez mentions "30 films with Latin American themes" for 1943 and says that in the first five months of "1945, 84 films dealing with Latin American themes had been produced" (Lopez 1993: 69). Many of these were genre films, and one pattern that emerged in films noirs such as Edward Dmytryk's *Cornered* (1945), Alfred Hitchcock's *Notorious* (1946), and Charles Vidor's *Gilda* (1947), was that of the stalwart American — Dick Powell, Cary Grant, and Glenn Ford, respectively — going south to encounter Hitler's henchmen. These noir films dramatize America's concern that the Axis powers would gain a foothold in Latin America.[4] Huston's source material reflects these concerns. In Williams' *The Night of the Iguana* (1961), the Reverend Shannon asks Maxine, "Aw — Nazis. How come there's so many of them down here lately" (1961: 15), and in Lowry's *Under the Volcano* (1947) Hugh Firmin tells Yvonne, "A Nazi may not be a fascist, but there're certainly plenty of them around" (1947: 299). They remain central to Huston's adaptation of Lowry's novel, but he omits them from the film version of *The Night of the Iguana*.

Critics have often discussed Huston's view of Mexico through the shaping narrative of the Anglo-American in Mexico. Richard Slotkin, in

Gunfighter Nation, provides one way of reading that narrative when he argues that "The delineation of 'Mexico' as mythic space in *Treasure of Sierra Madre* has had the strongest influence on subsequent treatments, because of the consistency with which Huston conflates Mexico and the archetypal landscape and images of *gringo* mythology," making Mexico "the scene of Americans' moral regeneration" (1992: 417–418). Daniel Cooper Alarcon (1997), working primarily with literature, develops a similar theory regarding the idea of the "infernal paradise," a view that presents Mexico as "a place of paradoxical extremes ... a symbolic backdrop against which a spiritual quest is played out" (1997: 40).[5] While Huston's habit of on-location shooting generally tends to give his films a very definite sense of place, that exploration of locale seems especially true of his Mexican films. Huston's general method often seems to be to throw his characters into situations that are unfamiliar, uncomfortable, and into locations that are unaccommodating, much the same way that he often treated his actors.[6] A conflict between character and environment is not, however, limited to Huston's Mexico pictures, and such films as *The African Queen* (1951), *The Misfits* (1961), and *The Man Who Would Be King* (1975), among others, offer ample testimony on that point, and a variety of critics have commented on this basic feature of Huston's filmmaking.[7] In this process, however, although Mexico may sometimes seem to function as exotic locale, the representation of the Mexican people is generally more subtle, with a broad sense of divisions and issues that affect their country.

In films set in Mexico, the border often becomes an emotional boundary, and crossing it means a confrontation with unexpected forces that trigger the opening of equally unexpected aspects of the self.[8] The characters in these border-crossing films usually begin by treating Mexico as a territory, a place that is different from home but still somehow delineated and understood as an extension of their previous experiences in their own country. Lewis Owens explains that "a territory is clearly mapped, fully imagined as a place of containment, invented to subdue the dangerous potentialities" (1998: 26). Because these border crossers think of Mexico as a place they can understand in terms they already know, they tend to believe they can negotiate the landscape and experience of the new land without making any significant changes or extraordinary effort. What they experience, however, is that Mexico becomes a frontier, a place without the familiar boundaries and divisions that have shaped their view of the world, a place for which their understanding of values and motives provides no map.[9] What sustained them before the crossing is hardly ever adequate once they are in another country, and often these outsiders simply try to impose their own values and views on as a way of restricting their experience to what they can understand and ignoring what they cannot. The conflict between their views and the demands that Mexico makes on them reveals the inadequacy of their defenses. In some cases their failure reveals these foreigners to be either comic or pathetic characters unable to benefit from their experience, but in more extreme cases they lose their lives. Huston's handling of his characters and his knowledge of Mexico make the situation more complex than generalizations about Anglo Americans in Mexico might suggest, and, most significantly, his views on the outsider in Mexico usually demonstrate nativist sympathies. Huston seems critical of these outsiders, and he takes some care to investigate the negative effects of foreign influences. As a result, his films sometimes critique communities within the Mexican population.

After such missteps as the unflattering stereotypes in *Girl of the Rio* (1932) and Wallace Beery's oafish turn as Pancho Villa in *Viva Villa!* (1934),[10] the 1939 film, *Juarez*, attempts to tell a much more sophisticated and inspirational story, in short, to make artistic propaganda. As Paul J. Vanderwood writes, "The movie was to stress the successful resistance of the hemisphere (actually Mexico) to past European intervention (supposedly due to the Monroe Doctrine) and was to urge new solidarity — under United States leadership — against the new threat" (1983: 19), and audiences were expected "to recognize that Napoleon in his Mexican intervention is none other than Mussolini plus Hitler in their Spanish adventure" (Vanderwood 1983: 20). Huston describes the film as "a conflict of ideologies" between "men of the highest principles" and explains that "the actual writing, when MacKenzie and I got to it, was by way of being dialectic," since Huston was "a Jeffersonian Democrat espousing ideals similar to those of Benito Juarez," while fellow scriptwriter Aeneas MacKenzie "believed in the monarchical system — perhaps even to the point of defending the Divine Right of Kings" (1980: 73).

Seen today, in spite of its focus on Juarez and his devotion to the character and principles of Abraham Lincoln, the film seems remarkable for its attempt at evenhanded presentation of the invader, Maximilian (Brian Aherne), who is both a puppet of Napoleon III (Claude Rains) and a dupe of the wealthy hidalgos. In fact, he emerges finally as a principled and even sympathetic fool. Asked to sign a decree that would, among other things, call for the execution of "anyone found in the possession of arms without authority of law," he comments that "The death penalty is not for those who act — however misguidedly — from principle." Later in the film, after Maximilian has abdicated and prepares to leave Mexico, Colonel Miguel López (Gilbert Roland) explains to the emperor that his supporters will be hunted down and killed. At first, Maximilian seems surprised, but then says, "I have been blind to my true responsibilities" and gives up his opportunity to escape. Finally, after Maximilian has been captured and condemned to be executed, General Porfirio Diaz (John Garfield) comes to tell him that that Juarez will not sign a pardon. Maximilian reflects, "So Benito Juarez is honest.... If he were otherwise — ambitious, self-seeking — he would have set me free and won the plaudits of the world.... But he is honest.... My dying proves that he is honest." The very last shot of the film shows Juarez standing over Maximilian's coffin, muttering "Forgive me," a sentence that Vanderwood explains was "blocked from the sound track on the film version released in Mexico, where Maximilian could hardly be forgiven for his intervention."[11] For many reasons, the film was not the prestigious critical or popular success in Latin America that Warner Bros. had hoped it might be, even though Mexico's president, Lázaro Cardenas, who in 1937 had "expropriated foreign oil holdings, among them substantial U.S. interests" (Vanderwood 1983: 28), now "made arrangements for the picture's opening in Mexico City's Palace of Fine Arts, the first time any movie had been so honored" (Vanderwood 1983: 36). Huston lays the blame on actor Paul Muni, who played Benito Juarez and "complained that he did not have as many lines as Maximilian." The result was that "a new writer — Muni's brother-in-law — was put on the script," and, writes Huston, "His changes did the picture irreparable damage" (1983: 73–74).

With his success as writer/director of *The Maltese Falcon* (1941), Huston gained far more control over his next pictures. Soon after directing *In This Our Life* (1942), he began negotiations to film *The Treasure of the Sierra Madre*. In fact, on November 17, 1941, the mysterious novelist B. Traven wrote Huston's agent, Paul Kohner, that he was interested in pursuing the project. Less than a month later, however, Pearl Harbor was bombed and America was at war. Huston spent the next few years making documentaries for the Army, but soon after the war he resumed contact with Traven, and began work on what was to be his second venture as both writer and director (Huston 1980: 138–148).[12] William F. Noland, one of Huston's early biographers, writes that "Having become accustomed to the rigors (and advantages) of location filming as a result of his wartime documentaries, Huston insisted that the studio allow him and his crew at least two months in Mexico on *Treasure*" (1965: 64).[13] Throughout his career, he filmed on location and claimed, with some pride, that "*The Treasure of the Sierra Madre* was one of the first American films made entirely on location outside the United States" (1980: 143).[14] In the context of the end of the Good Neighbor Policy films, *The Treasure of the Sierra Madre* stands out because it "was not the exotic Technicolor tourist fantasy of most movies, but instead a grim landscape of dusty oil towns, ramshackle villages, and scrub brush" (Sperber and Lax 1997: 337).[15] Along with John Ford's *The Fugitive* (1947),[16] also shot on location in Mexico, it is among the first post-war films to present a more critical view of Mexico. Robert Emmett Ginna, Jr. (2002) argues that "Huston's own knowledge of Mexico" makes *The Treasure of the Sierra Madre* "distinguished by the look and feel of the Mexican outback, and the Spanish spoken by the native actors heightens the realism of the film" (89).

The Treasure of the Sierra Madre begins on Valentine's Day, February 14, 1925, some months before his own first trip to Mexico.[17] Huston emphasizes the relationships between the three American treasure hunters by positioning them and repositioning them in several ways. As Stuart Kaminsky explains, "*Treasure* is a constant reorganization of the three partners in a single frame," a point emphasized by the repeated use of the word "partner" and by the "constant visual emphasis on the relationship of the three men" (1978: 53). Adding to this effect is the fact, noted by Naremore, that the film "has an oddly claustrophobic effect" because "Huston seems more interested in the physiognomy of his players and in the tight, three-figure compositions than in the environment itself" (1979: 21–22). Dobbs (Humphrey Bogart) and Curtin (Tim Holt), for example, are both down-and-out Americans in Tampico, who get jobs working in the oil fields for fellow American Pat McCormick (Barton MacLane), but they are cheated out of their money, and the two of them have to fight him in a bar to recover their wages. Howard (Walter Huston), by contrast, is an old hand, who knows Mexico, speaks Spanish, and is an experienced miner who warns them about the effects of gold.[18]

Midway through the film, after they have found the gold, Curtin goes into town for supplies, and their destinies separate in very definite ways. A fourth American, Cody (Bruce Bennett), follows Curtin back to their camp, and, when he ends up being shot by attacking bandits, it is Curtin who reads aloud the letter from Cody's wife. The letter is remarkable because it does not occur in the novel and because its description of the fruit harvest and the importance of family clearly echo Curtin's earlier dream of finding a place where he could experience the community and purpose that he did one summer picking fruit in the San Joaquin Valley. Howard suggests this connection at the end of the film when he gives his share of the proceeds from selling the hides and burros if Curtin will go find Cody's widow. Dobbs's fate, on the other hand, is connected with the bandit leader, Gold Hat (Alfonso Bedoya), who in Huston's film though not in the novel, appears three times in the film. He becomes the counterpart and nemesis to Dobbs; both are driven by greed. At the end of the film Gold Hat cuts Dobb's head off with a machete.[19] Again, by contrast, Howard's destiny calls him when the Indians ask him to cure a young boy who was saved from downing but cannot be revived. Huston films the curing session as though it were a religious event, with the boy on an altar and the congregation gathered around to witness the child's miraculous resurrection. When Howard leaves to rejoin the others, the Indians bring him back, and Howard has to trust the other two men to take care of his "goods," a carelessness about monetary wealth that he repeats at the end of the film, when he gives up his share and returns to an Edenic life with the Indians. His rejection of materialism and his acceptance of the simpler values of the natives is a significant choice, marking a clear contrast with Dobbs and Gold Hat. It is also a decision that has ramifications for other characters in Huston's films.

If these linked destinies amount to a somewhat different sorting out of characters than the infernal paradise model suggests, the role of the Mexican people is likewise more complicated. They are not simply the good Indians and the bad bandits. The Mexicans in Tampico, for example, tend to represent their specific occupations—the barber who cuts Dobbs's hair, the boy (Robert Blake) who sells him a lottery ticket, the young woman who smiles as she passes him on the street. The bandits, on the other hand, are images of the corruption brought about by an unscrupulous quest for wealth, and this is their primary connection to Dobbs, and, by extension, to people like McCormick who are in Mexico only to exploit its wealth. Gold Hat's mangled language, both in Spanish and English, is a signal of that same corruption.[20] His self-serving attempts at logic, when midway through the film he tries to coax Dobbs out of the rocks and later when he tries to talk Dobbs out of the burros and hides, make a stark contrast to the dispassionate logic of Cody. Most famously, when Gold Hat claims that he and his men are Federales looking for bandits, and Dobbs asks to see their badges, Gold Hat responds "Badges? We got no badges. We don't need badges. I don't have to show you any stinking badges." Cody negotiates in a very different way when he tries to convince them to include him as a partner and concedes quite dispassionately that their choices are to "kill me, run me off, or take me in with you as a partner," then proceeds to analyze each option.

A third group of Mexicans in the film are the citizens of the village near Durango where the miners buy their mules and where the bandits, after killing Dobbs, attempt to sell these same animals. As a group, the villagers are meticulous about records and legalities; as representations of law and order, they really provide the strongest contrast to the bandits. Huston is careful, for example, to show one of the men marking the brand beside the record of purchase for the mules. In the middle of the film, Cody explains to Curtin how these people are responsible for a very swift justice, and he describes the process exactly, to the point that his account is interrupted by the sound of the gunshots as the soldiers execute two bandits. At the end, the young boy who helped prepare the burros for sale is the one who alerts the village head that these are the same animals they sold to the gringos. Gold Hat incriminates himself when he does not know the brand, and again justice is swift. According to Huston, the entire episode was inspired by events on his trip from Acapulco to Mexico City (1980: 46–47). A final group is made up of the Indians who give Howard a place of distinction in their paradisiacal village and can easily be identified by the very different rhythm of their speech. They are soft-spoken and have an almost sing-song lilt in their language, markedly different from the way the citizens of Tampico or the villagers speak. They are over-polite and always concerned with the welfare of their guests or of those to whom they feel an obligation. Engell points out that "in both film and novel, the bandits serve a similar ideological function. They are the indigenous people ('Indians') tainted by the colonialist society's greed and institutionalized corruption. As a result they serve as foils for the primitively communalistic, unselfish Indians with whom Howard and (in the novel but not the film) Curtin go to live" (1993: 84).

Some fifteen years later, producer Ray Stark gave Huston a script for the Tennessee Williams play, *The Night of the Iguana*. Huston immediately changed the location from the commercialized tourist town of Acalpulco to the more remote Mismaloya, Indian land that had to be reached by boat from Puerto Vallarta. According to Madsen, Huston "felt the promontory better reflected the character's torment and the smothering atmosphere than Williams' stage Acapulco" (1980: 203).[21] Huston also thought the script Starke brought him "had too much sex and missed the real issue." For Huston, it was the story "Of a man, desperate and full of despair, at the end of his rope,"[22] the familiar notion of Mexico as refuge. He took Tennessee Williams' story of failure and turned it into a parable of salvation. Brill points out that, "Huston fundamentally changed the ending. The hopeful commitment of Shannon and Maxine (Ava Gardner) brightens Williams's more grudging version of a half-hearted promise from Shannon for a one-night stand" (1997: 93).[23] In addition, although the play begins with the arrival of Shannon and the tourists at Maxine's, Huston devotes the first third of the film to develop a background story for the Rev. T. Laurence Shannon (Richard Burton). In the opening scenes of the film, Shannon confronts his congregation over his seduction of a young Sunday school teacher. The film's credits appear over images of clouds passing over the moon and an iguana pictured against the sky with sea behind him. When the story resumes, the seeker of religious salvation is giving guided tours of Mexico and sitting outside a church drinking a beer which he hides in a hole in the wall when the group of American church women return. At this point Shannon seems cut off from his country and his religion, but, in fact, Huston develops a more significant transformation that Shannon must still undertake before he reaches the salvation that is his goal.

If Huston is seriously critical of anyone in the film, it is the American tourists. The women of the Baptist Women's College of Blowing Rock, Texas, are the foreigners who try to impose their map, their views and values, on Mexico. They are stereotypes of the bad tourist in Mexico. Other than the bitter Miss Judith Fellowes (Grayson Hall), only Miss Peebles, who is mainly characterized by suffering with "Montezuma's Revenge," really emerges from the anonymity of the group. In fact, the characters who are most assertive about their American identity — Charlotte Goodall (Sue Lyon), Hank Prosner (Skip Ward), and Miss Fellowes — become the antagonists in the film. Huston's sympathies clearly lie with Shannon, the recently widowed Maxine, and the spinster Hanna Jekles (Deborah Kerr), who has brought her grandfather, Nonno (Cyril Delevanti), the world's oldest poet, to the sea, "the cradle of life," as he calls it. Huston makes this spiritually and geographically displaced group the protagonists of the film.

Kaminsky says that Huston "fashioned a script eliminating the Nazis, turning Shannon into a comic character without eliminating his loneliness and doubt, and altering the character of Maxine so that she became not the source of evil but of salvation" (1978: 155). Some of that comedy is apparent in Huston's handling of the tourists. For example, as the women board the bus, Miss Fellowes has them sing "Happy Days are Here Again," a song about economic hard times, here made to apply to spiritual matters, significantly blurring the line between saving money and saving souls. When Shannon tells Hank to stop the bus on a bridge so the women can see "a moment of beauty, a fleeting glimpse into the lost world of innocence," children swimming in a shallow stream and women doing laundry on the rocky shore,[24] one of the tourists feels compelled to tell that her brother has a chain of Laundromats; "all he wants on his tombstone," she says, "is 'He liberated the women of Texas from the bondage of wash day.'" Soon, Miss Fellowes, no doubt inspired by the river view, begins a chorus of "Down in a River in an Itty, Bitty Poo." All of their associations neglect the reality of what they see out the window and reject Shannon's sentimental notion that the poor are somehow an image of innocence. They see things only in terms of their own cultural imperialism, an idea described by Dean MacCannell as "an effort of the international middle class to coordinate the differentiations of the world into a single ideology" and "intimately linked to its capacity to subordinate other peoples to its values, industry and future designs" (1976: 13). Another example occurs in the scene at the Hotel Paraiso, where they stop on the way to Puerto Vallarta. Charlotte slips into Shannon's bedroom to tell him that she loves him, so he does not need to worry about Miss Fellowes getting him fired, because her father has three Ford dealerships. Shannon mumbles, "Somehow I don't see a Ford in my future." Charlotte assures him that "Daddy" will give him a new church "in Thunderbird Heights." Meanwhile, Miss Fellowes is back in the room, lying in her bed apologizing to Charlotte for having slapped her earlier that day. When there is no response, she suddenly sits up, finds that Charlotte is not in her bed, instantly realizes where she must be, and comically runs down the hall to save her once again.

Charlotte, the blonde, blue-eyed pouty-lipped child-woman of the late 1950s and 1960s, a connection reinforced by casting Lyon, whose previous film was Stanley Kubrick's *Lolita* (1962), is the obvious focus for some of the comedy.[25] While she pursues Shannon, she is pursued by both Fellowes and Hank. Both she and Miss Fellowes retain strong connections to male authority figures back in the United States. Miss Fellowes's brother is a judge whom she has asked to investigate Shannon's past, and Charlotte often invokes her "Daddy." In a scene that Huston added to the play, Charlotte runs down to the beach cantina after Shannon rejects her and begins to dance provocatively with Maxine's houseboys. Huston shows the faces of the Mexican men and women at the tables, who are clearly embarrassed by the writhing girl. Suddenly, the Mexican bartender (Emilio Fernandez) lifts the arm of the ancient Victrola, stops the music, and tells her "we do not want our sons to know that young girls can be like you," and tells the boys to throw her out. Hank comes rushing up to save her, swinging wild punches, while the other tourists follow close behind. In this scene, Hank is the hero coming to the rescue of the fair damsel, or at least Huston makes it apparent that this is the way Hank understands his role in situation. He is completely unaware of how comic and ineffectual he really is. Interestingly, the scene clearly demonstrates the rejection of the tourists and all that they represent to the Mexicans. The boys easily dodge Hank's wild punches, but more than that, when the fight begins Fernandez puts on a 78 rpm recording of "Las Chiapanecas," also known as "The Mexican Clapping Song," and the boys dodge and punch to its rhythm. Meanwhile, the Mexicans seated at the tables clink their glasses together in time with the music. In effect, the Mexicans perform the communal role associated with the music and join to gently and comically expel the corrupting foreign influence. As Charlotte stands on the sidelines, shouting "Give it to 'em, Hank," Hank never lands a blow and finally falls to the sand after being twirled around until he is too dizzy to stand and becomes, at last, a fallen comic hero.

The real work of saving Shannon's soul takes place only after the American tourists have left, taking with them the values and conformity that contrast with the remaining protagonists. In the hands of the earthy widow, Maxine, and the spiritual spinster, Hannah, Shannon undergoes a rebirth, although he characterizes it as torture. Immediately after the tourists leave, Shannon runs to take "the long swim," his way of committing suicide, but Hannah and Maxine have the houseboys catch Shannon and tie him, cocoon-like, into a hammock. In the play, Shannon escapes from the hammock on his own, horrifies Hannah with the idea that the Mexicans torture, kill, and eat iguanas, and explains to Maxine that he is setting the animal lose.[26] Huston, instead, coordinates the series of epiphanies. Hanna releases Shannon, while Maxine gives up her swims with the houseboys, and Nonno completes his poem and dies, sitting in his wheelchair and facing the ocean. It is as though these characters could not reach clarification and completion until they have given up their past and, as Nonno's poem says, "Select a second place to dwell."

Huston based his last film set in Mexico on *Under the Volcano*, an almost unfilmable novel that nonetheless had attracted the interest of several writers and directors since its publication in 1947.[27] He met with producer Wieland Schulz-Keil and writer Guy Gallo in Puerto Vallarta to work on the script in April of 1983. According to Gallo, Huston believed the work was about "a man who suffers from dipsomania of the soul. ... the Consul's drunkness is a manner of perceiving the world. It's a response to all of it, not simply to his own personal disappointments but to a disappointment in Western civilization" (McCarthy 1984: 62–63).[28] Former British Consul Geoffrey Fermin (Albert Finney) stumbles through a day, beginning the evening of All Saints Day, November 1, 1938, before being shot to death by members of a right-wing militaristic faction at night on All Souls Day, November 2. For this film, Huston returns to a world that visually echoes the infernal elements of *The Treasure of the Sierra Madre*, adding vivid color and the permeating influence of the *Dia de los Muertos* (Day of the Dead), a celebration incorporating some uniquely Mexican attitudes toward death, which F. Gonzalez-Crussi characterizes as, "merrymaking and fatalistic impassiveness" (1993: 60). Huston's son, Danny, a recent London Film School graduate, shot the titles for the film, capturing images of the skeletal figures that abound in the Day of the Dead celebration and animating them by linking the images in an appropriately comic and macabre sequence (Grobel 2000: 239).[29]

Images of love and death play against each other throughout the film or join in unusual ways. The opening shots, for example, show Geoffrey, dressed in a tuxedo and dark glasses walking among families celebrating the Day of the Dead by leaving offerings at the graves of their loved ones. He passes a movie theatre where "Las Manos de Orlac" plays,[30] and Peter Lorre is saying

"I love you. You came to life for me." He arrives at a party, where his friend, Dr. Virgil (Ignacio Lopez Tarzo), asks about Geoffrey's absent wife, Yvonne (Jacqueline Bisset) and counsels, "no se puede vivir sin amar." The doctor convinces Geoffrey to go to a church and pray for his wife's return: "I'm dying without you. Come back to me, Yvonne." The next shot shows her on a bus coming to meet him. When she arrives, she recalls an appropriate Strauss song, "All Soul's Day," and a line from it, "return to me that I may hold you as once in May." Later in the day, Geoffrey, his brother, Hugh (Anthony Andrews), and Yvonne, pass by a performance of Don Juan Tenorio, a play in which the title character is being dragged to hell by devils until St. Inez appears to rescue him—a scene not in the novel. Later still, Hugh sings a song about men dying in the Spanish Civil War, and he afterwards jumps into the bullring to perform some veronicas before rejoining Geoffrey and Yvonne. The turning point in this sequence of situations occurs, however, when Yvonne suggests to Geoffrey that they leave Mexico and start over. Go off to Maine, live simply, "escape into the wilderness," replies Geoffrey, clearly anguished once more over the fact that Hugh and Yvonne had an affair. They could go further north each year, he says, getting to the North Pole, so when his brother visits he can "show proper Eskimo hospitality and give him my wife to bed down with during the cold northern night." Hugh asks what possesses him, and Geoffrey replies "Hell's my preference. I choose Hell. Hell is my natural habitat." Rejecting his last chance at salvation, Geoffrey crosses the bridge to the Farrolito, the one place he had been warned by Señora Gregoria (Katy Jurado) not to visit, and the place where he finds a satanic collection of oddities, perversions and death.[31]

Although the place is essentially a brothel that serves drinks, it is not sexuality or even drink that fuels the greatest sins. It is the contagion of the Nazis, who have infected the *sinarquistas*, a local semi-military group, responsible for a level of violence in Mexico that reflects the coming Second World War.[32] At first glance, the scene at the Farolito, where Geoffrey is shot to death by three Mexican men, conjures some of the same images present in the killing of Dobbs in *The Treasure of the Sierra Madre*, three Mexican men killing an obsessed foreigner. The point to make, however, is that these characters at the Farolito are clearly and deliberately established as not being representative of Mexico. An old woman, who appeared earlier in the film, tries to tell Geoffrey to leave the bar, since these men are "los malos." She says, "Estos hombres no son amigos de Mexico." They are exploiting Mexico and would put it at the mercy of the coming European conflict.

The sequence also concludes the sense of impending doom that pervades the film. Earlier, for example, Geoffrey challenged the German consul, asking whether the Nazis were financing these paramilitary groups. Geoffrey's half-brother, Hugh, is fresh from covering the prelude to World War II that was the Spanish Civil War. Hugh, Geoffrey, and Yvonne had also earlier seen a dying Indian lying at the feed of a magnificent white horse. As the man lies dying by the side of the road, it is a group of *sinarquistas* who ride up and announce that it is *prohibido* to do anything for the dying man. Climbing back on the bus, Hugh notices the *sinarchista* pin on the coat of one of the passengers who at that moment opens his hand to reveal a fistful of blood-stained money. At the Farolito, this same *sinarchista* is already in the bar when Geoffrey arrives. The other *sinarquistas* soon enter, one of them riding that same white horse. When Geoffrey stumbles outside and sees the white horse, which seems for a moment like the final symbol of innocence and salvation, he set in motion the final round of suspicion that leads to his own death and to Yvonne's tragic death as well, as she is drawn, once again to be near him and gets trampled by the white horse.

The death of both Fred C. Dobbs and of Geoffrey Fermin at the hand of a gang of Mexican men suggests some of the fundamental issues in Huston's recurring use of Mexico as subject and landscape, although the point is definitely not the obvious one that Mexico is somehow dangerous and that Mexicans are to be feared. In a number of Huston films, the obsessed outsider, caught in his own vices and foolishness, dies in a scene that emphasizes the inevitability of the action and, to some extent, the fact that the victim is complicit in his own death. That point seems as true of Daniel Dravot (Sean Connery) in *The Man Who Would Be King* (1975) as it is of the very different Rev. Samuel Sayer (Robert Morely) in *The African Queen* (1951). In terms of Huston's Mexico films, Fermin's death might easily recall the death of the Emperor Maximilian in *Juarez*, where again Mexicans, this time an official firing squad, execute a foreigner.

Expelling outsiders becomes a significant pattern in Huston's Mexico films, underscoring Huston's sympathies for the native against the foreigner. In the cases of Maximilian, Dobbs, and Geoffrey, the expulsion takes the form of an execution in each case by a group of Mexicans. In each case, the sense of being trapped by a series of bad choices culminates in one horrific and claustrophobic scene. In *Under the Volcano*, for example, the line of inevitability begins when Geoffrey questions the German consul about Germany's support of the *sinarchistas*, it flows to the appearance of the *sinarchista* organization that is present at the death of the Indian on the white horse, and then to the subsequent deaths of Geoffrey and Yvonne. The tourists, in *The Night of the Iguana*, are, of course, more mercifully expelled through the ritual of a mock battle set to music in what is ultimately a comic film. Huston also makes it a point to demonstrate that the more villainous executioners, the ones who seem to raise the issue of negative stereotypes, are specifically corruptions of the native temperament. Just as Gold Hat and his bandits are products of the corrupting influence of the commercial exploitation of Mexico, so the *sinarchistas* are presented as products of the corrupting foreign political influences. Conversely, those outsiders who reject the materialism that is most often associated with foreigners who would rob Mexico of its resources, are somehow elevated, as is the case with Curtin and Howard in *The Treasure of the Sierra Madre*, and, perhaps less obviously with Shannon and Maxine in *The Night of the Iguana*. Like Huston himself, they find that their time in Mexico yields something more valuable than treasures.

Notes

1. He won an Oscar for *The Life of Louis Pasteur* (1936) and received a Best Actor nomination the very next year for *The Life of Emile Zola* (1937).

2. In addition to Grobel's account of Huston's last years in Mexico, William Reed (2004) provides some interesting perspectives in his autobiographical *Escape to Paradise: A Mexican Odyssey*.

3. For the years leading up to the Good Neighbor Policy, see Delpar 1992. DeUsabel 1982 covers the period through 1951. Fein's essay, 2001, is a briefer treatment of some of the same issues from the point of view of the Mexican film industry. Pike 1995 provides a good overview.

4. Naremore (1998) suggests the complex set of factors when he writes that, "During the 1940s, noir characters visited Latin America more often than any other foreign locale, usually because they wanted to find relief from repression. This phenomenon was no doubt overdetermined by various geographic, political, and economic factors: California's proximity to Mexico; Hollywood's support for the Roosevelt government's 'Good Neighbor' policy the postwar topicality of stories about Nazi refugees in Argentina; the RKO-Rockerfeller interests in Western Hemisphere oil fields; the general importance of Latin American as an export market, and so on. But it also had to do with the purely symbolic value of south-of-the border settings, which provided a visual counterpoint to the Germanic lighting and modernist architecture in most varieties of dark cinema" (229–230).

5. The term comes from a Malcolm Lowry letter: "We can see it as the world itself, or the Garden of Eden, or both at once. Or we can see it as a kind of timeless symbol of the world on which we can place the Garden of Eden, the Tower of Babel and indeed anything else we please. It is paradisal: it is unquestionably infernal. It is, in fact, Mexico" (quoted in Alarecon 1997: 39).

6. Server (2006) writing about the filming of *The Night of the Iguana,* comments that "It was John Huston's delight to film under such circumstances, to bring a group of interesting people to an inhospitable, sweltering locale and watch the result. The actual stress and discomfort of the cast added to the reality of the film, and besides that it was fun to observe" (419).

7. According to Axel Madsen (1978), "John liked stories which arbitrarily threw together people for some purpose — idealistic, cynical, or downright criminal — and characters who, when they question their beliefs, come to realize how ambivalent things really are" (76). Lesley Brill (1997) adds that, "In virtually all his films, Huston chronicles his protagonists' attempts to discover, create, or recover themselves, to conceive and articulate their iden-

tities" (7), and John Engell (1993) says that Huston "believes that the individual must struggle with this place, this time, this world to achieve selfhood," an approach that he characterizes as "a kind of sentimental idealism" (92).

8. Pratt (1992) discusses this idea under the concept of the "contact zone," which she defines as "social spaces where disparate cultures met, clash, and grapple with each other, often in highly asymmetrical relations of domination and subordination" (4).

9. Owens (1998) distinguishes between a "territory" and a "frontier," so that a "frontier is always unstable, multidirectional, hybridized, characterized by heteroglossia, and indeterminate" (26).

10. Cortés (1997) calls *Viva Villa!* "violent, ludicrously macho"; García Riera (1987) in his *Mexico visto por el cine extranjero, Vol. 1, 1894/1940* (México, D. F. Ediciones Era, 212–220), describes Mexican reactions to the film, while Bruce-Novoa (2005), at the Thirtieth Annual Conference on Literature and Film at Florida State University, presented a credible defense of the 1934 film in a paper on the more recent Antonio Banderas film, *And Starring Pancho Villa as Himself* (2004).

11. It is important to note that the copy of the film available today is the reedited version of 1954. The dialogue quoted here is from the 1939 script published by Vanderwood (1983). See note 69 (255) on Maximilian's speech on Juarez's honest as justification for the execution and note 72 on the last line of the film.

12. Huston 1980: 138–148. According to Huston, Traven was a fan of Mexican actress Lupita Tovar, who was married to Kohner. Kohner, who represented Traven and Huston, was able to handle most of the preliminary negotiations. Producer Henry Blanke, who had given the *Juarez* assignment to Huston managed to get Warner Bros. to hold *The Treasure of the Sierra Madre* for Huston until after the war.

13. Nolan (1965) claims that, "In 1947 this was a revolutionary request" (64), but Henry King had shot *Captain from Castile* (1941) in Mexico, and Bogart's friend, producer Matt Hellinger, according to Sperber and Lax, 1997, had scheduled *The Naked City* (1948) "to be filmed not on a back lot but, in radical departure for Hollywood, on the streets of New York" (338). John Ford filmed *The Fugitive* in Mexico the year before, as Joseph McBride describes (439). Writing about *Kiss of Death* (1947), another on-location film, directed by Henry Hathaway, Agee, 1969, commented, "apparently if good technicians pay careful attention to the actual world, they can hardly help turning out a movie that is worth seeing; and the actors who have to play up to this world are greatly stimulated and improved by their surroundings" (275).

14. Comments about Huston's practice tend to hit the same theme. Regarding Huston's filming in Mismaloya, Ava Gardner (1990) writes, "Williams had set his play in Acapulco, but God forbid that John, whose motto clearly was, 'Do things the hard way whenever possible,' should ever consider filming there" (248). Server (2006), her most recent biographer, generalizes that "It was Huston's delight to film under such circumstances, to bring a group of interesting people to an inhospitable, sweltering locale and watch the result" (419). Bogart remarked about the on location shooting for *The Treasure of the Sierra Madre*, "If we could get to a location site without fording a couple of streams and walking thorough rattlesnake-infested areas in the scorching sun, then it wasn't quite right. We got to calling him 'Hard-Way Huston.'" (Grobel 289). Katherine Hepburn (1988), in *The Making of the African Queen or How I Went to Africa with Bogart, Bacall and Huston and Almost Lost My Mind*, gives a particularly charming account of the hardships on that filming.

15. Many of these Technicolor tourist fantasies were musical comedies featuring blonde American ingénues transplanted to exotic and musical Latin American countries and included such examples as Betty Grable in *Down Argentine Way* (1940), Alice Faye in both *That Night in Rio* (1941) and *Weekend in Havana* (1941), and Jane Powell in both *Holiday in Mexico* (1946) and *Nancy Goes to Mexico* (1950). Carmen Miranda made regular appearances in this genre, and she is in four of the five films listed.

16. Based on Graham Greene's *The Power and the Glory* (1940).

17. The script lists the date as August 5, 1924, which would have been Huston's eighteenth birthday. See Narremore 1979: 47.

18. Graebner (2004), in a psychoanalytic reading of the film, describes Howard's role in "a chilling experiment in economics and social behavior" (36).

19. The decision to add the three appearances of the bandits and to make Gold Hat Dobbs's nemesis came at the suggestion of B. Traven, who, according to Sperber and Lax (1997) mentioned in a letter to Huston "a sort of duel between Dobbs and Gold Hat" (342). Alphoso Bedoya's skills are a matter of some debate. Narremore (1979) calls him a "virtual amateur" (28), but Bacall (1979) says he is "a great Mexican actor" (153), and Madsen (1978) writes that he is "a matinee idol" (79). Nolan (1965) calls him "a nervous Mexican who was obviously approaching a state of panic" and suggests that Huston had to hypnotize him to get the performance (66). Huston (1980) himself says that "It was very hard to understand Bedoya's speech, and I had to work with him closely on each scene.... His was a bravura performance, but sometimes he just couldn't manage the English; the words wouldn't come" (146). Bedoya had been in some fifty Spanish language films, although mostly in small parts or as an extra, before working with Huston, and in 1946 he also appeared in Luis Buñuel's *Gran Casino* and in Emilio Fernandez's adaptation of John Steinbeck's novel *The Pearl*.

20. Pettit (1980), in *Images of the Mexican American in Fiction and Film*, characterizes his performance somewhat differently, writing that Bedoya "steals several scenes from Humphrey Bogart. Elevated to an existential hero who faces death with honor, Bedoya shows qualities of courage, wit, and pride foreign to the stock Hollywood bandido" (148–149).

21. Madsen 1978: 203. Gardner (1990) says it was just another example of Huston's impulse to "Do things the hard way whenever possible" (248).

22. From a letter Huston wrote to Starke, quoted by Grobel 2000 (530–531). Huston (1980) tells the story of making this film in his autobiography (306–312).

23. Server (2006) writes that "Huston believed the playwright's characterization of Maxine revealed his fear of women and, by the play's conclusion, his disdain for 'woman's place in the love life of a man.' Huston had a different view of the part, reshaped it in his script and cast accordingly. His Maxine was loveable, sexy, profane, funny, flawed, romantic. She was Ava" (413).

24. Brill (1997) comments that Shannon's remark "better describes the speaker's nostalgia for his own hopeful youth, however, than it does Mexican peasant society" (95).

25. Charlotte and Hank also bear some resemblance in this film to Sandra Dee and Troy Donahue, reigning teen movie idols of the time.

26. Williams (1964): "They're a delicacy. Taste like white meat of a chicken. At least the Mexicans think so. And also the kids, the Mexican kids, have a lot of fun with them, poking out their eyes with sticks and burning their tails with matches. You know? Fun? Like that?" (121).

27. Hagen (1991) reports that producer Wieland Schulz-Keil "read sixty-six completed screenplays ... dating from 1950 to August 1983" (142). Schulz-Keil summarizes the issues in an interview with Todd McCarthy (1984), "Cracking the Volcano" (60–63). Film reviewers, however, generally did not like the novel and did not feel much better about the film. Simon (1984) writes "Seldom have I found a famous novel so distasteful" (48); the film "is much more linear, logical, comprehensible than the book, but, alas, even more boring" (48–49). Kael (1985) says "I don't know whether the lack is in me or in the novel — I've never been able to get through it. But in the case of the new film version, directed by John Huston from a script by Guy Gallo, I'm reasonably sure the fault isn't mine (198).

28. See also Grobel 2000 (741).

29. Danny Huston also has film commentary on these scenes available in the DVD package from Criterion.

30. According to Hagen (1991), this film is actually "Karl Freund's remake of [Robert] Wiene's *The Hands of Orlac*, entitled *Mad Love*" (p. 141).

31. Joy Gould Boyum (1985), however, believes that the scene at El Farolito "is played not, as in the novel, for its emblematic value, but — what with Huston's much-publicized use of actual whores, a salacious dwarf, and the overstated performances of the Mexican villains — strictly for melodrama" (246).

32. *Sinarchistas* were a conservative group, founded in the 1930s in Mexico, who, according to Ramón Eduardo Ruiz, "trumpeted the virtues of Francisco Franco's Spain" (408).

The Discreet Charm of Huston and Buñuel
Notes on a Cinematic Odd Couple
NEIL SINYARD

John Huston and Luis Buñuel had a mutual admiration. When Buñuel's *Nazarin* (1958) opened in the United Kingdom at the Academy Cinema, London, it carried an endorsement from Huston on its poster: "Buñuel's film is a masterpiece which will live in film history." Similarly, in his autobiography *My Last Breath*, Buñuel spoke of his love of Huston's *The Treasure of the Sierra Madre* (1948) and described Huston as "a great director and a wonderfully warm person" (Buñuel 1983: 225). Although this admiration never extended to conscious influence — indeed Huston thought of Buñuel as one of those directors whose work is instantly recognizable whereas he saw no discernible pattern in his own output — their respective *oeuvres* have a number of distinctive similarities. They were roughly the same age and their lifetimes stretched the century: Huston, 1906–1987; Buñuel, 1900–1983. While their careers differed in terms of language and industrial contexts they were notably personal filmmakers who worked in popular genres and both continued to work until the ends of their lives — when they both achieved significant artistic success. They shared a relish for the absurd (which Huston said he inherited from his father and uncle); were each bored by realism; and found refuge in startling imagery. Both men explored a world of odd conjunctions between human and animal, and satirized religious fanaticism and the vanity of human wishes. Finally, both men lived for extended periods of time as exiles in Mexico, a setting that was to prove crucial to a number of their films.

In the work of each there is often an idiosyncratic mixture of horror and comedy. In Huston, it is at its most forbidding perhaps in *Wise Blood* (1979), which charts the grisly progress of a man whose denial of Christ's existence paradoxically has the fervor of an authentic believer. One can see it also in Marlon Brando's horse ride in *Reflections in a Golden Eye* (1967), which is pathetic but also pitiable and terrifying; and also in the scene in *Night of the Iguana* (1964), when Richard Burton's disbarred clergyman is so disconcerted by Sue Lyon's advances that he starts walking nervously around a room in his bare feet and treading unnoticed on broken glass that is strewn over the floor. It is a painful yet comical moment that crystallizes the man's mental agitation, and the film's theme of spiritual masochism is close to that of *Nazarin* (1959).

The following observations, then, are offered as jottings about two great artists with an affinity of style and attitude. They were individualists and owed nothing to each other but there were occasionally certain resemblances; and they fascinate partly because, to my knowledge, these resemblances have never been commented on by other critics and partly because it is one way (amongst many) of evoking Huston's distinctiveness from his Hollywood peers. No other Hollywood director of his generation who came through the studio system had this Buñuelian dimension. Billy Wilder might have come nearest but only perhaps in the blackly comic *Ace in the Hole* (1951), with its desert setting, its religious and sacrilegious imagery, and its evocation of a barren community that reminds one of the film that Buñuel had made a year earlier, *Los Olvidados* (1950). In Huston the similarities are much more pervasive, in terms of tone (impish irreverence), imagery (as we shall see, particularly of animal and natural life) and theme (the recurrence of religion, impossible love, and the dream state of some of their characters). I will illustrate these connections in a loose series of headings.

Artistic Formation

Huston and Buñuel had formative experiences as young men which were to affect and influence their subsequent artistic outlook. Buñuel discovered surrealism, which he said gave him the sense that man was not free, and the tenets of surrealism (its tone of anarchy, its fascination with the world of dreams, its love of the irrational) were to provide the basis of his work until the end of his life. In Huston's case, an important event of his young artistic life occurred when his mother returned from Europe and smuggled into America a banned copy of James Joyce's *Ulysses*, the Bible of the modern cinema, as Eisenstein was to call it, for its montage-like manipulation of mental time and space and its stream of consciousness experimentation. The work of James Joyce became a life-long passion, tempting Huston towards Ireland and perhaps towards affinities between literature and film, and culminating in his final work, that most sensitive and graceful of film adaptations, *The Dead* (1987), from the Joyce short story.

There are other incidental links, some more conscious than others.

Buñuel's cameraman on many of his greatest films (*Los Olvidados, El* [1953], *Nazarin* and *The Exterminating Angel* among others) was Gabriel Figueroa, and I have no doubt that when Huston chose Figueroa as cameraman for two of his films set in Mexico, *The Night of the Iguana* and *Under the Volcano* (1984), he cast him consciously because of the Buñuel association. Incidentally, it is also interesting to note that Buñuel was asked several times to film *Under the Volcano* and he resisted, wondering how you could film the inside of someone's head. Appropriately, it was Huston — his nearest American equivalent — who took up the challenge and made a superb job of it. In both directors Mexico was not just a background but a dynamic setting that is an important correlative to the action: an "infernal paradise" in Malcolm Lowry's phrase, or, as in *The Treasure of the Sierra Madre* and *Los Olvidados*, a hostile environment that can reduce its inhabitants to a spiritual and psychological aridity. Both directors made their own desert island films, Buñuel with *The Adventures of Robinson Crusoe* (1954), Huston with *Heaven Knows, Mr Allison* (1957), where a hard-won idyll will eventually be subject to invasion.

Buñuel became the director of dream sequences *par excellence* — one need only think of *The Exterminating Angel* or *The Discreet Charm of the Bourgeoisie* (1972) or the extraordinary mother-meat dream sequence in *Los Olvidados*, which Pauline Kael thought the best oneiric passage in all movies. Indeed, Buñuel would tell his producers not to worry if his films came in a little on the short side: he could always include a dream sequence. Man is not a rational being, Buñuel thought, but prey to impulses below the level of consciousness that he can barely control and understand (the rape and murder of the girl in his 1964 version of *Diary of a Chambermaid* is so horrific because it seems so unprepared, almost an afterthought of malevolence that sweeps over the character in a manner both unbidden and irresistible). How logical, or analogical, it is then that Huston will make a film about the century's supreme analyst and interpreter of dreams, the subconscious and the irrational, Sigmund Freud in *Freud: The Secret Passion* (1962), a film perhaps even trailed by his remarkable war documentary *Let There Be Light* (1945) where Huston sees how psychoanalysis and hypnosis can release tormented individuals from trauma. Huston's characters are often dreamers but they tend to dream by daylight and eventually have to wake up (or perish) in the harsh light of reality — like Stacey Keach's over-the-hill boxer in *Fat City* (1972), fantasizing about the future in dingy bars before stepping out into the harsh sunlight of the outside world, or the anachronistic cowboys in *The Misfits* (1960) who are left 'ropin' a dream" as one of them puts it. Buñuel rejected *Under the Volcano* as suitable material for the cinema, because he thought the inner conflicts of the characters could not be translated into effective images, but for Huston, in many of his films, that is precisely the challenge he relishes. He constructs external action as correlatives to, or metaphors for, internal conflict. His adventure films, like *The Treasure of the Sierra Madre*, or *The African Queen* (1951) or *The Man Who Would Be King* (1975), are grand physical spectacles on the surface but in each case the real journey is into the interior of personality.

A final point here might suggest that both men share a strange relationship with their respective national cinemas. Buñuel is identified as closely with Spanish cinema as Bergman with Swedish, and yet he made very few films in Spain, working mainly in Mexico and France and actually taking out Mexican citizenship in 1949. Equally, Huston is identified with a certain golden era of Hollywood cinema, but he made a considerable number of films outside America and was for a long time in virtual exile as a result of his disgust with the McCarthy era witch-hunts, finally ending up as an Irish citizen. The films of Buñuel and Huston raise complicated questions about conceptions of national cinema, its characteristics and its representatives.

Professional and Artistic Outlooks

It would be fair to say that Huston and Buñuel had an attitude to life verging on the sardonic. They looked at life from a jaunty angle. In Buñuel's *Phantom of Liberty* (1974), a personal favorite of the director's, Jean-Claude Brialy at one stage starts moving some objects on a tidily arranged mantelpiece because, he says, he is "bored with symmetry." It is a gesture remarkably echoed by Carol Burnett's alcoholic floozie in Huston's *Annie* (1982), when she notices a picture hanging straight and adjusts it so it looks awry and thereby implicitly corresponds more closely to how she sees things. Both directors see weirdness in the everyday and love the unexpected, or the crooked or out-of-line, whether it is found in the secretary's crooked teeth in *Annie* or in Lewis Calhern's apologia for the criminals he has to deal with as a lawyer ("Crime is only a left-handed form of human endeavour"). Both have a fascination for eccentric characterization: you feel there is a screw loose in all their major characters, which is precisely what endears them to their directors (which American director other than Huston could have made a film of *Wise Blood*?). No two directors had a greater love for so-called "ugly" faces in film: after all, it was Huston who made Bogart — a most unconventional leading man — a star.

In his book *Underworld USA*, Colin McArthur draws attention to the unusual features for the time of *The Maltese Falcon* (1941) which, he says, is characterized by "physical grotesques and sexual aberration" (86). That description could stand as a virtual definition of a typical Buñuel movie: think of the beggars in *Viridiana*, the terrifying blind man in *Los Olvidados*, the sexual fantasies of *Belle de Jour* (1967). Buñuel's characters invariably give way to obsession, like the religious hero of *El* suddenly thrown by the sight of a woman's leg, that is the first stage of his subsequent erotic delirium; but so too do Huston's characters, like the master-criminal (Sam Jaffe) in *The Asphalt Jungle*, minutes away from freedom but still unable to tear himself away from looking at the gyrating body of the young woman as she dances to the music of the juke-box.

"Sport is my term for Buñuel's bold manipulation of human frailties," wrote Parker Tyler once in connection with *Viridiana* (*Classics of the Foreign Film* 245). He was referring more to a tone than an attitude perhaps, but there is a feeling in both in a lot of their films that they are not taking things entirely seriously (whilst also not necessarily making a comedy). Simone Signoret fell out with Buñuel on *Evil Eden* (1956) because she thought he didn't really care about what he was doing; and when James Mason expressed some misgivings during the making of *The Mackintosh Man* (1973), Huston told him cheerfully that it might well turn out to be the worst film he ever made. Buñuel was an inspired artist sometimes, but he was anything but a perfectionist, never, he claimed, spending more than four days in the editing room and happily giving way to whim more than rationality when the mood takes him- like the moment in *Phantom of Liberty*, when Fernando Rey exits a scene after picking up a sack and putting it on his back: for no reason, Buñuel said, other than the fact that the moment seemed to work better with the sack than without it. There is the same love of irrationality in Huston's *Beat the Devil* (1954), a lark in which only half the cast seem to be in on the joke: as Harry Kurnitz remarked at the time, it was one of those films where, no matter where you came in on the running time, you still felt you'd missed half of the picture. A sense of sport and even carelessness pervades *Sinful Davey* (1968) or *Escape to Victory* (1981), neither being films where you would remotely suspect that the director at the helm was capable of greatness. Some of Buñuel's '50s films are like that. In both, you sense that film can be an art; but it can also be an expedient way of paying off your gambling debts. But the ostensible off-handedness is also a way of rejecting the facile fade-out, the obligatory happy ending, the over-tidy resolution that encourages complacency through the sense it gives of order being restored and all being right with the world. Buñuel's strategy for countering that is with the studied anti-climax that pulls the rug of moral certainty from under your feet, as in his greatest films, like *El, Nazarin, Viridiana* and *The Discreet Charm of the Bourgeoisie.*

Huston's equivalent for that is the unsettling sound of hollow laughter, which is the true climax of masterpieces like *The Maltese Falcon* and *The Treasure of the Sierra Madre*, as characters find their life's obsession blowing up in their faces at the point of achievement and realizing that their dearest dream has been scattered to the wind. So what did they care about?

Personal Themes and Motifs

"So much for auteurs," said Buñuel in his autobiography (131), reflecting on his experience during his early days in Hollywood of watching Josef von Sternberg at work, where Sternberg seemed to leave most of the placing of the camera to his set designers. Huston relished the role of chameleon more than that of auteur, and in his autobiography, said he could see no more consistency in his choice of films than he could in his choice of wives, whom he described as "a mixed bag — a schoolgirl; a gentlewoman; a motion-picture actress; a ballerina; and a crocodile." Of course it might be precisely this inconsistency, this unpredictability, which was the defining characteristic of Huston's life and films: a fatal attraction towards the impulsive, the impetuous, the irrational. Nevertheless, I would like to suggest three themes or motifs that regularly recur in Huston's films and, intriguingly, they do so also in Buñuel.

In his chapter on Huston in his book, *Underworld USA*, Colin McArthur gave short shrift to a review of *Reflections in a Golden Eye* in Issue 15 of *Movie* magazine, where Paul Mayersberg attempted to suggest some recurrent thematic concerns in Huston's films. However, I think Mayersberg made some valid points. One he noted was the recurrence of impossible love relationships where characters seem to fall for their polar opposites and which therefore means they are destined to fail: *Heaven Knows, Mr Allison, The Barbarian and the Geisha* (1958), even perhaps *The African Queen*, where the happy ending seems so unlikely that one is tempted to regard it as dream or wish-fulfilment. Certainly it is difficult to think of any of Huston's films where the conventional Hollywood happy ending, with its ideological thrust of the replication of the heterosexual couple, really applies. And Buñuel is very similar, expressing the theme as it relates to *L'Age D'Or* (1930), for example, as follows: "the irresistible force that thrusts two people together and ... the impossibility of their ever becoming one" (*My Last Breath* 117).

Another preoccupation which they share — and express their skepticism about in different ways — is religion. Buñuel's preoccupation with the theme hardly needs amplifying: it is at the core of nearly all of his major works. "Thank God I'm an atheist," he would say. For him, religious belief is invariably equated either with an ingenuous and impossible idealism that is doomed for disappointment, as in *Nazarin* and *Viridiana* (1960); or with an emotional inhibition that, if released, will explode with destructive force, as in *El*; or with the kind of disappointed experience of Robinson Crusoe on his island, where, unlike in the novel, belief in God is no help and his reciting of Psalm 23 comes back as a hollow echo. Religious zealots abound in Huston also, but they too are a frustrated, craven crew: the defrocked priest in *Night of the Iguana*, the crazed hero of *Wise Blood* with his founding of the "Church without Jesus Christ." He enjoys it when his reprobate heroes rub noses with the reverent and cause sparks to fly, as in *The African Queen* and *Heaven Knows, Mr Allison*. It is fascinating that both men reach in their films for an image of ultimate blasphemy, seen in Huston's whole conception of *Moby Dick* (1956) as being about a man who shook his fist at God; and unforgettably in Buñuel's *Viridiana* when he freezes an image of the beggars' party into a parody of Leonardo Da Vinci's "The Last Supper." Both men write thoughtfully about their religious non-beliefs in their respective autobiographies, and it is Huston who will be foolhardy enough to make a film of *The Bible ... in the Beginning* (1966), with himself as Noah, and then will have the audacity to play a villain of Biblical proportions in Roman Polanski's *Chinatown* (1974), where he will also be laying claim to valuable water supply, and who will have the resonant name of Noah Cross.

There could have been no more ideal role for Huston than Noah, for, like Buñuel, his films are full of animal imagery, and the animal kingdom plays an extraordinarily important part in his films, sometimes being at the absolute core of the films' meaning. This would take too long to list definitively: think only of the afore-mentioned white mare in *Reflections in a Golden Eye*; the white whale in *Moby Dick*; the tethered iguana in *Night of the Iguana*; the bloodhound that solves the crime in *The List of Adrian Messenger* (1963). In *The Misfits*, the soul-searing shattering of illusions that concludes the film is set inexorably in motion by a mustang round-up. In *The Roots of Heaven* (1958), a European in Africa declares war on the slaughtering of elephants; and the shooting of them becomes an Orwellian metaphor for imperialist and tyrannical human tendencies.

Huston made ecological and psychological dramas about the humanity of animals and the bestiality of humans. Buñuel's films are similarly teeming with animal imagery. A cat leaps on a rat at the conclusion of the nephew's seduction of the maid in *Viridiana*. The last shot of *Phantom of Liberty* is a close-up of an ostrich's head, an impudent and scornful comment on humanity's capacity to bury its head in the sand. One of the most beautiful moments in all of Buñuel occurs at the end of *The Adventures of Robinson Crusoe* when Crusoe, pulling away from the shore, hears a dog barking on the island. It is a reminiscence of the faithful dog, Rex, whom he encountered on his first day and whom he later had to bury; it suggests that Crusoe's heart has remained on the island and that he is mystically being called back. Arguably the single most beautiful shot in Huston's work also includes the animal world and is the last shot of *The Asphalt Jungle* when the farm-horses tenderly circle the fatally wounded body of Sterling Hayden's gangster at the point when his dream at returning to the farm he remembered from his boyhood is finally realized but only as his life expires.

I want finally, then, to look at two sequences from Buñuel and Huston, from what I think are their greatest films — respectively, *Viridiana* and *The Treasure of the Sierra Madre*— and where animal imagery is used with the utmost eloquence to express what is at the heart of the films.

Two Sequences

The sequence in *Viridiana* occurs midway through the film. Staying at her uncle's after his suicide and having renounced her vows when he claimed (wrongly) to have ravished her, the ex-nun Viridiana (Silvia Pinal) has taken in some beggars to give them shelter and food: are they genuinely grateful or just exploiting her kindness? Meanwhile her cousin (Francisco Rabal) is trying to modernize the estate. One day he sees a man driving a cart with a dog tethered to it: the dog is panting and struggling to keep pace. Dismayed by what he sees as an act of cruelty, the nephew buys the dog from its owner. As he takes possession of it, another cart passes in the opposite direction, with a dog tethered to its undercarriage.

Is this Buñuel's comment on charity? You might free one sufferer, but there is always another to take his place. Raymond Durgnat saw this incident as a Marxist critique of the parable of the Good Samaritan. Yet the scene can be interpreted in a number of different ways and seems in some way exemplary of the film's ambiguities. The nephew does at least free one animal, which is surely better than doing nothing, and it could be argued that his practical response to cruelty or injustice is preferable to that of Viridiana whose mission is the vague and impractical one of saving souls. On the other hand, one could suggest that, whereas the nephew is offering only a temporary materialist solution and that there is no implication that the driver of the cart who has accepted the money for the dog will feel any reluctance to repeat the cruelty at the next opportunity, Viridiana's goal is spiritual and psychological and might thus effect deep and permanent change. Who is right? That potent little scene with the dog, and the teasing questions it poses about charity — about how it is given, and to whom, and with what effect —

is a wonderfully succinct parable that goes to the heart of the film's irony and ambiguity.

There is an equally rich scene in the midsection of *The Treasure of the Sierra Madre*, where the theme is greed rather than charity but where again an animal plays a significant role in carrying much of the scene's symbolic meaning. The three prospectors, Dobbs (Humphrey Bogart), Curtin (Tim Holt) and the old man (Walter Huston), have struck gold, but have agreed to share it out daily, with each looking after his own share. This is partly in response to Dobbs's innate distrust. The feeling increases when he comes across Curtin about to lift a rock under which Dobbs's money is hidden. In fact, Curtin has had no idea that this was where Dobbs stashed his gold: he has actually seen a gila monster sneak under the rock and has been about to lure it out in order to kill it. However, when he tells Dobbs this, Dobbs does not believe him, seems ready to shoot him, and has to be forcibly restrained. Only then does Curtin roll back the rock to reveal the animal squatting on Dobbs's money-bag.

It is one of the most potent images in the film. The monster is not next to the bag but is actually on it, as if asserting ownership: this bag is mine. The monster and the money-bag are as one, and could be said to correspond metaphorically to the murderous suspicions Dobbs is harboring: the monster under the rock is a manifestation of the demons inside his skull. While the creature is palpably real (as is the dog in *Viridiana*) it seems also, in an unforced way, to be instantly symbolic, representing the sneaky and dangerous malevolence that gold can inspire. When Curtin taunts Dobbs by suggesting he put his hand under the rock if he does not believe him, he adds a description of what the monster does: it gets hold of a man and will not let go until it kills him. By association, it becomes a description of what this obsession with gold is doing to Dobbs's soul. Dobbs and the monster become synonymous: Curtin's reference to "chopping it in half" is, in retrospect, an unwitting premonition of the fate in store for Dobbs at the hands of the Mexican bandits. The whole incident is a superb dramatization of Dobbs's paranoia, which leads him to strike out wildly and unwisely when he feels someone is trying to put one over on him or that his manhood is being threatened. At the end of the sequence when he has been proved wrong and he feels totally humiliated, he goes over and squats on a rock, as if he were the gila monster on his money bag: a personification of defensive venom.

Conclusion

In sketching connections and correspondences in the work of Huston and Buñuel, I am aware that there are many other examples I could have cited and that each example would demand nuanced consideration of detail and context: material for a book perhaps more than an article. There is no intention of trying in any way to undermine the individuality of both artists who have their own distinctive styles and preoccupations: Buñuel remains the cinema's supreme scourge of the bourgeoisie, Huston its consummate ironist of human aspiration. Nevertheless, it is striking that although Buñuel has often been compared with Hitchcock (no doubt because of the Dali connection and the susceptibility of the works of both to Freudian interpretation), the comparison with Huston has tended to elude critical commentary and yet seems to me far more extensive in its potential application. Even in terms of personality, they seem much closer: instinctive anti-authoritarians who took nothing at face value, were skeptical of conventional morality, and were endlessly curious about the more mysterious pockets of human behavior. Do such comparisons matter? I would have thought they might be of interest to the dedicated cineaste. Does it change one's perception of Huston as a director? I think it could. It might not make him a better director in the eyes of some critics (not me), who will continue to see him as a more pretentious, less perceptive Howard Hawks. It might, however, make him appear a different one from that of common critical perception: not this shambling, sub–Hemingway personality with a penchant for over-reaching himself with adaptations of literary classics too heavy for the screen, but an altogether more variegated and subversive soul, with a touch of the surreal and with a twinkle in the eye.

Huston and the American South
The Night of the Iguana *and* Wise Blood
GARY D. RHODES

John Huston had a curious relationship with the American South. He was born in Missouri, a U.S. state with historical and cultural ties to the South, but also a state that sits geographically in the American Midwest. In some interviews, he fondly mentioned his birthplace Nevada, Missouri, but he never actually lived there. When he spoke its name, he pronounced it "Nevah-duh," as in the U.S. state, whereas its townspeople generally pronounce it "Ne-vay-duh."

Throughout his life, Huston possessed a strong admiration for Southern writers and playwrights, but he rarely addressed the South in his own films. When, for example, he tackled the Civil War, he did so through the eyes of a Northern writer, filming Stephen Crane's *The Red Badge of Courage* in 1951. Later, when Huston adapted Southern author Carson McCullers, he selected her novel *Reflections in a Golden Eye*. The resulting 1967 film featured actors like Marlon Brando affecting Southern accents; however, *Reflections* explored issues like adultery and repressed homosexuality that were not uniquely Southern. Nor did the film investigate the South pictorially, due in part to the fact that it was shot in Italy and in part to the unique colour scheme adopted by Huston and cinematographer Ossie Morris.

All that said, Huston did choose to make two films that dealt directly with Southern issues and themes. The first came in his 1964 adaptation of Tennessee Williams's play *The Night of the Iguana*, starring Richard Burton, Ava Gardner, Deborah Kerr, and Sue Lyon. The second was another adaptation, of Flannery O'Connor's novel *Wise Blood* (1979), starring Brad Dourif, Dan Shor, Harry Dean Stanton, Amy Wright, and Ned Beatty.

Grouping Huston films together is a difficult task of course. He remained proud of the fact that he could not "see any continuity" in his work; "what's remarkable," he added, "is how different the pictures are, one from another" (Huston 1980: 5). To be sure, *The Night of the Iguana* and *Wise Blood* are individually unique in many respects. For example, Huston recalled that the "tangled web of relationships among the ... principals" in *Iguana* generated more interest among the press than any of his other films (Huston 1980: 309). And *Wise Blood* is credited onscreen as *John Huston's Wise Blood*, making it the only one of his films to feature his name in the title. But the two films share important similarities as they present Southern characters who cannot mentally escape the South. The Bible Belt tightens around them, dictating their actions and their rebellions. Their lead characters look beyond Protestant Christianity within their increasingly modern worlds for salvation, but technology cannot save them; redemption can only be found in coming to grips with the past and by embracing the South. Together, *The Night of the Iguana* and *Wise Blood* form a coherent vision of the South and of redemption, a vision that stems as much from Huston as from the authors he adapted.

The Fantastic and the Realistic

In *The Night of the Iguana*, the Reverend T. Lawrence Shannon (Richard Burton) leads guided bus tours of Mexico; he has taken this job after having been literally locked out of his Virginia church due to "fornication and conduct unbecoming a minister of the gospel." In *Wise Blood*, Hazel Motes returns to Georgia after completing his military service in an unnamed war; he quickly leaves his small hometown for the nearby city of Taulkinham. Both of these men are from the South, and both are the sons of clergymen. The two characters struggle with their Protestant backgrounds. Shannon keeps his crucifix and collar nearby, and he continues to pray. Even though the tour group causing his troubles hail from a Southern Baptist college, their tacit leader Judith Fellowes (Grayson Hall) offers him no forgiveness when she tries to have him fired. In return, Shannon calls her the "Witch of Endor," in reference to the woman who predicts Saul's downfall in the Hebrew Bible. In exasperation, he claims that the "whole trip's been hoodooed," a subtle reference to a form of Southern paganism that includes elements of Christianity. The word connects to Shannon's final Virginia sermon, at which he suggests his flock have twisted Christianity into something else. He claims that they have "turned [their] backs on the god of love and compassion and invented for [themselves] this cruel, senile, delinquent who blames the world and all he created for his own faults."

Similarly, Hazel Motes lives under the burden of his Christian upbringing. He has flashbacks that reveal his father (played by Huston) was a fire-and-brimstone Southern preacher. He purchases clothes that, along with his intense expression, cause him to be mistaken for a preacher. In an act of rebellion, Motes creates the "Church of Christ Without Christ," taking to the streets with his sacrilegious message. But the shrunken mummy that Enoch Emory (Dan Shor) presents as the church's "new Jesus" enrages Motes. His adventures also uncover the hypocrisy of his fellow man. For example, Motes has little faith in Emory's alleged "wise blood" that grants special knowledge. He is disheartened when he learns that the blind preacher Asa Hawks (Harry Dean Stanton) isn't really blind, and is incensed when Onnie Jay Holy (aka Hoover Shoats, played by Ned Beatty) forms his own "Church of Christ Without Christ" just to earn some quick money.

In addition to their religious strife, Shannon and Motes experience troubles with three women who pull them in different directions. They both encounter a "loose" woman; for Shannon it is Maxine Faulk (Ava Gardner), and for Motes it is Leora Watts (played by an uncredited actress). They both encounter women coded as "moral"; for Shannon it is the artist Hannah Jelkes (Deborah Kerr), and for Motes it is his landlady (Mary Neil Santacroce). Thirdly, Shannon and Motes become entangled with very young women. The underage Charlotte (Sue Lyon) vigorously pursues Shannon during the bus tour, declaring her love and her intention to marry him. She even visits him in his hotel room in the middle of the night; when Ms. Fellowes catches them, Shannon's job is thrown into jeopardy. Later, Shannon calls Charlotte a "Jezebel." Similarly, the under-aged Sabbath Lily (Amy Wright) gives Motes the "fast eye" at their first meeting. Later, she tempts him while they are in the woods ("Ain't my feet white though?"), and then sleeps with him at their boarding house.

"We live on two levels," Shannon declares in *Iguana*. "The fantastic and the realistic are the two levels in which we live." Coincidentally, those two words — "fantastic" and "realistic" — are the very words that Michel Ciment used to describe *Wise Blood* when interviewing John Huston in 1984 (Long 2001: 138). In their experiences with religion and with women, Shannon and Motes oscillate between the fantastic and the realistic levels. The same could be said of their struggle with the past.

"I Remember the Night and the 'Tennessee Waltz'"

Time and remembrance mark the bizarre incidents that Shannon and Motes experience. As both a place and a culture, the South exists in a clear narrative of time: Antebellum, and Reconstruction. "Once I was lost, now I am found." Nevertheless, a closer examination reveals how the past continues to encroach on the present. The South will rise again, even if merely to raise a Confederate flag (as can be seen at the opening of *Wise Blood*) or to contaminate modern minds with racism, the ongoing legacy of slavery. Conversely, a powerful nostalgia can arise for the Old South, an allegedly idyllic place removed from the ills of modernity.

Shannon and Motes exist on a linear timeline, but they cannot escape the past and struggle with the modern world. They are caught in a liminal state, grappling with the realistic and fantastic. For example, Shannon has been inactive in the church "for all but one year since [he] was ordained," the impression being that many years have passed since that time. However, the film makes absolutely no effort to age Richard Burton's appearance from Shannon's final Virginia sermon to the date of the bus tour. The passage of time appears not to have passed.

Another example of the past-present conflict occurs when Ms. Fellowes leads the tour group in a chorus of "Happy Days Are Here Again," a song that immediately invokes an earlier age. After Franklin D. Roosevelt used the tune during his 1932 presidential campaign, it became forever linked with the Democratic party. The historic ties between the South and the Democratic party run deep, ranging from the Civil War to the production of *Iguana*. The connection was strong enough to have given rise to the phrase the "Solid South," a block of Southern states that once voted overwhelmingly for the Democrats. The camera captures the women from the Baptist college singing the old song in a single shot that tracks down the aisle of the bus; the camera stops on Shannon, who responds with a single word: "fantastic."

In attempting to tame the modern world, Shannon wrests control of the tour first by driving to the unplanned destination of Mismaloya and then by stealing the bus's distributor head. The distributor head represents the fact he remains in charge even as Ms. Fellowes and the other tourists undermine him, but his control over technology is short-lived. The remote hotel in Mismaloya has a newly installed phone, which allows Fellowes to call her brother, a Texas judge. Then Charlotte steals the distributor head from Shannon's pocket.

Even though Shannon is unable to fend off modernity, he understands its ills, telling Hannah: "We've poisoned [God's] atmosphere. We've slaughtered his creatures of the wild, we've polluted his rivers. We've even taken God's noblest creation, man, and brainwashed him into becoming our own product, not God's: packed, stacked, and canned." Happy days are not here again, certainly not for Shannon.

The world of Hazel Motes is also plagued with the problem of time. For example, a series of black-and-white still photographs at the beginning of *Wise Blood* evokes the rural South of the early twentieth century. After numerous images of this kind, Huston shows a photo of a 1970s Dairy Queen fast food restaurant; though shot in black-and-white, it is — given that the film was made in the seventies — a "modern" image. But underneath the restaurant sign is a religious message, which echoes the messages seen in the other photographs. The Dairy Queen photograph is not then a sign of linear time progression, but rather the overlap of the old and new.

After the credits, *Wise Blood*'s visuals continue to suggest a conflation of time periods. The trees are largely bereft of leaves, but occasional spots of green signal the shift from one season to another. The Motes family home still stands, but it is empty and its windows are boarded. Motes travels to the modern city, but does so on a train powered by an old steam engine. He drives a 1950s car, while other automobiles on the street are from the 1970s. He wears a suit and hat that evoke an earlier era, but he uses a clip-on necktie. Most telling of all is a scene where Motes preaches on the street in the aged downtown. His activity mimics street preachers of earlier generations, but just over his shoulder is a sign for "contact lenses"; along with commenting on his inability to see clearly (as does his nickname "Haze"), the sign shows the intrusion of modernity into his world.

The coexistence of the past and present are also apparent in the belief systems of film's characters. The repeated use of the word "nigger" invokes the ugly history of racism in the South, while the monkeys at the zoo and the live appearance of "Gonga" the gorilla subtly introduce ideas of science and evolution. But Motes does not turn to those answers, nor does he appreciate the Arab mummy that Enoch steals. The mummy is "foreign," which is something he does not want his new "Church of Christ Without Christ" to be. After all, as Motes tells his landlady, his new church is still Protestant. Severing ties to Christianity proves impossible; Christ is present in his church through his stated absence.

Flashback sequences also vividly bring Motes's past to life. He recalls his early contact with sin: he saw a topless woman at a carnival sideshow wriggling her legs suggestively while lying in a coffin. But impure thoughts lead to darkness and damnation; he also remembers his father's powerful sermons. At one of them, Motes urinated in his trousers out of shame and guilt. "Time does fly, don't it?" a lady on the train tells Motes. But even if the years have flown by, the flashbacks have a powerful effect on Motes when he is both awake and asleep.

Perhaps the past encroaching on the present is best represented in *Wise Blood* by Alex North's use of the 1947 Redd Stewart — Pee Wee King song "The Tennessee Waltz." Though heard instrumentally, the famous lyrics speak to a past that cannot be lost or forgotten. North's repeated use of the song underscores that theme, as does his choice of instrumentation. Initially played on rustic banjo, "The Tennessee Waltz" is later performed on a modern synthesizer. This is no mere aural progression of time, however, because even after the synthesizer is heard, the banjo returns.

"Everything is just the same as before," Motes's landlady reassures him in the final act of *Wise Blood*. But everything is not the same as before for Motes or Shannon. Motes's father lies in a graveyard in his hometown, and Shannon is no longer in Virginia. Time has passed, even if the past has not passed. Change, rather than stasis, causes a conflict between the new and old, between the fantastic and the realistic. Motes and Shannon fight these problems, and the battleground is the American South.

"Back Home My Daddy's Got Three Ford Agencies"

The American South is a place that remains difficult to define geographically. From the Antebellum period, there is the "Old South," which refers to states like Virginia, North and South Carolina, Georgia, Delaware, and even Maryland. There is the "Deep South," which includes states like Mississippi, Georgia, Alabama, Arkansas, South Carolina, Louisiana, and Florida. And there were the eleven Confederate States of America, which included Tennessee and even rump governments in Missouri and Kentucky. Aside from specific states, there is also Dixie, a term which stems from Northerner Daniel Emmett's 1859 song "I Wish I Was in Dixie" and which is as much about a state of mind as about a particular U.S. state or states.

Shannon's Virginia is indeed a place that becomes a state of mind. Huston begins the film in Virginia for a brief, pre-credits scene of Shannon at his Episcopal church. As pictured in widescreen black-and-white, it is a sad, mournful place. The camera tilts down the building to reveal a sign that mentions Shannon's name and his sermon on "The Spirit of Truth." The surroundings are grey; rain pours out of the heavens.

Inside the church Shannon is seen in his robe and collar. Huston pictures him from a low angle as he delivers some lines in a sermon that quickly falters. He attempts to justify his sins by mentioning a "collateral branch" of his family tree. They were men who went into the wilderness, outside of the civilized South. They were men "with men's hearts.... They knew hunger, and they fed their appetites, appetites that I have inherited." As the credits begin, the film's setting leaves Virginia. The title sequence features an Iguana, representing the primordial, the uncivilized, the "foreign." In those respects, it is not dissimilar to the shrunken mummy and gorilla that appear years later in *Wise Blood*.

Following the credits, Huston again has his camera tilt down a church.

"The skies above are clear again," as the lyrics of "Happy Days Are Here Again" will ironically suggest. No rain falls, and the sun shines. This time there is no sign announcing Shannon's sermon. Instead the camera stops on a man with a newspaper covering his face. It is the Reverend Shannon sans collar in sunny Mexico, waiting in the outdoors as his tour group explores the church. The image identifies what happened in Virginia: he was locked out of his church, and he has left the South for a place he calls a "jungle."

But the South will not leave Shannon. He no longer wears his clergyman's collar, but he keeps it with him at all times; he also vigorously maintains that — even if he was forced to leave his church — he was not technically defrocked. Indeed, his position with Blake's Tours promotes the fact that travellers will see Mexico under the care of the "Reverend T. Lawrence Shannon." And though he claims "there's nothing lower than Blake's Tours," Shannon desperately clings to his job. Thanks to it, he maintains a connection to his religion and to the South, as he acts as guide to Southern tourists.

The job also tethers him to the South via his employer's location in Texas. Texas is of course a state that — like Missouri — has curious ties to the South. Its history, culture, and geographical size mean that it also has ties to Mexico and to the Southwest. However, Texas was a member of the Confederacy, to which it provided soldiers and supplies during the Civil War. And Texas, especially East, Central, and North Texas, continues to share much of what might be considered Southern culture.

Shannon also has his memories of the South. When he sits alone in his hotel room in Mismaloya, Shannon's mind turns to the state he had to leave. He recites lyrics from Stephen Foster, the famed Southern songwriter of the nineteenth century. "Nelly was a lady, last night she died, Toll the bell for lovely Nell." But even his happy nostalgia is interrupted, as the Southern girl Charlotte has already quietly entered his room. Much to his chagrin, she completes the lyric, "My dark Virginny bride."

Physically of course Shannon has been in Mexico for some years. He has made friends with Maxine Faulk and her late husband Fred. He relishes the chance to watch the Mexicans on the beach, stopping the tour bus to examine what he calls the "lost world of innocence." It is a world that harkens back to that "collateral branch" of his family, a world that exists apart from the South and apart from religious judgment and guilt. It is the world of Tierra Caliente, the "hot land" where Ms. Fellowes claims he had an inappropriate *tête-à-tête* with Charlotte. It is a world he enters again briefly when swimming with Charlotte after the bus's tire goes flat. But it is also a world in which he cannot stay. Ms. Fellowes angrily calls him back to the beach and chastises him for being a "beast."

Most of the time Shannon's life in Mexico is hardly tranquil. When he drives the bus, he does so with reckless abandon. The surroundings seem to engulf him, with the foliage reflecting so heavily on the windshield that it is difficult to see his face through the glass. The vehicle's gears squeak, and its passengers shake. In the only oblique angle seen in the film, the tour group's luggage — a sign of their Southern homes — falls from the baggage compartment. The shakes of the bus mimic Shannon's condition. Threatened with the loss of his job and all that it means, he drifts into what he calls a "panic." Charlotte offers to get him a job at one of her father's Ford agencies, but he knows that Fords aren't in his future. The border he has crossed is less a geographic border than the "border of sanity."

Shannon attempts to write his bishop a letter of "complete capitulation" in order to return to his Southern church. Here Huston captures Shannon from a high angle image, the inverse of how he appeared during his sermon at the beginning of the film. He struggles with the letter, wadding up a sheet of paper in frustration. A long, dark shadow is cast behind him. As Hannah learns, Shannon has difficulty wearing his clergyman's collar, but he also has difficulty trying to force the crucifix from around his neck.

Like the Reverend Shannon, Hazel Motes is unable escape the South. "The Tennessee Waltz" plays on the film's soundtrack as he returns to the state of Georgia, the conflation of the two states suggesting that *Wise Blood* occurs less in an individual city or state than in "The South." After the black-and-white photos shown during the opening credits, the film begins at a country crossroads, evoking Southern folklore that suggests such a place is the meeting ground of two realms. It is the realistic and the fantastic, the old and the new, the righteous path and the road to ruin.

Motes has returned to the South after completing his military service. Without any hesitation, he throws away his soldier's uniform and purchases a civilian suit in his hometown. "I'm going where I'm going," he declares, planning to wear the new suit to the city. But Motes does not cut all ties with his small hometown. He does not sell his family's home or land; in fact, he places a note on the "shiffer-robe" in their house that threatens to kill anyone who steals it.

The city of Taulkinham, Georgia (a city which doesn't actually exist) appears rather small and typical of most Southern towns. Old buildings, ranging from the local bank to the movie theatre, constitute the downtown. It also features the requisite museum and large statue of a prominent Southerner. Deteriorating wooden homes combine to form aging neighbourhoods. Taulkinham may not be Motes's hometown, but it is still The South. As Motes walks the city streets, Huston pictures him in lengthy tracking shots that anchor him firmly to the environment.

Walking soon leads to driving. Motes hopes the old automobile he purchases will be his "house"; it represents movement and the possibility of escape. But car problems keep him from leaving the city on a number of occasions. The first results in the car momentarily stalled on the highway, with an impatient trucker calling his "house" an "outhouse." Motes drives back to Taulkinham, telling the trucker that he doesn't "have to run away from anything." Later, the car won't restart in the countryside; thanks to help from a mechanic, Motes and Sabbath are finally able to drive back to Taulkinham. Then, during his third attempt to leave, a policeman kicks the car into a pond. Once again on foot, Motes walks back to the city he has tried to leave. Escape seems impossible.

As Asa Hawks has told him, "You can't run away from Jesus." To be sure, even when Motes preaches the "Church of Christ Without Christ," a neon sign towers over him announcing "Jesus Cares." Eventually, Motes embraces the South and the religion he has spurned. Rather than writing a letter of capitulation, Motes blinds himself with lime, achieving in fact what Hawks has only faked. He walks with rocks in his shoes, and he literally fences himself in to the Bible Belt by wrapping barbed wire around his chest. When policemen return him to his landlady's home at the end of the film, he is seen through the bars on her window. As his father said in a flashback "Jesus will have you in the end." And in the end, Motes—like the Reverend T. Lawrence Shannon—remains tied to the South.

"Man's Inhumanity to God"

John Huston's films frequently adapted pre-existing literary works: short stories, stage plays, and novels. Even years before his directorial debut with Dashiell Hammett's *The Maltese Falcon* in 1941, he struggled on the script for a 1932 version of Poe's *The Murders in the Rue Morgue*. Decade after decade, a hallmark of Huston's filmmaking was a sincere attempt to be faithful to his literary source material. For example, when bringing *The Red Badge of Courage* to the screen, Huston began the film with an image of Stephen Crane's book opening. After speaking about Crane and his book, documentary-style voiceover explains that the film's narration is taken from "the book itself."

A case could be made that Huston's adaptations of *The Night of the Iguana* and *Wise Blood* are largely faithful to the works of Tennessee Williams and Flannery O'Connor. And it is true that some of the similarities found between the two films stem directly from the Williams play and O'Connor novel. However, taken together, the two films represent a coherent vision of the American South and its emphasis on Protestant Christianity. The vision — even if unintended — is largely Huston's, in part because he chose to direct both films. But there is also the crucial fact that Huston actively participated in changing the endings of both stories.

For *The Night of the Iguana*, Huston reworked the conclusion even while Tennessee Williams was present on the set. As biographer Lawrence Grobel wrote,

> Williams had a far more cynical attitude toward his characters than John wanted to give them, especially at the end. Williams saw the Reverend Shannon as a broken man, destroyed finally by Maxine. But John saw the Ava Gardner character as providing Shannon with his salvation. It seemed more fitting and uplifting [Grobel 1989: 536].

Huston told at least one interviewer that Tennessee Williams maintained that Huston's ending was a "mistake" (Long 2001: 160). Mistake or not, Huston's ending offers Shannon redemption.

When Nonno (Cyril Delevanti) reads his final poem in *Iguana*, he speaks of a "second history" and a "second place to dwell," words that suggest redemption. But the words do not mean an escape from the past. After all, Hannah claims, "Home is between two people, not a place." Even at the end of the film, Shannon remains tied to the South. He gives Hannah his crucifix to pawn, but she will send him the pawn ticket so that he can retrieve it later. Moreover, Shannon's choice to stay with Maxine also speaks to his past. She is herself a Southerner, a point underscored both by Ava Gardner's Southern accent (which she hardly restrains in the film), as well as by her dialogue (from "cotton-picking" to "ya'll") that uses Southern words and phrases.

In *Wise Blood*, Motes quietly leaves the landlady's home after she proposes marriage; policemen later find him lying in some mud. In the O'Connor novel, Motes dies in the police car on the way back to landlady. But Huston offers a different, or at least more open-ended conclusion. In the film, when the police find Motes, they comment on the fact he is still alive; indeed, Motes speaks briefly. Huston does not include the drive in the police car. He shifts immediately to the landlady's home, where she says, "Well, Mr. Motes. I see you've come home. I knew you'd be back, and I've been waiting for you." He does not respond to her, but no dialogue or visual cue suggests he is definitely dead. If Huston has not changed O'Connor's ending, he has at least obscured it. As a result, Huston grants Motes the possibility of redemption on earth or in death.

Redemption, despite what Shannon calls "Man's inhumanity to God." Thanks to Huston, Shannon and Motes have access to salvation, even if they have been blasphemous. But salvation does not come in the form of escape;

the South has too tight a grip. After all, Maxine Faulk is a Southerner, and Motes's landlady has bars on her windows. The Bible Belt will not be unbuckled; even taking the boy out of the country cannot take the country out of the boy. In *The Night of the Iguana* and *Wise Blood*, Huston permits redemption and forgiveness, but he does not allow forgetfulness.

Re-Visioning the Western
Landscape and Gender in The Misfits
GEORGIANA BANITA

For John Huston, part of the attraction of embarking on a film project was the novelty of the idea in relation to his past work. There was little he would ever balk at, be it theme or genre, especially if the making of the film itself presented an extra perk of excitement and human entertainment. As a result of this adventurous spirit, there is little that his films share, and even less that they owe to standard film archetypes or strict genres, either in narrative or technique. When he claimed, five years before the release of *The Misfits* (1961), that he preferred to bend genres rather than retain a consistent style in all his films but would never dare to put his brand on the Western (Long 2001: 17), it was still too early for him to foresee that he would eventually tamper even with this "noble convention": *The Misfits* brings all the patterns of the Western into disarray. The so-called "cinema novel" supplied by Arthur Miller as shooting script and Huston's adaptation occasion a unique blend of genre revision and redefinition of gender roles, by inscribing sexual difference and tension into the majestic imagery of the Western's visual canon, spanning a bridge between the spectacle of its scenery and the visual display of femininity.

Huston's *The Misfits* traces the gradual evolution from naivete to empowerment of Roslyn (Marilyn Monroe) — arguably the most sympathetic female character in Miller's work (Savran 1992: 45). This heroine, who steps out into the center so forcefully in the film, is reconceived as a larger-than-life figure through Monroe's Method[1] acting style, which Huston's preference for self-performance in his actors surely encouraged. An abundance of feminine and masculine signifiers layers the film, while the subtle, projecting gaze of the camera eroticizes the Western landscapes at the same time as it undermines the male codes that dominate them and stresses the indeterminacy or codelessness of the female mode best reflected by the "negative signifier" of the desert. Notions of deprivation, death, and decay support this extension of the natural environment of barren Nevada to the emotional and sensual lives of characters that never really convince as human beings but instead give voice to isolated, self-justifying principles, blinded to what lies outside their mental perimeters. This absence of sympathy in fact permeates the whole film. Even the viewer is immunized against all compassion by the solipsistic tone of the dialogue and the disconnection between words and image: the overstated Western myth versus an only superficial interest in landscape, the prurient camera focused on Monroe's physical assets versus the deceived (and deceiving) child she is supposed to personify. Although initially the female figure and the wilderness seem to appeal to the male in equal measure and thereby create a competitive tension, the woman and the desert share a more discrete connection highlighted by the film's ending and the interpretations it fosters with regard to the winners and losers of this game, where sexual and generic codes alternately trump one another. Even after the end of the last scene there can be no consensus as to who has emerged victorious,[2] as to the moral motives of the people involved, or whether Roslyn's "gift of life" has any chance of materializing through the act of giving birth. I will argue that in Huston's interpretation of the script a subversive side of the female character, skillfully rendered by Monroe as a self-conscious impersonation of herself, nuances the overstressed femininity of Miller's Roslyn and brings to light the role of the desert in the film's revision of gender roles.

This chapter will analyze Roslyn's image in the various stages of the plot and the connection the female character bears to the setting of the film by focusing on three dimensions of her screen persona. A sense of the absence that the female character is supposed to fill dominates the first part of the film (initial encounter), revealing in the second episode the complexity of Roslyn's "strangeness"—which never wears off although she seems to adapt herself to her human and natural surroundings. The final act (the mustanging scene) relieves the tension by bringing about the paroxysm of femininity—as a frantic breakdown more typical of a film noir than a Western—exposing the void at the core of the male fantasy of Woman and the true emptiness of the Western myth, literally disintegrated into the dust of arid salt flats. The connection between femininity and landscape in this film is partly based on the non-canonical role both the woman and the desert play in *The Misfits*, or in other words, Roslyn and the salt flats in Reno collectively destabilize the underlying Western pattern of the film. It is debatable, however, whether we are dealing with a Western at all, partly because the script—Miller jokingly referred to it as an "Eastern Western" (Miller 1987: 462)—exceeds the average intellectual requirements of the genre. Also, in Huston's hands, the film seems more of a star vehicle than a genre piece:

the cursory examination of the characters' lives offered by the threadbare plot fits perfectly with the screen personae of the lead actors. In keeping with the ideal of masculinity described in *The Misfits*, Huston himself spent his life perfecting the macho role canonized before him by Ernest Hemingway, some of whose works (*The Killers, To Have and Have Not*) he adapted for the screen. Bearing this in mind, it comes as no surprise that he should have found the nostalgic cowboys in Miller's piece very appealing, just as it cannot be an accident that *The Misfits* recounts "an adventure shared by desperate men that finally came to nothing" (Viertel 1992: 389–90). But this nothing may in the end be the woman, a volatile, improbable creature of nondescript affability, whose personal lack of direction and substance is mirrored by the desert scenery and overall emotional dryness of the film. This aridity reflects Huston's anti-decorative, terse style, whose flatness and monotony achieved their best realization in such films as *The Asphalt Jungle* (1950) and *Fat City* (1972). Although virtually every word in the film was written by Arthur Miller, and the plot is entirely his, the volatile set of tensions among characters and the consistent avoidance of any controlling point of view are hallmarks of Huston's own distinctive style. This essay pursues the assumption that *The Misfits*' most intriguing feature, namely the canny juxtaposition of gender and landscape tropes, has its origin in an underlying pattern of visual and verbal estrangement on which uneasy and expedient liaisons are based, a style of deliberately alienated acquaintanceship for which Huston's title *We Were Strangers* (1949) can serve as an overarching catchphrase (Jameson 1980: 30). It is through Huston's anti-heroic reading of Miller's play as well as in his female casting choice that the original script exceeds its intensely personal tensions and achieves a rare harmonious balance of its aesthetic components (camera, soundtrack, cinematography) but also a fascinating misbalance in terms of gender compartmentalization. Much of the film's impetus lies within Miller's own plot and the complex performance by Marilyn Monroe, who may have delivered in this film the most mature interpretation of her career. For purposes of brevity and coherence, I will restrict myself to those aspects of the film's multiple scenarios that appear to signal clearly the establishment of a Western aesthetic which is then questioned and unsettled by the interference of a feminine element with the film's heroic masculinity, both in terms of content and cinematic style. My intention is to single out the desert landscapes of the film as the key entry point of this transgression.

Absences

The feminine symbolism of the film is rooted in a dialectical interplay of presence and absence, life and death. Gay (Clark Gable), Perce (Montgomery Clift), and Guido (Eli Wallach) all refer to idyllic times in their lives marked by the presence of women whose disappearance — through betrayal or misfortune — seems to have stopped time in its tracks and roped the men to their pasts like wild mustangs to tires. In a conscious bid to cure their bereavement, all three men come together in the "leave-it-state" of Nevada, paradoxically looking for fulfillment by giving everything up:

> The leave-it state. You want to gamble your money, leave it here. A wife to get rid of? Get rid of her here. Extra atom bomb you don't need? Just blow it up here and nobody will mind in the slightest. The slogan of Nevada is, "Anything goes, but don't complain if it went!" [Miller 1981: 30].

The conflict between masculine and feminine forces revolves around the sense of a home, which the modern-day cowboys simultaneously long for and reject, in that they act according to a work ethic that posits an essential homelessness, but turn to women and to a feminized landscape as emotional stand-ins for actual domesticity. Home itself becomes a gendered concept sustained by the presence or conspicuous absence of a woman: for Perce home is the place where his mother lives and a number that he dials long-distance; for Guido home is equal to his wife, whose death leaves the house uninhabitable and in ruins. Sexual and geographical "belonging"[3] coincide to the point where the promiscuity that slowly envelops the characters — all three men wooing Roslyn and causing friction among themselves — is reflected in the house that no longer seems to have a definite owner anymore ("Roslyn: 'This is my house ... or Guido's.' She laughs. 'Well, it's a house anyway.'") The woman herself is situated strangely at the border between wilderness and society: she is both the desert and the heliotrope garden, both "God's country" (as Nevada's vast expanses are described) and something to be pursued and ultimately possessed. Herself a sad woman, Roslyn lifts the mood of those around her by making them oblivious to their own faults and giving them more credit than they would ever give themselves. Her energy rises out of her idealizations of the others. Thanks to her nurturing ways — she sobs over Perce's recklessness and head injuries at the rodeo — she has the three men nestling in the hollow of her hand within minutes. Lover to Gay, mother to Perce, surrogate wife to Guido, Roslyn becomes a flexible, almost empty signifier. She never appears alone in a scene and is often the subject of comments by the other characters, as if she were absent, set apart or somewhat in need of interpreters between herself and her audience. Half the things we find out about Roslyn — both informative and descriptive — are revealed by others. Often shown as a mirror reflection and always through other people's eyes, Roslyn hardly seems to exist at all: she is a projection made up of imagined, unfitting fragments (as in the opening credits) of the male imagination.

Although she is present in the room, she stands for everything that the men lack, so the persona that her sensitive actions suggest is overshadowed by her role as a poultice to their wounds. Aided by the biographical undertones inscribed into the narrative by Miller, Huston plays with Monroe's screen image, occasionally even breaking the continuity of her portrayal. Nonetheless Huston ultimately creates a fantasy almost as clichéd and idealized as the West itself. In his attempt to objectify a pre-existing idol called Marilyn, Huston underestimates Monroe's original contribution to the part and ignores (or forgets) her lack of regard for her public image, which she took every opportunity to dismantle, this film being no exception. While Monroe admittedly cherished her work with Huston and treasured her part in *The Asphalt Jungle* as one of her most successful, by the time she slipped into the character of Roslyn she was already going to great lengths to shed an itchy public persona that never allowed her anything beyond sexual allure. Even though Huston's Roslyn still owes more to such stereotypical portraiture than the actress would have preferred, Monroe manages to sublimate her charm into an atmospheric sensibility that goes beyond Huston's earlier seductresses. While women are indispensable to most of Huston's films, most of these productions are explicitly hostile to them, with the occasional exception of strong-willed women, who remain, however, at a wanton or infantile stage — Monroe's own nubile mistress Angela Phinlay (in *The Asphalt Jungle*) among them. Like Anjelica Huston's Greta in Huston's last film *The Dead*, Roslyn displays a certain sadness or a secret which makes her privy to the dark unknown spaces or hidden corners of domesticity, thus exceeding the confines of Huston's earlier female stock characters.

The Double Woman

Roslyn exudes a femininity that we cannot account for and certainly cannot place in the otherwise bland sexual environment of the film. The lines she is given are those of a poorly educated, half-witted angel waif, who lavishes undiscerning sympathy (but never any passion) onto her companions. Despite her tender body language, there is a restraint about Roslyn that the men detect and refer to as a blank behind her friendly image:

> GUIDO: "She's kind of hard to figure out, y'know? One minute she looks dumb and brand new. Like a kid. But maybe he caught her knocking around, huh?" [Miller 1981: 25].
> ROSLYN, almost laughing: "You think I'm crazy?"
> GAY: "Uh-uh. I just look that way 'cause I can't make you out."
> ROSLYN: "Why?"
> GAY: "I don't know" [Miller 1981: 39].

PERCE: "I can't place you, floatin' around like this. You belong to Gay?"
[Miller 1981: 75].

The script forces Monroe to wear her sex on her sleeve, readily available to the men as if it were all part of a game subsumed to the condescending joy of the cowboys taking the child-woman out to "have some fun." They protect, court, and dismiss her all at the same time. They fall under the spell of her extremely feminine charm, marked by defenselessness and the courage to take life on unarmed. But from behind this imposed mask, Monroe is occasionally aflame with rebellion against the passivity and intellectual helplessness of her character, who must resort to a fit instead of logical arguments to prevent the massacre of the horses.[4] While she is forced to exaggerate her childlike innocence and joie de vivre, Monroe still undermines the masculine fantasy that she is supposed to incarnate by subtly revealing her true sexuality and independence. She is much more in control of the situation than she seems to be and she quickly learns to manipulate the men by mirroring their behavior: independence and subdued desire towards Gay, motherly tenderness towards Perce, sympathy for Guido's sensitive nature, bruised by misfortune and war trauma. Not only does she put on her femininity as masquerade,[5] but she adapts it to what the various masculine egos demand from her. The schematic nature of Miller's characters makes it easy to relate the patterns of masculine demand and feminine response in the cowboys and Roslyn, especially since Huston does little to elaborate on the script material, still faithful to his proclaimed intention not to interpret and put his stamp on the original text. The air of formula in Roslyn's way of speaking also betrays the contrived nature of her "act": she often uses stock phrases expected from housewives eager to please their husbands (such as "Let's have some fun today" to Gay and an insistent "Smile!" to Guido while dancing.)

Monroe makes ample use of the screen persona she acquired through her previous performances, dexterously enacting this image once more and deconstructing it in the process. She gives a camp performance of what the Western code emulates as ultimate femininity: naiveté and naturalness. Roslyn is naïve to the point of stubborn defiance, and natural in mirroring the vast emptiness of the landscapes that surround her. She flaunts the signifiers of femininity in a subtle performance that has come a long way from her earlier camp persona. In her attempt to seem helpless and innocent, Monroe's mannerisms (such as looking confused and asking questions) become so extreme as to resemble the performance of a female impersonator. In turn the men display equally degenerate Western masculine codes, derailed by technology and confused about the opposite sex, which they simultaneously despise and covet. It may well be that Miller never intended the masculine code of independence to be so radically undermined in the film. To him, the cowboys represent "the last really free Americans" (Nolan 1965: 180), and the original cowboys on whom the short story was based most probably were.[6] But the nagging question throughout the film is whether "freedom" was properly understood,[7] which is hardly surprising for a director as intensely preoccupied with the question of heroism and failure as Huston was (Rubin 1993: 137). The final answer is negative, whereby the masculine (and canonical Western) codes are replaced by the non-assertive dominance of the woman. Many inconsistencies can be invoked to support the thesis that the film developed well beyond Miller's initial ideas, due to Huston's encouragement of his actors' natural proclivities and a certain carelessness with Miller's stereotypes which gives the film its depth and subtlety. Miller's concise account of the plot in his autobiography reads as follows:

> Three men who cannot locate a home for themselves and, for something to do, capture wild horses to be butchered for canned dog food; and a woman as homeless as they, but whose intact sense of life's sacredness suggests a meaning for existence" [Miller 1987: 438–9].

Although she herself becomes the home the cowboys lack, Roslyn is even more disillusioned than they are and very secularized by her down-to-earth demeanor—a significant deviation from Miller's intent and one that owes a lot to Marilyn Monroe's performance.

The reception of Monroe in *The Misfits* is affected by the catalogue of her previous appearances, most of which are blurred by fantasy into a streamlined version of the "American doll," as she was packaged and marketed by the studios. "I carry Marilyn Monroe around me like an albatross" (Weatherby 1976: 45), the actress conceded: yet in *The Misfits* she carries it easily and exploits her image. The role of Roslyn is impinged on by Cherie in *Bus Stop* (1956) and The Girl in *The Seven Year Itch* (1955),[8] but the influence also applies in reverse, in that Roslyn sheds new light on Marilyn's earlier roles: it seems that the male imagination has made an ideal of what can be possessed in Monroe (i.e., her sexuality), whereas a less palpable aspect, the psychological bundle of her motivations, is ignored, since it becomes threatening in its volatility. According to Laura Mulvey, the cinematic gaze reveals a contradictory image of the woman, both as object of desire and source of anxiety (Mulvey 1989). Miller's polysemic image of Roslyn—seconded by Huston's attentive camera that belabors both the woman's body and her melancholic absent-mindedness—tries to do justice to this duality, but is armed with the same preconceptions of male fantasy. Short on substance but strong on suggestiveness, Monroe's role as Roslyn may not be that different from her earlier work: as in many of her roles, her mental abilities are embryonic when compared to her sexual appeal. Or as Theresa Russell impersonating Marilyn Monroe in Nicolas Roeg's film *Insignificance* (1985) bitterly remarks on her generic persona, she is "a what not a who," a figment of men's imaginations. The script's biographical references to Monroe seem designed to fit the ubiquitous stereotype: Roslyn is a mannerist hologram of the successful showgirl Marilyn Monroe, both in content (she is a beautiful former stripper with a broken marriage and a mother who "was not there") and presentation. The camera often lingers on her attractive body usually filtered through a male perspective: Gay watches her rear fondled by the saddle as they ride together, the same rear that almost caused a scandal with Monroe's nude *Playboy* photo shoot. Her breasts stand out in several scenes, one of which was eventually deleted shortly before the film's release, despite the actress's wish to keep it in as it would have perked up the otherwise anemic passion of her morning-after scene with Clark Gable. She may well have been right, but her attempt to defend the full display of her sexuality may have been too strong an act of rebellion for mainstream expectations, since a bared breast would have destroyed Roslyn's infantile sex doll persona.

As for the woman herself, she seems to be at a turning point in her life. With her arrival in Reno Roslyn enters a liberated state, also shown in her sartorial behavior in the course of the film. From the black dress cut typically low to the virginal cherries on a figure-hugging white dress and finally the jeans and white shirt at the end, she goes through an emotional transformation that brings her closer to her goal of locating her own identity, as Isabelle (Thelma Ritter) implies in her question to a shining Roslyn coming out of the house she now shares with Gay: "Darling, you look so lovely! You found yourself, haven't you?" While she tries to untie the knots of the relationships in which the others are entangled—she suggests bringing Isabelle back together with a former cowboy lover—Roslyn becomes the bone of contention in a three-way tug of war between the men over her sexual favors, all the more enticing for their ambiguity. Roslyn oscillates between energetic effervescence and dreamy somnambulism, reminiscent of the "inspired, narcissistic moods" that Cecil Beaton captured in his photo shoots with the actress. It is only in her final moment of crisis that we glimpse the energies churning within her and a certain tension that was contained in earlier scenes. Less a character and more of a sensitive organ, she acts as a moral and emotional barometer in the film as she carefully watches everyone, her eye a projection screen for her emotions. She also listens intently, slowly taking everyone in. This personality and aura is meant to contrast with the sterility of the cowboys' existence. However, her overstated gestures, her rituals of femininity, the verve and abandon she displays in everything she does erase all credibility of the character and paint a fantasy woman as devoid of life as the wilderness whose myth she was supposed to reanimate. Isabelle shares the impractical sentimentality of Roslyn, but a certain serenity coupled with resignation in the face of disillusion make her believable as a character yet totally invisible to the men around her. The cowboys' quixotic search for the frontier[9] can be extended to a similarly delusional quest for an ineffable femininity that they proceed to elevate to an ideal that they promptly gun down. Roslyn's gentle and melancholy nature seduces them, but her happiness remains insecure, always in suspense, liable to be smashed the next minute. Moreover, everything that is creative in her is used to fructify the male: she turns Gay's life on its head by re-channeling the emotions he used to squander in frivolous affairs, inspires Guido to dance and banishes memories of his late wife, then prompts Perce to release the mustangs as a gesture of his newly regained sense of morality and respect for freedom other than his own. Gay regards her with a mixture of ill-concealed contempt and fear and attempts to resist her influence, although, like the rabbit Gay tries to execute for consuming his lettuce, Roslyn does not know any better: she cannot compromise and accept that societal norms have "turned it around"—i.e., made traditional killing-for-a-living into an ethical sin — her protectiveness towards all living things is instinctive. What she completely lacks is self-protection, which makes her past experience seem unreal: no-one can imagine Roslyn going through a marriage with a man whom she never loved enough to bear him children, and finally through a divorce caused by something resembling lack of communication. Or perhaps this is the mystery of a character who cannot be made to feel sorry for her husband, but cringes at the thought that a rabbit might get killed. This is far from being the only contradiction concerning the heroine. Roslyn reintegrates the men into an almost familial world, a bond that she soon afterward rejects by turning a deaf ear to Gay's requests for marriage and children:

> He grasps her hand, preventing her from leaving. "Would you ever want a kid? With me?"
> She pats his hand, starting to turn away. "Let me just turn the lights off in the car." He raises up, struggling to get on his feet. "Whyn't you sleep now..." "I don't wanna sleep now!" He staggers to his feet, swaying before her. "I asked you a question! Did I ask you to turn the lights off in the car? What are you running away from all the time?" With a wide gesture toward windows and walls that nearly tumbles him: "I never washed the windows for my wife even. Paint a fireplace! Plant all them damn heliotropes!" [Miller 1981: 83].

Roslyn is at the center of the disconnected plot, enthralling the men by her soft, sentimental ways, but as a character she is something of an afterthought rather than a heroine. A lot is suggested about her, but very little becomes clear in the film. We do not know how or why she falls in love or what the intensity of her emotion really is, and even her conversation with Gay after their night of love does not rise above the level of one-night-stand small talk. In addition, the passion that this encounter is supposed to show is excised by the incestuous overtones of their relationship, further complicated by Monroe's lifelong idealization of Clark Gable as the father she never met. Roslyn and Gay end up living a domestic, decompressed life, but it is never clear whether this was also her wish or she was merely talked into it, or she simply settled down into the idea of joining this lonely man following an uncanny sense of compassion or emotional escapism:

> They laugh quietly. He works the ground. She looks off now at the distant hills. She is almost content; she knows she might well be content but something gnaws at her, and she listens to it.
> "In Chicago everybody's busy."
> He glances at her; he doesn't quite understand what she means, but the feeling is a welcoming one, so he lets it go [Miller 1981: 43].

Woman as Lack: A Gendered Desert

This is not to imply that Roslyn is anything less than disturbing. While very attractive, her seduction, apart from her physical ampleness, does not seem to come from fullness, but rather from a lack or an inner void. Gay, Guido, and Perce wallow in their personal torments, and while Roslyn acts as the still point to their irresolution, yet her inner peace rests on the absence of emotion and not on her ability to keep her feelings in check. It is for this reason that her eruption in the middle of the desert surprises the men and the viewers: coming from nowhere, her tirade seems unjustified, since she provided no ground to believe that she is a paragon of morality, or to suspect that anything might irritate her at all:

> Forty yards away, she screams, her body writhing, bending over as though to catapult her hatred.
> "You liars! All of you!" Clenching her fists, she screams toward their faces: *"Liars!"* ... Man! Big man! You're only living when you can watch something die! Kill everything, that's all you want! Why don't you just kill yourselves and be happy? ... I pity you all. ... You know everything except what it feels like to be alive. You're three dear, sweet dead men" (Miller 1981: 111).

Roslyn is a melancholy woman permanently in need of company and support. Her extreme sensitivity leads one to expect that everything can unbalance and hurt her, that everything can shatter her weak grip on life. In fact, nothing does: she quickly forgets Gay's refusal to let the lettuce-munching rabbit live, she equally forgives the men after their drinking bout and rude behavior, and she and Gay soon reconcile after their dispute over the mustangs. The many conflicts gradually dismantle her hopes for "just living" with Gay, but her mood rises again as they drive home and consider having a baby. It is only an effaced personality that can take so many setbacks, as if Roslyn had nothing better to return to and little to look forward to in the future, beyond the meandering affectations of the cowboys. The Nevada desert around her illustrates the scarcity of opportunities available to her. She has nothing to leave in the leave-it state except herself. Norman Mailer was the first to suggest that Monroe's sex appeal depends on the existence of a void (Mailer 1973: 34). In his imaginary memoir of the actress, he describes her as lost in thought over the "space" in her expression in one of her own photographs (Mailer 1973: 138).

In *The Misfits*, this vacuous availability is in keeping with the sensual boredom of the setting, a combination of glitter and dust not unlike Nevada itself. Roslyn appears all of a sudden, surrounded by the waste of her previous life of which little to nothing is revealed. She moves slowly, without purpose, as if in a state of stupor, often repetitive in her gestures as she plays with a paddleball and jumps in and out of the house trying out the new step: in fact, one of the film's opening motifs is her remark that she always ends up back where she started, in a circuitous, childlike merry-go-round effect. Often described by her co-workers as a somnambulist, walking as if ten feet under water, and with the reactions of a person surrounded by a wall of thick cotton, Monroe is very much in her element as a slightly bewildered woman floundering around with no direction. The desert is for her and for all the other characters not the frontier of the mythic wilderness but a granular view of the illusions they discarded in their attempt to fulfill the American Dream. Instead of perpetuating the Western myth of masculinity, the three cowboys wander around confused and aimless: they stake out no goals and have no ambitions. Their only target is the woman, which, in the context of a Western, might be seen as a debasing development, and indirectly reduces the value of the woman herself— except that Roslyn is hardly a woman at all, or, as Mailer put it, she is a "presence," an "essence," a "visual existence" (Mailer 1973: 151) very much like an illustration or background landscape. Incidentally, Monroe herself began her modeling career with a photo session in the desert with the Hungarian photographer André de Dienes. The cheesecake idol of America that he and others photographed appears here as nothing less than an epiphanic harbinger of truth. The men's encounter with this envoy takes the form of a series of seductions, which are nevertheless not strictly sexual. Roslyn unsettles the men, but it is important to remember that as far as overt actions are concerned, it is they who seduce her and not the other way around. Their methods of seduction reflect their respective attitudes towards the wilderness and the Old West: Gay is honored to (still) be a cowboy, he has internalized the prospective, gradual time of nature (love growing like a habit "as time goes by"), and its peacefulness. Guido needs immediate gratification, mostly of a concrete nature (money or Roslyn), for his pursuits. Perce is an honest, sensitive man whose only defense against pain and injustice is a set of self-numbing pastimes from which he emerges in a state of stupor, bandaged, broken, and drunk. The rodeo and the mustangs have no significance to him beyond a short distraction from his personal troubles. The same can be said about his interest in Roslyn: he seems not to notice her, but merely uses her to purge his soul by confession and by verbalizing his supposedly amorous feelings for her or at least the maternal image that she happens to personify. After her magical visitation, all three men realize at last how airless and dead their lives have been. The desert represents the emptiness they have inhabited and the wasteland that Roslyn will fertilize, perhaps literally, by giving birth. The salt flats mark the transition from the farce that has passed for freedom hitherto towards a new understanding of this concept: willful belonging to a desired home. The flats thus function as a liminal space, in which the characters come together at dusk — a liminal time. In consequence, the lakebed fits Gilles Deleuze's description of an "any-space-whatever" — a rarefied void which serves as a point of transit for the characters in the process of reconfiguring their lives:

> Any-space-whatever is not an abstract universal, in all times, in all places. It is a perfectly singular space, which has merely lost its homogeneity, that is, the principle of its metric relations or the connection of its own parts, so that the linkages can be made in an infinite number of ways. It is a space of virtual conjunction, grasped as pure locus of the possible [Deleuze 1986: 109].

The openness of the desert also points to the absence of psychological barriers in the characters' understanding of what "being alive" truly means. The spiritual barrenness of the "three dear sweet dead men" reaches the bottom of its downward spiral in the desert. When they leave, it looks as if they would never return. For a chamber piece reduced to slow, stagy scenes and only five characters — not real people but shadows of their own doubts — the salt flats also act as an ideal minimalist setting. The props of the drama are all whittled down to a minimum, and even the female lead is stripped of the sexual artifice Monroe had otherwise employed. The black and white cinematography additionally serves to increase the impact of the blank surroundings, as Huston felt that color would intrude on the harsh qualities of the story.

It is not only Roslyn who ideally fits the barren backdrop: so do the cowboys. Strangers to their own lives, which have little to offer except humiliation (or "wages"), they take refuge in the desert and thereby retreat from life itself, or, as Miller put it, "I had set out to create the feeling of a few isolated, lost and lonely people on the vast mythic plane of existence" (Miller 1987: 463). Still, cinematographer Russell Metty dismissed the Nevada setting as "scenery" that no one would pay to see, and showed little interest in Miller's exegetic comments on the thematic function of the setting. Most of the alkali flats footage was actually a filmed track added to studio process shots done in Los Angeles, which makes a genuine interconnection between setting and characters rather implausible. Huston, however, was not new to such techniques of artificial juxtaposition and could derive symbolic significance from even such stark incongruity. If in *The Maltese Falcon* Huston had used stock views of San Francisco in order to contrast the conventionality of an iconographically familiar city with the evil mystery presented in the film, the distant mountains and salt flats pasted on *The Misfits* seem to reinforce the cardboard flatness of the characters' wrecked dreams, the stage-prop artificiality and brittleness of their ideals. In Miller's view, compared to the theater, film is "a far lesser medium, because of the simplicity of its distances and the passivity of its audience" (Bradbury 1997: 215). But a subtle drama whose main theme *is* distance (physical and psychological), would be better off on the screen, since the camera eye can duplicate human distance in the wide exteriors the plot is set against. Also, *The Misfits* often makes use of embedded space, such as endless stretches of desert seen through car windows, or Roslyn framed apart from the men, looking tired and anguished, to point out the contrasting sensibilities of man and woman.

Despite its somewhat overstated symbolism, the landscape reveals itself indirectly to the camera, a representation perhaps derived from Miller's decision to write the script as the prose version of a film that only existed in his imagination, so that *The Misfits* might be described as the film of a film:

> It was as though a picture were already in being, and the writer were recreating its full effects through language, so that as a result of a purely functional attempt to make a vision of a film clear to others, a film which existed as yet only in the writer's mind, there was gradually suggested a form of fiction itself, a mixed form if you will [Miller in Murray 1972: 77].

It is as if the wordiness of the dialogue also took hold of the visual level, so that the images are not immediate but filtered through the level of discourse: although gritty, devoid of color, and anything but lush — as they would normally be in old-fashioned Hollywood Western style — the desert images and all other exterior shots seem extracted from a conceptual repertoire of symbols. It is almost as if Huston, whose reticence about character symbolism was notorious (Jameson 1980: 42), had decided to compensate by rendering the desert setting in broad metaphorical brushstrokes. What these images (like the entire film) lack is the cinematic descriptivity of places and characters. Imbued as it is with ideas and memorable phrases, the film misses out on the surface level of its images: Monroe is always filmed in soft focus,[10] which gives her contours a fluid, dreamlike shape, while the landscapes never seem to really connect with the people and events, in the same way that the complex personalities adumbrated in the dialogue never seem to come to life in the figures we see on the screen. Miller admittedly aimed at an "immediacy of image" and was involved in frequent debates with Huston over how this could be achieved. The variable subjective viewpoints that the screenplay correlates work differently on the written page than they do on screen. However, some cinematic techniques taken over from the screenplay remain very effective: the plotlessness of the film — often described as "formless and directionless" (Palmer 1997: 203)[11] — mirrors the languor of the setting (which was intended by Miller, see Murray 1972: 79). In a similar fashion, the tempo of the film itself is in step with the two different speeds of life in the wilderness: a long, static monotony in the first two parts of the film and the rapid violence of the struggle for survival during the mustanging scenes.

Russell Metty's black and white cinematography sustains the light/darkness contrast that accompanies Roslyn, and points to the shifting centres of power. The sparse light vampirizes her shuffling, unsteady figure in the dancing scene which shows her embracing a tree trunk in a phallic gesture of sexual availability. Daylight, on the other hand, clings to the woman, her skin, and her garments like an aura, but a mystifying one, suggesting illusion and ignorance rather than pure clarity. It is precisely in the light that Roslyn seems more shadowy than ever. While preserving her mystery, the camera regards the female subject worshipfully, catching each of her quivering smiles. The gradual revelation of character, both male and female, is mirrored by the expansion of locations from relatively cramped interiors to broad, exterior shots. The shift from Guido's house to the desert also widens the breach between the characters. As Roslyn and Guido arrive in the desert, the first bloom is already off their relationship, while tension among the men also begins to mount. But it is the woman who comes into her own once the natural space widens. This is not the first time that setting was used to enhance the effect of Monroe's performance. In *River of No Return* (1954) — Monroe's first Western film — spacious, prodigious scenery reflects the physical attractions of the female lead, while in her film noir collaboration with Joseph Cotten, *Niagara* (1953), the waterfalls look as beautiful and menacing as the murderous wife that Monroe is (atypically) impersonating. In the desert, i.e. a setting that is exactly the opposite of Niagara, Monroe takes over something from the texture of her surroundings. Her lush eroticism in *Niagara* is replaced by the dry, evanescent attraction pervading the atmosphere around her in *The Misfits*. It is a similar aridity and spiritual dehydration that the male characters are steeped in and under which they suffer. Moreover, even the silence of the desert takes on erotic overtones: "You can hear your skin against your clothes," a sensuous Roslyn remarks, gently loosening the white, starched collar of her shirt.

Despite such seductive scenes, it often happened that John Huston fell asleep in the director's chair on the set of *The Misfits*, finally conquered by long nights of drink and gambling. However, the lumbering pace of the film is not only the result of his chaotic involvement with the project, or of the general disinterest that settled over the entire crew once the film went over budget and began to try everyone's patience. The slow motion allows more room (and time) for the character-borne narrative to spread. Alex North's soundtrack, a welcome exception to Huston's frequent misguidedness or sheer indifference in terms of musical score, also strikes subtle nuances of character: Roslyn's musical symbol, superimposed on her elegant choreography, acts as background to her "dream ballet" (Alex North, in Henderson 2003: 164). Her nostalgic theme is carried by strings, while its instability indicates the psychological liability of a woman who is not only lonely and insecure, but also goes through a rollercoaster of emotions over the course of the film. The grand melodic sweep of the main title seems appropriate to the pathos of the landscape discussed above, especially during the mustanging scenes, heading with a crescendo of foreboding towards a tipping point that never comes.

The entire film, in fact, conveys this impression of a regrettable absence or loss, although one cannot be certain what exactly was there in the first place. Miller continually sets hopeful signposts and good omens for the future, while at the same time undercutting his characters' trust in anything at all: Roslyn's belief only in "the next thing that happens" is nothing but a concealed indulgence in the past. According to the lax philosophy of this film, which, as a Western picture, should have provided a solid ground for the proliferation of traditional Western ideals (such as virility, freedom, or transgression), it is not fair to expect fairness, and it is not consistent to demand consistency:

> ISABELLE: "You're too believing, dear. Cowboys are the last real men in the world, but they're as reliable as jackrabbits."
> ROSLYN: "But what if that's all there is? Really and truly, I mean. ... Maybe you're not supposed to believe anything people say. Maybe it's not even fair to them."
> ISABELLE: "Well ... don't ask me, dear. This world and I have always been strangers — deep down, I mean" [Miller 1981: 25].
> PERCE: "What the hell you depend on? Do you know?"

ROSLYN: "I don't know. Maybe...." She is facing the distant horizon, staring at her life. "Maybe all there really is is what happens next, just the next thing, and you're not supposed to remember anybody's promises" [Miller 1981: 76].

Even this might be taken for a form of humanism in itself, if only of a transitional kind. Miller achieves this acid dissolution of values firstly through the intervention of a woman and the transformations the male figures undergo in its wake, while Huston pins this story to a dead and deathly scenery, wide enough to ease an irreversible spill of morals and humanity, but also open enough to give a clear view of what went wrong and to what grave extent the fabled Frontier has been abused and misunderstood.

Notes

1. The Method is a form of acting out inner emotions. The actor becomes acquainted with her own emotional depths and takes control of them so as to better gain control of her role (see Strasberg 1987). Each of Monroe's earlier films brushed in one way or another against a persona that strikingly resembled the "genuine" Marilyn or what has gone down in film history as such: a childlike, vulnerable creature, sensitive and self-deprecating at the same time. In *The Misfits*, however, through a concurrence of circumstances (intensive work with the Strasbergs, the influence of John Huston, a role written out for Monroe, and last but not least her growing lack of control — even in the sense of theatrical discipline) Marilyn became herself, or, in Huston's words: "She wasn't acting — I mean she was not pretending to an emotion. It was the real thing. She would go deep down within herself and find it and bring it up into consciousness. But maybe that's what truly good acting consists of" (Huston 1988: 287).

2. The film leaves out a decisive exchange between the protagonists, which reinstates the male supremacy that Roslyn had temporarily suspended.

3. "Belonging" points to sexual possession in Roslyn's reply to Perce as to whether she belongs to Gay: "I don't know where I belong" (Miller 1981: 75). Roslyn does respond to the advances of all three men and seems to vacillate between the one and the other, and it was indeed only towards the end of production that Miller and Huston conjointly decided to pair her with Gay.

4. "I convince them by throwing a fit, not by explaining anything. So I have a fit. A screaming fit.... And to think *Arthur* did this to me.... If that's what he thinks of me, well, I'm not for him and he's not for me" (quoted in Steinem 1986: 79). Early critics typically labelled this behaviour as "hysteric" and dismissed Roslyn's views (e.g., Kauffman 1961: 26).

5. Seminal ideas on femininity as disguise and neutralization of a possibly traumatic experience of female sexuality were first formulated by Joan Riviere (1929). For a related article discussing the fetishistic abuse of Monroe's feminine attributes see Kaplan 1993.

6. The plot was suggested to Miller by his six-week stay in 1956 in a rented cabin at Pyramid Lake, 50 miles north of Reno, while awaiting a divorce from his first wife.

7. "Gay deludes himself into thinking that he has forged a frontier beyond that economy by following the cowboy code. Yet far from connecting him to the reality of his experience, the Western myth insulates Gay from it" (Press 1980: 42).

8. The overblown attention given to Monroe as a public figure seeps into her own films, where she is mentioned in the script as the ultimate showgirl (*The Seven Year Itch* [1955]),

while in *The Misfits* posters of a glamorous Marilyn are pinned to the inner side of a wardrobe door.

9. The caption of the short story for first publication in *Esquire* was "The Last Frontier of the Quixotic Cowboy."

10. Also because close-ups would otherwise have betrayed Monroe's exhaustion.

11. Norman Mailer's view is less favourable: "It was a script so delicate in the drift of its emotions and so taciturn in its story that the daily problem must have been to decide what motive they could offer the actors for a line" (Mailer 1973: 192).

Ethical Commitment and Political Dissidence
Huston, HUAC, Hollywood and Key Largo
Reynold Humphries

John Huston's 1948 film *Key Largo* represents, both in theme and character, certain values Huston (who wrote the script in collaboration with Richard Brooks) held publicly in his opposition to the investigation of the House Committee on Un-American Activities (HUAC) via his co-founding with director William Wyler and writer Philip Dunne of the Committee for the First Amendment (CFA). These values dated back to the 1930s when they were shared by liberals, radicals and Communists both within Hollywood and throughout the nation. We shall see that the limpid values of the past became controversial and unacceptable in post-war Hollywood.

The plot follows former Army Major Frank McCloud (Humphrey Bogart) as he travels down to Florida to inform Frank Temple (Lionel Barrymore) of the circumstances surrounding the death in action of his son George, who served under McCloud during the war. Temple owns a hotel at Key Largo where McCloud meets not only his daughter-in-law Nora (Lauren Bacall) but also a suspicious group of unsavory characters who, it transpires, have taken over the hotel so that their boss, gangster Johnny Rocco (Edward G. Robinson), can hide there prior to leaving for Cuba to escape arrest and deportation to Italy. McCloud also runs into Sheriff Ben Wade (Monty Blue) and his deputy who are looking for Indian brothers who have escaped from jail and are assumed to have returned to Key Largo. The deputy becomes suspicious of Rocco's men and is killed by them. Rocco blames the Indians and the Sheriff shoots them both down when they attempt to flee. Realizing how dangerous Rocco and his men are, McCloud agrees to take them to Cuba in his own boat to protect Temple and Nora. In fact, McCloud intends to use the situation to force a showdown. He picks the gangsters off one by one and finally kills Rocco. He then returns to Key Largo where Nora Temple is waiting for him.

My most persistent memory from a first viewing of the film over thirty years ago is the scene at the end of the film where Nora, realizing that McCloud is safe and is coming back for her, throws wide open the shutters of the hotel (kept closed because of a storm that rages during part of the action) and lets the sunlight stream in. It was unbelievably corny then and it remains so. As we shall see, however, the context renders the shot polyvalent — it is massively over-determined — and it is this context that needs to be addressed first.

I propose to begin by discussing the possible significance of the two Indians. In the film's opening sequence a police-car stops the bus transporting McCloud to Key Largo and asks the driver if he has seen two Indian brothers who have broken out of jail. The driver tells McCloud that the Indians always head for this part of the country. During *their* first conversation Temple informs McCloud that George and the Indian brothers grew up together, that the brothers got drunk and "tried to take back Florida." This is said with humour, but in the light of what we see later, where the Indians trust Temple as completely as the Sheriff does, something else is at stake. George and many like him died in Europe to take the continent back from the Nazis and make it safe for democracy. As McCloud says, enlisting was not just a question of duty. Thus the film introduces the theme of the struggle against fascism, a struggle that united very different people and groups in the 1930s, both in the United States and abroad. For the Indians, however, there can be no justice, no taking back of Florida for the Indian nation. As Nora points out, they're reduced to "selling sea shells by the sea shore."

Given that George fought fascism because he believed such a struggle to be necessary, it can be argued that Huston and Brooks are implicitly carrying us back to before World War II and that (henceforth symbolic) anti-fascist struggle the failure of which helped precipitate the conflagration: the Spanish Civil War. In the light of the active participation of Hitler and Mussolini on Franco's side and the passivity of so-called European democracies in the face of fascist aggression (a simple continuation of their indifference faced with Mussolini's invasion of Ethiopia in 1935), *Key Largo* suggests that there is an unbroken continuity from the mid–1930s to the late 1940s and that certain conclusions need to be drawn.

Significantly, the Indians do turn up to surrender to Temple who, for them, represents the United States. It is clear from Temple's violent diatribe against Rocco later that he had inculcated anti-fascist values into George over the years and that, since Rocco is a "throwback" to the 1930s, Spain would have been the touchstone for the old man. It is at this point that Rocco, who has shot down the deputy, misleads the Sheriff who confronts the brothers and shoots them. When McCloud hears of this, Huston cuts to a shot of his face, the very picture of horror and despair. This shot recalls an earlier Bogart and Bacall movie, *To Have and Have Not* (1944), when Bacall is slapped by the fascist Captain Renard, sparking a strong response from Bogart. The scene in the Hawks film is eloquent and potent but the implications are more explicitly political in *Key Largo*: a woman getting slapped by a thug in a position of power and authority is not the same as two innocent men being killed by a decent, well-intentioned man who represents socially-legitimated power and authority. McCloud's look suggests that what has happened — thanks to Rocco — confirms his worst suspicions of the way post-war society is moving: for him, more than just two Indians have died, however deplorable their deaths may be. For McCloud, the Roccos of the world can now walk the streets freely: liberal values of justice and dignity have been sacrificed. As we have seen, Rocco is hiding in Key Largo prior to escaping to Cuba, but little is made of this apart from his simply being there. It is as if his presence bothered nobody, except people like McCloud and the Temples. The sheriff has the impression that he recognizes him but does not pursue it when Rocco replies: "I don't think so." This takes on another meaning. The sheriff is so busy chasing the Indians that he cannot see what he has under his nose.[1]

The sheriff's concern with tracking down the Indians finds a parallel in the post-war witch-hunts, which seek phantom "Reds" while the really dangerous elements in society — hoodlums in both the film and real life — are free to come and go as they please and do what they like. Huston and screenwriter Brooks are suggesting that the sacrifice made by people like George Temple will have been in vain if the democratic values extolled and shared in the 1930s are replaced by those of the hoodlum, another symbol of the same decade.[2] Just what Rocco symbolizes, however, is complex. He is furious at being treated badly by the government, "as if I was a dirty Red," and is outraged at being considered "an undesirable alien."

These remarks have a peculiar and particular resonance in the context of Hollywood. *Key Largo* evokes the Prohibition, "the good old days" for Rocco, when gangsters dictated policy to politicians (and Rocco brags about placing politicians in positions of power). We can see here a reference to Hollywood in the 1930s, the control by gangsters of the sole union, the International Alliance of Theatrical Stage Employees (IATSE), the complacency and complicity of the studio bosses, ever ready to pay protection money to keep studio hands in their place (Horne 2001; Nielsen and Mailes 1995). People like Rocco were encouraged to lean on the Reds — and it was a Communist trade unionist, Jeff Kibre, who led the struggle against the corrupt IATSE (Ceplair 1989) — so we can appreciate the irony of the situation and Rocco's indignation (perfectly sincere, in the light of Hollywood in 1948, as we shall see later) at suddenly finding himself subjected to the same treatment. Similarly, being looked upon as an "undesirable alien" outrages Rocco, not because he is of Italian origin — he has always received far better treatment at the hands of politicians than the Indians ever did from successive American governments — but because he is being assimilated to Reds. Perhaps, indeed, to one particular individual: San Francisco trade unionist Harry Bridges. Because he led the successful longshoremen's strike on the West Coast in 1935, Bridges had long been a thorn in the flesh of big business and its supporters in Hollywood and in the press nationwide. He was considered to be a Communist by the government and J. Edgar Hoover who tried to deport him for over twenty years as he was an Australian (the Supreme Court definitively put at end to such attempts in 1958). Within a year of *Key Largo*, Hollywood was offering its own version of Bridges: the Communist Party thug Vanning (played by Thomas Gomez) in *The Woman on Pier 13* (1949). This was part of the film community's appeasement of HUAC, whose 1947 hearings had resulted in the Waldorf-Astoria Statement where studio bosses declared they would never hire Communists. Interestingly, Gomez also plays Curly, one of Rocco's henchman and, that same year, appeared in a major role in the film that came to symbolize the Hollywood Left: Abraham Polonsky's *Force of Evil* (1948). Was he offered the role of Vanning to make sure he was not "tainted" as a result of working with Polonsky? The insidious implication was that anyone who defended Communists was a fellow traveller. The only way to disprove this from 1951 on was to name names before HUAC, but playing a Communist thug in an anti–Communist film got those "tainted" off the hook once Hollywood started making anti–Communist films in 1948. Similarly, Frank Lovejoy, who acted in another major contribution by the Left to *film noir*, *The Sound of Fury* (1950), appeared in the anti-labor and anti–Communist movie *I Was a Communist for the FBI* in 1951 (Humphries 2006).

McCloud hates Rocco, not as an individual but as a symbol of everything he and people like him (or like Rick in *Casablanca* [1942], before settling in Morocco) had fought since the 1930s. Now he refuses to shoot Rocco when he has the chance, knowing that to do so would get him shot in turn by one of Rocco's henchmen. This decision upsets Temple: it is as if McCloud were backing down and letting fascists take their revenge, as if he were now of the opinion that past struggles were in vain (akin to Rick in *Casablanca*, albeit in *Key Largo* this sense is inflected with a profoundly political and historical charge as opposed to an emotional one characterizing *Casablanca*). To a certain extent McCloud is throwing in the towel and hence the crucial shot of his reaction to the death of the Indian brothers: now he must do something. Thus these totally unnecessary deaths come to symbolize the failure of everything McCloud and George fought for in Europe (and died for in the case of George and so many others), just as Rocco's life symbolizes the victory of those forces Hollywood's liberals sought to stop before, during and after the war. As Temple says, in a remark whose ramifications are considerable: "When you're a fighter, you can't walk away from a fight."[3] Which brings us to the Committee for the First Amendment (CFA). It is important to remember that the CFA was formed as soon as HUAC announced that it would be holding hearings in Washington on Communist infiltration of Hollywood. This chronology, I would argue, is important for showing that liberals were quickly aware of the possibilities of censorship, given that the most right-wing elements of the Republican Party, as well as racist Southern Democrats, controlled the committee: the attempt to smear the New Deal as Communist was very much the trademark of HUAC Chairman in 1947, J. Parnell Thomas. However, his philosophy — more business in government and less government in business — only echoed that of his mentor, Democrat Martin Dies, who launched mini-hearings in Hollywood in 1940 to investigate those stars his informers had denounced as Communists: Bogart, James Cagney and Fredric March. Dies is on record as making the following recommendation to March: "Never participate in anything in the future without consulting the American Legion or your local Chamber of Commerce" (Pomerantz 1963: 15). The full significance of this "paternalist" advice was to become abundantly clear after the war and we shall return to it in due course.

Throughout the war, of course, liberals, radicals and Communists were united, and never more so than in mid–1944 when the anti-union forces of the Hollywood Right created the Motion Picture Alliance for the Preservation of American Ideals, a body far more interested in opposing "crackpots" of the radical or Red persuasion than in the ongoing fight against fascism (the war, of course, was not over).[4] The existence of the MPA was experienced as an insult and an attack on democracy by Hollywood as a whole. On June 28, 1944, the Council of Hollywood Guilds and Unions, at a public meeting attended by 1000 delegates, unanimously voted through a motion "to combat anti-democratic and anti-labor activities in the motion picture industry during and after the war."[5] By founding the CFA Huston, Wyler and Dunne were continuing to defend the values expressed in the motion quoted and were joined by several hundred Hollywood personalities, including Bogart and Bacall who were among those who flew to Washington to sit in on the hearings, both as a token of support and to represent the film community. As we now know from a variety of accounts, the confrontations between writer John Howard Lawson and the Committee shocked many members of the CFA who returned to Los Angeles in disarray (Horne 2006: 184–9).

Bogart and Bacall quickly disavowed both the Hollywood Ten and the CFA, a gesture which elicited reactions from two very different quarters. Not surprisingly, the Communist Party's journal the *Daily Worker* (October 31, 1947) attacked both Bogart and actor Paul Henreid for recanting in the belief that "they can deflect the wrath of men like Parnell Thomas with the plea 'We are just as anti–Communist as anybody else.'"[6] And Democrat Representative from California Chet Holifield wrote to Bogart (December 9, 1947). In his letter he evoked the "red smear which will be the chief weapon in the coming campaign against liberal, progressive American candidates' to Congress.[7] These were prophetic words indeed, but Holifield was very much a man preaching in the wilderness. The dominant tone and point of view — not only in Hollywood but also in the Republican Party and those journals which supported it — could be found in the pages of *The Hollywood Reporter* whose conservative editor and publisher, W.R. Wilkerson (notoriously His Master's Voice when it came to echoing the views and interests of the studio bosses and their financial backers), wrote on November 10, 1947, about "causes that looked innocent and needy on the face of them, but were fund raisers for the bums who are trying to upset our government and our way of living."[8] Wilkerson voiced his anxiety about films losing money — the ultimate heresy for the Right — because of the Communist controversy and called on Hollywood to "start something," his way of supporting HUAC's demand that Hollywood "clean house."[9] Just two weeks later, on November 24, 1947, the studio bosses, their lawyers and East Coast financial backers met in the Waldorf-Astoria to launch what was to become a real but unofficial blacklist.

On December 18, 1947, red-baiting journalist George Sokolsky published in the Bridgeport, Connecticut, *Post* an article entitled "Who's Behind the Committee for the First Amendment?" This was a purely rhetorical question, whose form already provided its own answer: Reds. It was to become a favorite device of witch hunters in the years to come, where innumerable associations would be denounced as Communist fronts (a smear tactic already implicit in the Wilkerson quote given above), enticing the complacent, the naive and the dupes into the Red fold under the guise of defending liberal, humanitarian causes. Implicit, of course, was the accusation that any cause supported by the Communist Party was un–American. I refer to Sokolsky's article as it condenses much that is central to this study of *Key Largo*. In the course of his article the journalist referred to Dunne and Huston calling on France to abandon its policy of non-intervention and to allow the purchase of supplies by Loyalist Spain. The co-founders of the CFA were quoted to this effect in *New Masses*, a CP periodical.[10] Two syllogisms over-determine each other here: anyone quoted by a Communist journal belongs to/is sympathetic to/is bringing succor to the CP; as Loyalist Spain (the republican forces opposed to Franco's fascist coup d'état) received support from Stalin and various American organizations in which Communists played a part, Loyalist Spain was Communist. And so on, *ad nauseam*.

Of all the causes that brought liberals, radicals and Communists together, the Spanish Civil War uniquely marked an entire generation and became the symbol of everything the Right was determined to crush: an ethical, as opposed to a purely opportunistic, opposition to fascism, an acute sense of justice and a belief in solidarity and collective action. This in turn meant fighting for the welfare state, civil rights and trade unions, all Red bogeymen for HUAC. If it is clear that the Indians serve a dual purpose in *Key Largo*— they simultaneously stand in for the Negro and symbolize a sense of history and the past, absolutely crucial for Huston and Brooks — we must not forget an equally important element, so patent that it may pass unobserved: McCloud is a war veteran and George, were he alive, would be at his side now, as during the war in Europe. The question of veterans was a burning one in the immediate post-war years. The CFA drew attention to the voting record of HUAC members Rankin (Democrat) and Parnell and Mundt (Republican): they were opposed to subsidies for housing for war veterans.[11] The equation was an ideological one: subsidies = government intervention = Roosevelt's New Deal = socialism = Communism. Of particular interest here is the film *Till the End of Time* (1946), directed by future member of those to be called The Hollywood Ten, Edward Dmytryk, and written by Allen Rivkin.[12] Described as "a fist-swinging attack on anti–Semitism" (Buhle and Wagner 2002: 387) because the heroes take on a fascist veterans' association that refuses admission to Jews, Catholics and Negroes, the film anticipated, in a more radical mode, the far more celebrated *Crossfire* (1947) the following year which was also concerned "about the wave of potentially murderous anti–Semitism and violence quotient that still persisted among veterans and warned of an American-style Hitlerism" (Buhle and Wagner 2002: 231).[13]

Till the End of Time both captures the climate rife in real-life incidents and contains a striking parallel with aspects of *Key Largo*. Rep. Chet Holifield had the occasion to use language identical to that of Buhle and Wagner quoted above. On November 24, 1947, he had inserted into the Congressional Record information he had found in a local, Californian paper concerning a group of armed men "wearing veterans' uniforms" entering forcibly a private home in Montrose, California, and intimidating citizens, who were registered Democrats. Asked Holifield: "Are we on the verge of storm-trooper incidents throughout America?"[14] It turned out that one of the armed men was none other than the Commander of the local post of the American Legion. Given the remark by Martin Dies quoted above, the registered Democrats had clearly not demanded permission to congregate from the American Legion![15] *Till the End of Time* includes a sequence where the film's heroes meet up with the fascist veterans' association, one of whose members says to them: "15 percent of every pay check you get goes to those foreign-born labor racketeers." This at once betrays a reactionary hostility towards any trade union activity, smears every unionist leader as a gangster,[16] and introduces surreptitiously the theme of anti–Semitism via the epithet "foreign born." The fact that anti–Semites tended to equate Jews and Communists — which played a crucial role in turning conservative Jews such as the Warner Bros. against their radical employees[17]— returns in the script of *Key Largo* in the form of Rocco's outrage at being, in his own scheme of things, equated with Reds because his name designates him as one of the foreign born. History steps in here, in the form of a remark made by a real-life gangster, and like Rocco an Italian: Al Capone. Just as Rocco's remark implies that he at least is a true patriot, so does Capone's:

> Bolshevism is at our gates. We can't afford to let it in. We have got to organize ourselves against it, and put our shoulders together and hold fast. We must keep America whole and safe and unspoiled. We must keep the worker away from red literature and red ruses; we must see that his mind remains healthy [Pomerantz 1963: 42].

As John Steinbeck wrote in *The Grapes of Wrath*: "A red is any son of a bitch who wants thirty cents when we're paying twenty-five." I quote this, since Capone's remark could be that of an anti-union capitalist.[18] Although the source does not give the date on which Capone made the remark, it perfectly sums up the climate and the witch-hunting of the Cold War period, a climate which led director Wyler to denounce how the MPA and HUAC had provided the "groundwork designed to keep all liberal and progressive persons off the Hollywood pay rolls."[19] On January 16, 1948, progressive Senator Taylor (D) asked that the article in *Screen Writer* where Wyler made this remark be inserted in the appendix of the Senate Record. Huston at the time was in the throes of making *Key Largo* and we know that he greeted Bogart furiously on the set for disavowing the CFA. Let us return now for the last time to the scene where McCloud chooses not to kill Rocco. First of all, is it a true choice or a gamble? McCloud can shoot Rocco, knowing he will himself be killed immediately. Or he can lower his gun, feeling that Rocco's not worth dying for. This is, however, not necessarily an either-or situation, as McCloud cannot be sure Rocco won't have him gunned down the moment he lowers his weapon. McCloud, consciously or not, is still taking a risk, but it's one where he will have lost the chance forever, should Rocco prove vindictive and decide he's too dangerous to live.

I would argue that this scene parallels what befell Bogart in real life, just as he was starting to shoot the film with Huston. If Bogart backed down after the ill-fated flight to Washington undertaken by more than a score of the members of the CFA, that did not end the affair. We know that Bogart was given a dressing-down by none other than Jack L. Warner, hence the actor's caving in to pressure. But more than this was demanded of the star: he had to renounce defending the Ten — for to do so was to condone Communism — and, for good measure, indulge in a piece of self-criticism which, with retrospect, looks suspiciously like a mild run-up to the public acts of humiliation — naming the names of former friends and comrades (Navasky 1980) — imposed on the friendly witnesses from February 1951 on when HUAC returned for the great house-cleaning.[20] For Bogart, then, it was no more an alternative between supporting or not supporting the CFA than deciding not to kill Rocco was, for McCloud, a simple alternative to shooting him. If we continue with parallels between the film and real life, I would point to a case of sacrifice (for McCloud would have sacrificed himself, had he shot Rocco) that highlights the insufficiencies of the scene. I am thinking of how French Resistance member Jean Moulin, captured by Klaus Barbie of the Gestapo, endured being tortured to death rather than speak. He too had a choice — of sorts: not talk and die horribly or talk and survive. But would Barbie have let him live? And what would the consequences have been for his fellow anti-fascists if he had broken down? The unsatisfactory nature of the confrontation between McCloud and Rocco stems from the fact that the film cannot fully convince us that Rocco is worth dying for in the way that a democratic Europe was worth dying for in the eyes of George and countless others.

Temple clearly believes that the risk was worth taking, because he equates Rocco and his values with the fascism that George died to prevent spreading. And Temple is right to consider that those values were in danger of winning the day in the United States. Indeed, they were well on their way to victory by 1948. The ambiguity of the film would seem to lie in the fact that Huston and Brooks could not make up their minds as to how best to fight the mortal danger facing liberal values. It is in this context that we can return to the shutters I mentioned in my opening remarks and attempt to analyze their significance, one that goes beyond the simple symbolism of light and dark, good and evil, etc. When McCloud has completed his account of George's devotion and courage, Nora closes the shutters of the room the three of them are in. We can take this as symbolizing her sense of grief over a loss and the film's indicating that, in the wake of World War II, another storm is gathering — the film's storm is clearly both symbolic and motivated by the needs of the script — bringing darkness with it. However, to get beyond that "corny" dimension, we must not forget the very ending of the film. On hearing McCloud has got the better of the gangsters, she throws open the shutters and the sunlight floods in: let there be light, so to speak.[21] She also makes a most interesting remark: "He's coming back to us."

It has been clear from the outset that Nora is attracted to McCloud who therefore stands in for George in every possible way, at least in her fantasies. The remark is therefore not just simply a hackneyed happy girl gets boy ending. It is also a form of wish fulfillment: if only McCloud were George, if only George were standing there now. In that case, George is returning from across the sea to take up the cudgels again to protect democracy, but this time within the United States, against the Roccos and the witch-hunters who are Rocco's objective real-life allies. It is also as if Huston and Brooks were representing Bogart as what he once was, as if Bogart-as-McCloud returning to Key Largo were a sign that there was still hope, still a chance of protecting Hollywood from HUAC after the studio bosses gave in.

Unfortunately, there wasn't. Huston was forced to recognize this two years later when he came to make *The Asphalt Jungle* (1950) which "can be interpreted as Huston's lament on the disappearance of New Deal liberalism and the death of civic culture" (Munby 1999: 135), an homage to "a specific community that could no longer maintain its Depression-era faith that America would someday evolve into a socialist democracy" (Naremore 1998: 130). The CFA was moribund by 1948, the year *Key Largo* appeared. It is as if the he of "he's coming back to us" were John Huston himself, a sort of unconscious lament for his own failure, but in an inverted form where failure miraculously becomes success.[22]

Notes

1. This bears a striking resemblance to an anecdote involving J. Edgar Hoover and the FBI: "The Top Hoodlum program was inaugurated in November 1957, just days after Hoover had been disastrously upstaged by a state trooper in Apalachin, New York. The attentive trooper had noted an unusual number of long black limousines pulling into the gates of a nearby estate. What he had detected, and later disrupted, was a convocation of more than one hundred of the most powerful organized crime figures in America. For more than three decades, Hoover had assured America that no such organization existed. Not only did the Bureau not know the mobsters were going to meet, they didn't even know who they were" (Fariello 1995: 93n10).

2. Robinson played the character of Rico in *Little Caesar* in 1931.

3. This is the progressive version of the equally noble but profoundly individualistic values expressed in certain Budd Boetticher/Burt Kennedy/Randolph Scott Westerns: ... There are some things a man can't ride round, ... etc.

4. Already by January 1944 right-wing intellectuals were predicting an inevitable confrontation with the Soviet Union after the war. See Lora 1974.

5. Howard Estabrook Collection, Academy of Motion Picture Arts and Sciences, Mar-

garet Herrick Library, Beverly Hills, folder 398. Estabrook was a liberal writer who, by the early 1950s, was praising HUAC to the skies for its fight against Communism. By then, of course, he was once again in the majority.

6. Paul Henreid Papers, Margaret Herrick Library. Readers will remember that Henreid played the anti-fascist Resistance leader in *Casablanca*.

7. John Huston Collection, Margaret Herrick Library, Box 8, HUAC folder. Holifield was one of the 17 Congressmen who opposed citing the Ten for contempt. For the complete list, see Bessie, 1967: 248.

8. The HUAC hearings had made public what was well known in Hollywood, namely that the Ten were Communists. They and Communists in general are, of course, the "bums" being referred to.

9. William Wyler Collection, Margaret Herrick Library, folder 591 (CFA). It is interesting to note that, just two years earlier, on November 5 1945, Howard Estabrook had published in *The Hollywood Reporter* a full-page polemic against Wilkerson under the prophetic title "Freedom of Repression," where, on the ironic mode, he chides Wilkerson for his opposition to Hollywood's writers for their liberal and radical opinions. Howard Estabrook Collection.

10. William Wyler Collection, MHL, folder 591.

11. William Wyler Collection, folder 592.

12. Like most liberals, Rivkin quickly turned against his former comrades and helped eliminate Communists from the Screen Writers' Guild by becoming part of an "All-Guild slate" in 1947 (Navasky 1980: 176).

13. Also directed by Dmytryk, *Crossfire* was produced by another member of the Ten, Adrian Scott and written by John Paxton (a non–Communist who was unable to find work in the 1950s because of this collaboration with the proscribed pair). In the original novel, the victim of the psychopathic racist played by Robert Ryan was not a Jew but a homosexual. Richard Brooks was the author of the novel. Homosexuality, of course, had been taboo on the screen since the early 1930s, so Scott, Dmytryk and Paxton exploited the momentarily liberal climate, due to the revelations about Nazi atrocities and the concentration camps, to remind their fellow citizens of a few necessary truths, to combat amnesia, and to sound a timely but unheeded warning.

14. John Huston Collection, MHL, Box 8, HUAC folder.

15. The American Legion was notorious for picketing films involving those the Legion considered to have connections with Communist fronts, such as actress Katharine Hepburn. In 1951 it pinned its Medal of Merit on the chest of General Franco. J. Parnell Thomas had close ties with Franco and the Veterans of the Abraham Lincoln Brigade (the Americans who had fought Franco in Spain, including future member of the Hollywood Ten writer Alvah Bessie) were persecuted by J. Edgar Hoover and put on the Attorney General's list as members of a Communist front (Caute 1978: 351, 178).

16. As we saw earlier, this was to be the tactic of *I Was a Communist for the FBI*. In *The Woman on Pier 13* Communists look and behave like gangsters (when they're not intellectuals).

17. On this delicate and complex issue, see Gabler 1988, especially Chapter 9.

18. It is worthwhile reminding readers that the person responsible for the Waldorf-Astoria Statement, Eric Johnston (who had come to Hollywood in 1945 to head the Motion Picture Producers and Distributors of America), was a former member of the Chamber of Commerce. As one writer has succinctly put it, he "was the sign of an emergent order ... espousing the ideals of liberal corporate consensus" (Munby 1999: 168–9). On this consensus and the Left's response to it in their films, see Humphries 2004.

19. William Wyler Collection, folder 591.

20. The actor gave the press an appropriate interview under the title "I'm No Communist" (Ceplair and Englund 1980: 291).

21. I write this, not only because of a possible reference by Huston to his documentary of 1946, *Let There Be Light*, but also because of the quasi-religious aspect of the shot whose ironic dimension I comment on in my concluding remarks.

22. See the previous note.

King Adapter
Huston's Famous and Infamous Adaptations of Literary Classics
PAGE LAWS

> *To reproduce a mighty book, you must choose a mighty theme. No great and enduring volume can ever be written on the flea, though many there be who have tried it.* — Herman Melville's *Moby-Dick* (1851/1996: 482)

> *Looking back now, I wonder if it is possible to do justice to Moby Dick on film.* — John Huston's *An Open Book* (1980: 251)

Let no one ever accuse John Huston of wasting his time or talent on fleas. To make the first epigraph directly applicable to Huston, simply substitute the word "film" for Melville's word "volume." Because Melville uses the Platonic term "reproduce" (rather than the expected "produce") there is no need to modify the quotation any further. It fits John Huston's career ambitions like the custom-tailored riding pants Huston favored (according to Ray Bradbury in his tell-all *Green Shadow, White Whale*) on hunt days in Ireland. The second epigraph, by Huston himself, reflects him in a more wistful mood. One pictures him temporarily chastened, not by one of his frequent horseback riding falls, but by the mixed reception of what turned out to be his most ambitious adaptation ever: *Moby Dick*.

John Huston. Did ever a director's person and persona lend itself better to great book and article titles? Two of my favorites — "Call him Ishmael" and "The Man Who Would Be Ahab"— are cited in Robert Benayoun's 1985 book *La grande ombre de l'aventure*. My current title, "King Adapter," was devised as a play on biographer William Nolan's *King Rebel*, while my working title — "'Thar he blows'— was a lame allusion to Huston's Leviathan ego — the *chutzpah* he repeatedly demonstrated in his choice of challenging literary peers: James Joyce for *The Dead* (1987); Flannery O'Connor for *Wise Blood* (1979); Rudyard Kipling for *The Man Who Would Be King* (1975); Tennessee Williams for *The Night of the Iguana* (1964); Stephen Crane for *The Red Badge of Courage* (1951); even God, the presumed author of *The Bible: In the Beginning...* (1966).

Huston was, of course, equally outsized in his epic personal life. How else can one explain the *six* books in which he appears as a fictionalized character, including the two best-known: Peter Viertel's 1953 novel *White Hunter, Black Heart*, itself adapted into a film directed by and starring Clint Eastwood, and Ray Bradbury's 1992 novella *Green Shadows, White Whale*. The other four books, as listed by Cohen and Lawton (1997: 412–413), are Niven Busch's *The Actor* (1955), Charles Hamblett's *Crazy Kill* (1956); Theodore Koszak's *Flicker* (1991) and David Thompson's *Suspects* (1985). They are an interestingly entitled lot, as well.

The title of *Reflections in a Male Eye*, a collection of critical work on Huston both reflects a major theme of his work—his love of Hemingwayesque masculinity—while also playing on the title of his adaptation of Carson McCullers' famous novel. And I am also fond of the title of an article included in that collection, "Mastery through Masterpieces" by Virginia Wright Wexman. Wexman writes about the art masterpieces in Huston's *Moulin Rouge* (1952), but the word "masterpieces" works just as well for books.

Huston's career can be "read" as an attempt to "master" or dominate various literary masters, by recreating their work in a wholly different medium. In one sense, it's just a matter of one artist—the filmmaker—choosing a specific "signified" for another artist's "signifier." But there's nothing simple about that, as poststructuralism tells us. The process of creating a film adaptation is as tricky and complex as withdrawing the narrative DNA from one organism and reintroducing it into a different species: a chimera sometimes results. As Huston says of his famous mechanical Moby Dicks when they changed media: "When they were placed in the water, their behavior changed radically. Most of them went straight to the bottom" (Huston 1980: 252). I shall return to this idea of mastery, DNA manipulation and other metaphors for the adaptation process, for these metaphors are a chief interest in this study. But for the moment it might help to recall the sheer quantity of adaptations in the Huston canon. Leslie Brill's count puts it at 34 films of the 37 he directed (1997: 5). Indeed Brill calls Huston "Perhaps the most resourceful adapter of complex literary texts in the history of American and British cinema" (1997: 5). Martin Rubin (1993: 137) has similarly called Huston "the supreme littérateur of classical American cinema."

Why Huston chose these *particular* books and plays to adapt is an irresistible topic for speculation. Lawton cites "biographical bias" as one leitmotiv in the Huston canon. He calls Huston "a conscious promoter of his own mythology" (Cohen and Lawton 1997: 1–2), a fact other critics have observed of many other artists in many other ways. Psychoanalytic critics such as Norman Holland might speak of Huston's search for his "identity theme' in the books he chooses to adapt. Doubtless Harold Bloom would have regarded Huston as reading and then creatively (Oedipally) misreading his literary fathers (and mothers) in an effort to find his own voice. In short, Narcissus looks into many ponds — even oceans — but always finds his own reflection.

Huston's pervasive themes are indeed well known. Lawton, for example, speaks of one group of films about quests: "the quest that is initially for riches or glory, then turns sour, and proves to have been subconsciously animated by less tangible motives." The "soured quest" group includes *The Maltese Falcon* (1941), *The Treasure of the Sierra Madre* (1948), *Moby Dick* (1956) and *The Man Who Would Be King*. Lawton's second group includes films about "misfit heroes, exiles [and the] ... self-destructive." Here he places *Beat the Devil* (1953), *The Misfits* (1961), and *Under the Volcano* (1984). Group three is characterized by mismatched couples: *The African Queen* (1951), and *Heaven Knows Mr. Allison* (1957). Group four illustrates Huston's preoccupation with death, especially his own: *Under the Volcano*, *The Dead* (1987). Add a word about Huston's love for "essentially masculine groups," his "absurdist thread" and his penchant for Promethean figures like Ahab (Cohen and Lawton 1997: 31), and one has a fair survey of the most familiar Huston themes. Many films fit in two or more categories. *Night of the Iguana* is about misfits, mismatched couples *and* death. All Huston films are quest films of a sort. And *Moby Dick* spans all categories. What are Queequeg and Ishmael, if not a mismatched couple who rise above gender and race to form a marriage of true minds?

We can return to Melville himself for another felicitous term by which we can grasp Huston's personal and artistic *ethos*: it is the phrase "desperado philosophy" found in the following passage from the novel *Moby Dick*. Ishmael says:

> There is nothing like the perils of whaling to breed this free and easy sort of genial, desperado philosophy: and with it I now regard this whole voyage of the *Pequod* and the great White Whale its object" [1996: 241].

Moby Dick—the book and the film—provides an oceanic reservoir of Hustonian privileged themes. For Robert Benayoun, "*Moby Dick*, en ce sens, est la justification complète de Huston ... le sommet de son expression et de sa pensée"(1985: 61). ["Moby Dick, in this sense, is the total justification of Huston ... the summit of his expression and his thoughts."] Benayoun calls the White Whale the key to "tous les symboles qui hantent son oeuvre" (1985: 58) ["all the symbols that haunt his work"] and I heartily agree. But first let us consider some more metaphors for the adaptation process itself.

Open Books

Huston alludes to his love of books in the title of his autobiography: *An Open Book*. Certainly he means that his life was unusually public — open to others who would "read" him. But the title also recalls his prodigious appetite for reading, for always having books close at hand. Huston was not above using the hoary old device of showing an open book under his opening credits or having still illustrations come to life on the screen. He does both in *The Red Badge of Courage*. And the opening credits of *Moby Dick* are all run atop illustrations from whaling books. Indeed it was the look of old whaling book illustrations that Huston was striving for visually throughout the film — thus his specially devised use of two superimposed film negatives — one in black and white and the other in color.

Huston seems to have experienced reading a great author, writing a screenplay and directing, as one continuous ongoing creative process. Gideon Bachmann recorded Huston's following remark:

> The directing of a film to me [Huston], is simply an extension of the process of writing. It's process of rendering the thing you have written. You're still writing when you're directing ... [sic] a gesture, the way you make somebody raise his eyes or shake his head is also writing for films" [after Long, 2001: x].

Huston is equally well known for saying it's the idea, the "inbred idea" (Long, 2001: xiv) of a book and then the film he makes out of it that truly matter. Robert E. Long likens Huston's use of the word "idea" to the Henry Jamesian term "figure in the carpet." More than a casual thought, a Hustonian "idea" is a controlling metaphor, even a fully-fledged allegory, in some instances. And Huston speaks of mentally holding on to such "inbred ideas" (sometimes for years) inevitably bringing the notion of gestation or pregnancy to mind. Here is the pertinent passage, again in Huston's interview with Bachmann for *Film Quarterly*: "Most of my pictures begin with this kind of inbred idea, something that lives in me from long ago..." Huston continues, a few lines later, "I let my films make themselves" (after Long, 2001: xi).

From metaphors of indwelling or pregnancy — the adaptation conceived of as a "child" of its original author and the adapter — we move, in the latter quotation above, to the related idea of adaptation as possession of the adapter by the source author. In *Green Shadows, White Whale* Bradbury speaks of his experience writing the script of *Moby Dick* directly as a form of "possession" by Herman Melville. Huston was impressed, and perhaps, from Bradbury's perspective, a bit jealous that "Herman" visited Bradbury and not Huston.

For, after all, the overriding metaphor for adaptation to which Huston and other speakers of the English language probably most often subscribe is that of love, romantic love between the source author and his or her adapter. Consider the very words critics or even casual film fans tend to use. We say Huston (or whoever the adapter might be) was "faithful" or "true" to the original — Melville or Crane — as a lover is faithful or true to his beloved. There is an implied, almost mystical marriage of author and his/her adapter in a romantic — even sexual — union. If this sounds overstated, consider the following description by Wieland Schulz-Keil of Huston writing and later directing a scene:

> He seemed to disappear in the thoughts and images brought about by the writing, his face would light up, he would laugh, sometimes he would almost start crying.... In a mysterious way, he dissolved into what was before him; became, body and soul, one with the scene" [in Cooper 1994: 209–209].

In an interview with Edouard Laurot, also reprinted in Long's collection, Huston, (probably unaware some critic would someday call him on his double entendre), says proudly, "I do believe that my interpretation penetrates to the deepest parts of Melville" (Long 2001: 13–14). From this passionate lover's perspective, it is no wonder Bradbury and Huston clashed during the writing of the *Moby Dick* screenplay. They were involved, along with Herman Melville, in a homoerotic triangle. It is particularly ironic that the real rift between the collaborators, so carefully charted in Bradbury's *Green Shadows, White Whale,* occurred at Huston's insinuation that Bradbury was a closeted gay.

Leviathan Love: Adapting Moby Dick

> *We wanted people to confront a human experience, not to have them listen to the text of a book reproduced on the screen.*— Huston to Michel Ciment, in Long 2001: 146

> *Lose the whale, lose me!*— Huston, having climbed upon his last remaining mechanical whale, *Open Book* 1980: 257

We have already mentioned common themes in the books Huston chose to adapt: soured quests, male-bonding, etc. Given these penchants, Huston must have found Melville utterly irresistible. Consider the allure of this line from the novel as Ishmael surveys the men eating their chowder: "A curious sight; these bashful bears, these timid warrior whalemen" (1996: 33). Of course the *Pequod* is male-bonding heaven. But the attraction of Melville obviously goes deeper than that. It's Melville the Existential Joker whom Huston loves — Melville the Language Lover caught up in an eddy of alliteration. New Bedfordmen, writes Melville, "give whales for dowers to their daughters, and portion off their nieces with a few porpoises a piece" (1996: 35). It's Melville the Allegorist, writing more than once in the novel *Moby Dick* the cryptic words, "This is full of meaning" (1996: 42–43). It's Melville the Humorous Humanist who proves so irresistible to Huston. But it's also these very same alluring qualities — the philosophical passages, the intangibles, the tone — that make the adaptation nigh on impossible.

Negative appraisals of Huston's film usually place it above previous adaptation efforts — the *Sea Beast* (1926) and *Moby Dick* (1930) — in which the whale, in the words of Brandon French, has only "a cameo role" and there's an inexplicable happy end. French continues,

> After all, what could Hollywood do with a whale who allegedly represents nature, all evil, the invisible forces of the universe, truth, the white soul of America, the superego, and God? [1997: 53].

This is not to mention Ahab who needs to be a blend of "Adam, Prometheus, Don Quixote, Ulysses, Jonah and [his Hebrew namesake] Ahab" (French 1997: 52). No wonder Gregory Peck had a few problems.

Another naysayer, critic Vivian Sobchack, warns us about all film adaptations in which "that which is different pretends to be identical" (1980: 285). She likens the illusion that a book can be made into a film to falling for false cognates in the study of a foreign language. What sounds like the same word, isn't. Though she has some good things to say about Huston's efforts — he does create an "autonomous aesthetic work" and he does provide a "penetrating critical interpretation" of his source (1980: 289) — Sobchack tends to mistrust all adaptations as "ideological structures." She, like Walter Metz, sees Huston's take on Melville as a product of its own Cold War time period: 1956. But at least Sobchack doesn't relegate Huston's *Moby Dick* to the "same status as Classic Comics" (Sobchack 1980: 287).

Brandon French has calculated that Bradbury and Huston cut 135 chapters (724 pages in the Library of Literature edition he used) into "54 plot elements over 148 pages of screenplay" (1977: 53). Milton Stern, in his generally negative appraisal, believes the large number of deletions "cut the story loose from its moorings" destroying the nuances of Melville's inherently ambiguous moral stance. Stern fusses about the emphasis on adventure, calling Huston's version "a salty, wet western" (1956: 472). He describes as "unjustifiable" (*ibid.*) the dismissal from the screenplay of the novel's character of Fedallah — a point to which I will return. He says furthermore that the screenplay plus Richard Basehart's performance reduces Ishmael "to a country bumpkin" (*ibid.*). He finds Peck equally miscast. Stern's twelve questions exposing the differences between the novel and the film are somewhat useful for teaching both works in the classroom, but his appraisal seems overly harsh. It is more helpful to discuss the adaptation process in terms of elements that lend themselves to adaptation (we might put these under the heading "Herman Helps") and elements that do not ("Herman Resists").

The principal processes at work during the adaptation process seem to me much akin to the processes operating in the human mind to transform latent desires into the manifest content of dreams. The Freudian dreamwork — like the would-be adapter — functions by cutting, cutting and cutting our memories, based on experiences, then disguising unacceptable, repressed elements by various tricks: displacement and condensation chief among them. But first, a word on qualities inherent to Melville's novel that lend themselves well to the adaptation process.

Herman Helps

The themes in Melville that must have attracted Huston have already been mentioned: the doomed quest, the brotherhood of men, etc. But there are narrative elements on the level of structure that also make Melville highly adaptable. Firstly Melville uses visual symbols that can be transferred quite effectively to the visual medium of film. Consider the painting of the whale impaling himself on the ship's mast at the Spouter Inn and foreshadowing, in part, the *Pequod's* doom (Melville 1851/1996: 11). Huston and Bradbury wisely follow Melville's description and then include the resulting visual — the painting actually realized by some artist or prop man — within the film. Other visual symbols from the novel such as Father Mapple's pulpit shaped like the prow of a ship also transfer quite readily. So does the rope ladder that Father Mapple (Orson Welles) ascends to reach the pulpit, pulling it up behind him. Melville *tells* us that it symbolizes Mapple's otherworldly power and status when he preaches, but we may well have gotten that without being told; Huston *shows* us the rope ladder. He has his Mapple ascend it and pull it up — in a long shot lasting several moments. Then Huston's Mapple gives his sermon — quoted at unusual length directly from the novel. Most important in evaluating the emphasis given this scene in the film is that fact that Huston gives the sermon to his most formidably gifted actor, Orson Welles. He nailed its delivery — production legend has it — in just one extraordinary take.

Auditory (sound) symbols can also transfer nicely from print onto a movie soundtrack. Consider the sound Ahab's whalebone peg leg makes on a wooden deck. The sound symbolizes the deep, still reverberating injury done to his body and soul. Huston likes the sound so much that he actually contradicts his source Melville in order to feature it more prominently than Melville in the original. He takes Melville's assist, in other words, and then runs with it. Realizing the power of sound in a film, Huston allows the ominous thump, thump of Ahab's leg to become our very first sensory introduction to the character. We *hear* him, outside the Spouter Inn, even before we see him. Melville, of course, does not let Ahab fully appear to his readers — other than by hearsay allusions — until 126 pages into the novel, by which time the suspense is overwhelming both to Ishmael and to us as readers. Sacrificing this more obvious opportunity for suspense, Huston lets *his* Ishmael see *his* Ahab — albeit at a distance, in a long shot through the window of the inn — much earlier in the plotline, before he and Queequeg have gone on board the *Pequod*. For the sake of the same sound symbol, Huston takes another large liberty with his source text. Melville says that Ahab *avoids* walking the deck of the *Pequod* when he knows that the crewmembers are sleeping just below (see Chapter 29). It is one of his rare but significant humanizing traits, going on a very short list in the novel that includes two brief mentions of his wife and child, plus his concern for Pip. Huston's Ahab, by contrast, stomps around — we are to imagine nightly — in the person of Gregory Peck. We repeatedly hear the haunting sound POV (really POH — Point of Hearing) of Ishmael and Queequeg whose hammocks are slung only inches below the deck (by Huston) expressly for that very purpose.

Besides providing the would-be adapter with useful visual and sound symbols, Melville goes so far as to dramatize certain sections of his novel — stage directions and all! On a first reading, one is astonished to find these stage directions that have seemingly made an incursion from some wholly different genre — a play or, to contemporary eyes, even a screenplay. Melville includes them without the least apology for his sudden shift in generic expectations. The stage directions certainly suit Melville's Shakespearean tones — his allusions to *King Lear, Hamlet, Macbeth, Richard III* and *Othello*. One extraordinary example should suffice. Melville (1996: 173) actually writes the following lines said by Ahab. For their exuberant theatricality, the lines could just as well have come from the lips of Iago or Richard III as from Ahab. Melville actually prefaces the lines in question with the word "Aside" in brackets:

"[Aside]
 Something shot from my dilated nostrils, he has inhaled it in his lungs. Starbuck now is mine; cannot oppose me now, without rebellion" [1996: 173].

Melville's sudden and frequent forays into dramatic writing within the confines of a putative novel, *Moby Dick*, seem less surprising when one remembers that the work is really a radically mixed generic entity throughout. After all, we have drawings of the wall plaques in the Chapel (words surrounded by what we now call "text boxes"). We have a picture of Queequeg's mark that looks like the sign for infinity: a figure "8" on its side. (Huston interestingly turns it into a drawing of a whale.) We have cetology galore in every conceivable form: whale recipes, whale anatomy, whale journals, whales in literature via quotations, etc., etc. We even have whale songs (sung by the men, not the whales) and whale dancing — the genesis of several operatic and other stage adaptations of the novel. What genre is Melville's *Moby Dick*? That's a question best answered by Shakespeare's Polonius when he is asked what the actors newly arrived in Elsinore can perform. He famously answers "tragedy, comedy, history, pastoral, pastoral-comical, historical-pastoral, [tragical-historical, tragical-comical-historical-pastoral]" (*Hamlet* 2.2.385–388). At any rate, parts of *Moby Dick*— especially visual and sound symbols and scenes already written by Melville in dramatic form — certainly do lend themselves to a film adaptation. Other elements of Melville's art, just as surely do not.

Herman Resists

The sheer size of the novel — the quantity of incidents and musings rendered — has already been cited as perhaps its most daunting characteristic for a would-be adapter. Huston and Bradbury frequently allude to it in interviews and in Bradbury's book. This led, no doubt, to the many and necessary cuts in the text, but also to accompanying condensations and displacements (or substitutions) — some more successful than others. It is not surprising that Huston and Bradbury cut several ships that the *Pequod* meets at sea and combined their various symbolic functions into those of just two ships for the movie: the *Samuel Enderby* and the *Rachel*. Cuts invariably lead to such substitutions. Likewise Huston and Bradbury cut Nantucket from the movie and have New Bedford stand both for itself and the missing Nantucket. At a first glance, there is little lost by this switching of one famous whaling town for another. We do, however, suffer collateral damage. In the novel, Queequeg heroically saves a drowning man who falls overboard from the boat that takes Ishmael and Queequeg out to Nantucket. That act of heroism is lost, as are so many nuances — including homoerotic ones — in the ripening friendship between Ishmael and Queequeg. Melville's chief metaphor for their first night together as bedfellows is, after all, honeymooning.

Melville gives a bemused tone to his first person narrator Ishmael that cannot easily be conveyed in any medium other than its native element: words. The novel is ALL about tone, and many of Melville's most delicate strokes are completely missed in favor of the adapters' quick snapshots and underdeveloped Polaroids (to introduce still another loaded set of metaphors). Melville, for instance, writes about Queequeg's athletic prowess with the awe of a sportswriter. His Queequeg is the Michael Jordan of the long boat, the Tiger Woods of the try pot. And there's that name of his, the subject of one of the few out and out hilarious passages in the novel. The Quaker captains who co-own the *Pequod* and enlist our heroes by playing good cop/bad cop cannot quite get the Pacific Islander's decidedly ethnic-sounding name straight:

> We must have Hedgehog there, I mean Quohog, in one of our boats. Look ye, Quohog, we'll give ye the ninetieth lay, and that's more than ever was given a harpooner yet of Nantucket [Melville 1851/1996: 95].

Huston wisely retains the enlistment scene, including Queequeg's impressive demonstration toss of his harpoon. But he can't fully capture the humor of the original. Huston's actor — Friedrich Liedebur — is an Austrian after all, and not a true South Seas exotic. Like the Quaker owners of the *Pequod* who rechristen Queequeg first "Hedgehog" and then "Quohog" after the name of one of their native clams, Huston finds it necessary to substitute Queequeg's true and alien nature with something more familiar: his European friend Liedebur. Liedebur, a nonactor, is not bad. He suggests the harpooner's friendliness and sometimes his stoicism; but we never believe him for a moment to be a cannibal. Richard Basehart, likewise, does a creditable job conveying Ishmael's friendliness and perhaps a glimmer of his flippancy. But we miss out on the darker shadings of Ishmael's character. The novel is told by a man who has already suffered the death of all his shipmates. Huston's film, true to its own nature as film, is always and irrevocably present tense even when using the convention of flashback. And there is no possible way to convey on film the way Ishmael and the omniscient narrator who occasionally intervenes in the novel melt and bleed into one another — for all the world like Ahab's "torn body" and "gashed soul" are said to bleed into one another (1996: 195) after the White Whale takes his leg. It's a problem unsolved — and probably insoluble — by any adapter.

Equally challenging, and perhaps equally insoluble, is the problem of Ahab, the paradoxical character at the heart of the novel. The first substantial description of Ahab by Melville sets him up as a walking paradox: "he ain't sick; but no, he isn't well either ... [he's a] a queer man" but "a good one." The speaker, Ahab's friend Captain Peleg, continues, "He's grand, ungodly, god-like man, Captain Ahab." The train of paradoxes stretches on: "Ahab's been in colleges, as well as 'mong the cannibals ... [he's] named for a vile king, but 'innocently named'" (Melville 1996: 85). To make things even more difficult for the actor destined to play him, Ahab is, in Melville's terms, insane. Following his mutilation, writes Melville, "Ahab's full lunacy subsided not, but deepeningly contracted" (1996: 196). What's more, Ahab knows that he is unhinged. "Now, in his heart, Ahab had some glimpse of this, namely: all my means are sane, my motive and my object mad" (*ibid.*). Shortly after this we get the strange admission that even Ishmael cannot begin to fathom Ahab: "[A]ll this to explain, would be to dive deeper than Ishmael can go" (Melville 1996: 198), says ... someone. At this point in the novel, the astute reader can see that the narrator, Melville's own persona, has had to quietly take over from Ishmael to save him from metaphorically drowning.

Pity the actor who must make his character an oxymoron. Such was the thankless, impossible task of Peck. And if Ahab is impossibly surcharged with metaphorical meaning, consider his nemesis Moby Dick. Melville devotes a whole chapter just to the mythological meanings of the animal's color. Moby Dick is freighted and weighted with the symbolic charge of all beasts — mythic and real, metaphorical and literal — who have ever tormented mankind. No wonder his mechanical FX counterparts sank! For the Derridean Transcendental Signified, no mere single Signifier could ever suffice. As T.S. Eliot famously complained about *Hamlet*, there's no objective correlative within the play to account for the emotions evoked. The novel *Moby Dick* has a similarly supercharged aura, an aura that cannot be captured on film.

While it is possible to unravel many of Huston and Bradbury's shifts in dialogue and clever scene combinations, some of their efforts — such as the cutting of Fedallah and the change in the various prophecies seem harder to explain. Fedallah, the "tiger yellow" Asian who serves as Mephistopheles to Ahab's Faust is missing and missed in the Huston/Bradbury adaptation. Fedallah's prophecies about the two hearses that Ahab will see (one of American wood) seem rather silly to a contemporary reader, but certainly no sillier than the variations handed over by Huston and Bradbury to their own Elijah figure. Melville's other prophecy, "Hemp only can kill thee" delivered by Fedallah (Melville 1996: 525), sounds strikingly like those tricky statements made to Macbeth by those pesky witches: "No man born of woman," etc. While it is admittedly more dramatic to have a drowned Ahab — instead of Melville's drowned Fedallah — wave to us from Moby Dick's back, the cutting of Fedallah necessitates the other string of changes in the prophecies already reported and seems, in retrospect, more trouble than it is worth. It might have made sense to cut Fedallah's "yellow" fellow crewmen: the super rowers whom Ahab smuggles on board. But Fedallah himself should not have been cut. Ray Bradbury never really explains his loathing for the character, even in the space of a whole book devoted to the rigors of the adaptation process and his jaded views of Huston as a friend.

Conclusion

> *I am Herman Melville.* — Bradbury's
> *Green Shadows, White Whale* 1992: 227

> *No way to describe it. You'll see it on
> the screen someday.* — *Ibid.*, 233

One metaphor for adaptation that relates to possession but bears mentioning on its own is that of the source author as a departed spirit, even a god. It is also the implicit metaphor we use every time we suggest that a director of an adaptation may have changed some things but was faithful to the *spirit* of the original. We are faithful not only to lovers, but to God.

Although he didn't hesitate to make changes to source materials, Huston's quasi-religious reverence for great writers is clear in most of his aesthetic choices and, as mentioned, in the sheer number of good books he adapted into films. The film version of, for example, *The Red Badge of Courage* is as much about its author Stephen Crane as it is about Henry, the Everyman soldier played by Audie Murphy. The voice-over narration at the beginning makes it clear whose *Entwicklungsroman* (or *Entwicklungsfilm*) it really is. Huston has his narrator say, "Stephen Crane wrote this book when he was a boy of 22. Its publication made him a man."

Huston's film version of *The Man Who Would Be King* likewise keeps its source author Kipling's spirit alive and present throughout by retaining the framing premise that Peachy (Michael Caine) is telling the story to Kipling, after the loss of Peachy's Masonic brother/best friend (played by Sean Connery). In this case, Kipling also has a corporeal form, played in the film by Christopher Plummer.

Though the source author's Holy Ghostly presence may not be that obvious in every Huston film adaptation, one still gets frequent shivers at the sight of authorial spirits hovering close at hand. Bradbury — despite his differences with Huston over who would be Alpha Adapter — speaks eloquently about Huston's deep-seated love for Melville (and, by inference, his other great sources). Bradbury's thoughts can be found in a poem entitled "Old Ahab's Friend and Friend to Noah, Speaks His Piece," reprinted in an 1992 article by Steven E. Kagle. The poem is so revealing because it works as either the thoughts of Bradbury or of Huston himself.

In the former reading of the poem, we are encouraged to see Bradbury himself (or a Bradbury persona) as the first person speaker of the poem. Bradbury is, after all, or at least started out as Old Ahab's (Huston's) friend, a friend to Noah (played, of course, by Huston in *The Bible: In the Beginning*). But Huston has become the domineering spirit that haunts Bradbury's dreams. Huston is Bradbury's White Whale, his nemesis. He has been Huston's equal, his writer-kin, his collaborator on the screenplay. Huston, however, has treated him condescendingly — as a feeble son or, worse, a male wife, with the homosexual overtones that term implies. In the poem, and even more clearly in the novel *Green Shadows, White Whale,* Bradbury strikes back, demanding his full masculinity and a place out of Huston's shadow.

But the poem can also be read with Huston as the first person speaker. Then it is he who is haunted by the White Whale — the Impossible Adaptation. Even if Melville takes him as an equal, his writer-kin, Huston is haunted by feelings of weakness. He is merely a "feeble" literary son, effeminate by comparison with the great Melville. And yet their marital union as husband and "husband wife" is fruitful: we have the film *Moby Dick,* their offspring. Like other adapted progeny, it carries traits of both its parents, but it is an independent entity. In the case of John Huston's *Moby Dick,* it may not be perfect, but it certainly deserves its great title, the equivalent of its family name. It, like Huston's other adaptations of great literary works, is a truly *sui generis* work of art.

The Melodramatic Conscience of *In This Our Life*

VICTORIA AMADOR

In his 1980 autobiography *An Open Book*, John Huston states, "I never cared for *In This Our Life*" (81). He barely discusses the 1942 film, his second directorial effort at Warner Bros. and the first after *The Maltese Falcon* (1941), giving it only three paragraphs. While the film was a major career opportunity for Huston and starred Bette Davis and Olivia de Havilland, two of Warner Bros.' most popular female stars, Huston wasn't mad for Howard Koch's screenplay. Adapting Virginia novelist Ellen Glasgow's 1942 Pulitzer Prize winner, Koch altered much of Glasgow's grit and to an extent created another "women's picture." Nevertheless, the film was Warner Brothers' highest grosser for 1942 and Davis' biggest hit to date, earning over $1.7 million (Spada 1993 [2005]: 260), although it wasn't nominated for any major awards and the reviews were mixed.

Yet this picture presented important societal concerns to its audience, mirroring Ellen Glasgow's novel more than Huston acknowledged. Glasgow was one of the founding members of the Equal Suffrage League, and most of her works attacked the South's "coloured spectacles of evasive idealism" (Glasgow 1941: 136). Glasgow's view of the novel's world was grim. Asa Timberlake, her central protagonist, decides that "man is not a rational animal. He may have invented many social philosophies, but he remains incurably biological" (*ibid.*: 157). The other characters also find no peace or moral certainty.

In the film, Koch shifts the emphasis to the two daughters of Asa, played by Davis and de Havilland. Asa (Frank Craven) is a quiet, aging Virginian who has lost his tobacco business interests to his wife Lavinia's brother, William Fitzroy, a powerful and unscrupulous businessman. The Timberlakes have two daughters, Stanley (Davis) and Roy (de Havilland), presumably named thus because they had no sons — another failure for Asa. Stanley is spoiled and headstrong, while Roy is quiet, hardworking, and living in her parents' home with her surgeon husband. On the eve of Stanley's wedding to her fiancé Craig Fleming (George Brent), a civil liberties lawyer, Stanley runs away to Baltimore with sister Roy's husband Peter Kingsmill (Dennis Morgan). They marry, but Stanley treats Peter badly and he commits suicide.

When Stanley comes back home, she discovers petulantly that Roy and Craig are a couple. A young black man, Parry Clay (Ernest Anderson), is working in Craig's law office. Resenting the new couple's happiness, and angry because her rich uncle William will not help her leave town, Stanley drives too fast and accidentally kills a young girl and injures her mother. Stanley blames the accident on Parry, but when the truth finally emerges, she tries to escape the police and is killed in a car accident; screenwriter Koch appended that divine justice to the plot, for in Glasgow's novel, Stanley lives, unrepentant.

Despite Huston's reservations, the film maintains many of Glasgow's lessons in social conscientiousness while giving audiences a Bette Davis melodrama. The mixture is not incompatible, for "melodramas open space prohibited by the so-called classical realist film text, which is restricted to oppressive patriarchal norms" (Kaplan 2000: 52). The film certainly brings attention to a variety of negative patriarchal constructs in its 100-minute running time: the complexities of family relationships, particularly the challenges of loyalty and forgiveness; the importance of personal responsibility and culpability; the tension within the culture concerning profit for personal gain versus community contribution; and most importantly, the racism inherent in American society of the time.

It also demonstrated "the seeds of Huston's social conscience" (Pratley 1997: 50), his commitment to political and social commentaries in his films, his ambitions "to exceed the set limits of American genres" (Thomson 2002: 424), and his ability to make moral statements even within the generic limitations of melodrama, thereby engendering simultaneous diversion and debate.

Family Ties

As noted above John Huston was not overly fond of *In This Our Life*, perhaps in part because he had accidentally killed someone with his car in the 1930s and the plot was too familiar for comfort. Yet he did acknowledge some family feeling within the turbulent production. That feeling is certainly reflected in the ambivalent presence of screenwriter Howard Koch, in the on-set relationships, and in one of the film's major themes — the complexity of family associations.

Huston had recommended to producer Hal Wallis that he hire Koch, whose "first assignment at Warner Bros. was *In This Our Life*" (Huston 1981: 80–1). Huston said, "I didn't like the script, but Koch was there on my say-so and I couldn't very well shoot down his first effort" (*ibid.*). Huston's loyalty to Koch led him to "put aside [his] reservations and [try] to make the best picture [he] could" (*ibid.*).

Huston also recognized that "there were some good things about it," not the least of which being that "it was very flattering for me — a director with only one picture behind him — to be given a picture with Warners' top stars: Bette Davis, Olivia de Havilland, Charles Coburn, George Brent and Dennis Morgan" (*ibid.*). That Warners gave the young director such a major production and cast demonstrated the family feeling which the studio system promoted, and Huston conceded, "I will remember this film mostly for what it shows about the old 'dictatorial' studio system: how much sympathy and latitude could be granted even to someone as inexperienced as I" (*ibid.*).

Family feeling went even further in the film. Huston cast his father, Walter, in a brief unbilled role as a bartender deeply annoyed with Bette Davis' Stanley. Davis herself had to miss several production days because her husband Arthur Farnsworth was ill with pneumonia in a Minneapolis hospital. She was also working again with George Brent, her co-star in eleven films, another Warners contract player, and an on-off lover for years.

Meanwhile, Olivia de Havilland was engaged in one of her many "familial" battles with the *pater familias* of Warner Bros., Jack Warner, over her contract expectations and even her costumes (Higham 1986: 138–142); this would lead her the next year to take Warner to court for contract abuses and eventually resulted in the landmark de Havilland Decision, which changed the studio star system forever. She was also tiptoeing around Davis, with whom she became close friends later but who had ignored her completely during filming of *The Private Lives of Elizabeth and Essex* (1939). Higham notes that the "picture was saturated with neurotic strains" (1986: 140), rather like a dysfunctional family.

Further on-set family feeling resulted from Huston's intense and doomed love affair with de Havilland, about which he and the actress maintained necessary but painful discretion, for Huston was married at the time to his second wife, Lesley Black. In fact, Huston doesn't discuss de Havilland in his autobiography but instead simply includes two photographs of the two of them fishing and singing together, letting the images express the poignancy of their years-long, on-off relationship.

Thus, family loyalties, and the love and grief which can result, drive the central conflict of the film and the novel. The two Timberlake sisters' masculine names, Stanley and Roy, represent a freedom increasingly common in war time for two young women but which, when mishandled and unappreciated, results in family dysfunction. Roy (de Havilland) is the responsible, beleaguered sibling, working as an interior decorator and living in her parents' home with her husband Peter to help her family. When Craig compliments her on her intelligence, she replies, "That's a trait every man admires — in another man," adding a distinctly feminist, New Woman note which reflected societal ambivalence concerning strong women.

Stanley contrasts Roy as the prodigal son/daughter, much more traditionally feminine, yet driving carelessly, seducing Roy's husband and driving him to suicide, and then trying to win back her jilted fiancé Craig. Considering the time of the film's production — they were shooting retakes when Pearl Harbor was attacked on December 7 — the financial independence of women implicit in Roy's work ethic and Stanley's sexual transgressions represent the gender tensions which were about to become manifest within the shifting configuration of the American family.

Roy could easily appear to be weak in her forgiveness of Stanley's murderous actions, yet through de Havilland's restrained and mature performance, guided by Huston to such an extent that Davis complained he was giving her too much attention, Roy's selflessness appears believable. Her inner strength, reflects the same sort of credibility that de Havilland achieved as Melanie in *Gone with the Wind* (1939); tolerance and loyalty become strengths to be admired.

Roy is like her father Asa in her capacity to love and forgive. Asa's wife Lavinia sees him as a failure because he has been cheated out of his wealth by her brother, William. She is a permanent invalid as a result, and as portrayed by Billie Burke, poignantly pathetic. William Fitzroy (the ineluctable Charles Coburn) has stripped Asa of his stature in the community and of his business, and yet he is still welcome in the Timberlake home. Stanley even mocks Asa to her uncle when, after hearing how he cheated her father, she declares, "I call it smart." Yet Asa welcomes Stanley home after Peter's suicide, an event for which she takes hysterical responsibility only briefly to earn sympathy.

Roy and Asa's family compassion is mirrored in Minerva Clay, played by Hattie McDaniel, and her son Parry, portrayed by Ernest Anderson. Minerva works as a housekeeper for the Timberlakes and is intimate enough to dryly note, "Poor Mr. Craig. ... the gentleman what gets Miss Stanley gets a handful." Her son, Parry, valets Stanley's car — a gift from her rich uncle. However, his law aspirations are given substance when Roy secures a clerk's position for him in Craig's office. Minerva and Parry are a part of the Timberlake family as far as Asa and Roy are concerned, as was common with many blacks working for whites in the South at that time.

These representatives of the ideal family feeling are challenged constantly throughout the film by those who would exploit them, and Ellen Glasgow's initial judgments of that exploitation are vividly illustrated by Huston and Koch in the depiction of William Fitzroy and his Doppelganger, Stanley.

Surely Huston enjoyed the depiction of two very greedy, very amoral characters who eventually get their comeuppance. William even acknowledges that greed when he tells Stanley, "What we want, we go after. And what we go after, we get." Stanley in turn proves she is her uncle's niece when she calls him to his face "the goose that lays the golden eggs."

The amorality of both is best expressed by the disturbing note of incest in their relationship, presented quite literally and spicily by Huston and crew. Played as "something slightly obscene" (Crowther 1942) by Charles Coburn, Uncle William clearly has unhealthy affection for Stanley. When he gives her a huge check for her wedding to Craig, he declares, "You're not going to turn your face away this time," seeking her lips for a kiss but being thwarted. Of course, she cashes the check and buys a phonograph despite leaving Craig at the altar.

Later, after Peter's death and her return home, she "wins a chuckle from him with the brazen admission: 'Guess I'm kill or cure'" ("New Pictures" 1942). Stanley flirts shamelessly with him to get money, nestling against him on the couch, encouraging him to drink, and telling him, "You've never looked better — or younger." When he calls her a "rascal" and a "little devil" for stealing Peter from Roy, she teases, "Was it moral indignation? Or jealousy?" He in turn suggests she move in with him and says, "We'll take trips together." Clearly his interest is not avuncular, and clearly she exploits this to the boundaries of becoming his mistress. Huston's direction encourages this wicked subplot and the lascivious playing of both Coburn and Davis, a daring choice for the time.

His direction also manages to give Bette Davis the opportunity to create a character who is so dreadful one cannot stop watching her in fascination. Alexander Walker noted, "Deceit becomes Davis marvelously: it sharpens her femininity. She never seems more desirable than when she is lying her way out of a crisis with a ready tongue and, if that fails, falling back on wiles and pleas that are pitched at the male she basically mistrusts and despises" (1995: 110). Huston said of her, "Bette fascinated me. There is something elemental about Bette — a demon within her which threatens to break out and eat everybody, beginning with their ears. The studio was afraid of her ... demon.... Over their objections, I let the demon go; some critics thought

Bette's performance was one of her finest" (1981: 81). Although Davis was nominated for an Oscar that year for *Now, Voyager* (1942) her fire as the demented southern belle and bad sister Stanley is equally memorable and due in great part to Huston's guidance.

Personal Responsibility

Huston's film also addresses another of his pet themes — the idea of personal responsibility for one's actions. It's no surprise that in Huston's *oeuvre*, there must almost always be payment for guilt and sin of some kind. Brigid O'Shaughnessy must be turned in by Sam Spade in *The Maltese Falcon* (1941). Audie Murphy's frightened Civil War soldier returns to the front in *The Red Badge of Courage* (1951), and Sean Connery's *Man Who Would Be King* (1975) dies for his grandiosity over others. *In This Our Life* portrays the sense of entitlement in wealthy white Americans, resulting in an expectation that personal happiness is everything, and individual culpability is antiquated. However, Huston also offers the hope that eventually, scores are settled and some people still think of others.

Asa Timberlake reflects upon entitlement when Stanley cries petulantly, "I can't bear to see other people happy when I'm — when I'm so miserable" He responds with dry irony:

> In my day, we didn't talk much about happiness. If it came, we were grateful for it, but we were brought up in the belief that there were other things more important ... oh, old fogey, fantastic notions such as duty and personal responsibility.

Roy summarizes Stanley's selfishness when she says, "All she wants is to be happy, no matter what it costs someone else." Koch's script foreshadows the narcissism of future generations of Americans who have taken the notion of "life, liberty and the pursuit of happiness" to the greatest extremes imaginable.

Asa has remained responsible for Lavinia, who does absolutely nothing but wear peignoirs and demand her medicine. He has accepted that his home and his business and his prospects are lost due to William's machinations and his own weaknesses. Roy too bears responsibilities by giving Parry work, forgiving her sister and burying her ex-husband. She also encourages Craig to help Parry further, telling him:

> I've just talked with a colored boy.... He's going to be a lawyer. No woman or nothing on earth's going to stop him. You've got everything that boy wants, and you sit here feeling sorry for yourself.

Craig in turn rejects William's offer of business when William insists he stop helping the poor, telling Fitzroy, "I couldn't afford to ... they can't pay much, but they're very good clients."

Parry and Minerva share the responsibilities of life in that both work, and Parry gives part of his salary to his mother Minerva to help pay their rent. The only treat he buys himself is "a book I've been wanting to get at the second hand store ... Blackstone's Commentaries, Foundation of Common Law and Modern Jurisprudence."

However, with the exception of these characters, the other major characters of the film do as they wish in the belief that their own desires are paramount. There is no sense of collective morality or community. When Peter asks Stanley strickenly, "Do you realize what we've done? All the unhappiness we've caused? If we don't make up for that in our own happiness, heaven help us," her response is to run up bills, and drive him to drink and suicide.

Her greatest abnegation of personal responsibility occurs when Stanley blames the hit and run accident she has caused upon Parry. She fully expects that Parry, a black man, will take the blame for her; if he will "just say you took the car," he can go to jail for a few years and then Uncle William and Craig will "give him a fresh start." She also fully expects everyone to believe her innocence, dismissing with blatant racism Minerva's assertion that Parry was home during the accident: "Whenever they're in a tight spot, they always lie for each other."

Bette Davis attacks her role the way Stanley attacks the world, with frightening, narcissistic vigor. Walker notes that "her Stanley Timberlake is ... morally stone-deaf ... no use using the voice of conscience against her eardrum" (1995: 115). Of course, she represents for both Glasgow and Huston the ethical void of many white southerners.

Interestingly, in Glasgow's novel, while Parry is freed, his spirit is broken. Meanwhile, Stanley only receives a slap on the wrist and is released, unpunished and presumably unchanged. Huston's film leaves us with a similar disaffected sense of justice, but the thought of some kind of karmic balance provides a suggestion of hope for the viewer. Stanley is dead in the iconographic car which represents everything she is — shiny, fast and dangerous. William is dying and has six months to live. Roy and Craig, the good guys, get the closing shot.

Private Gain and Public Commitment

In This Our Life presents an ambivalent perspective upon American commerce and cultural expectation, symbolized primarily by William Fitzroy.

Uncle William is a clever businessman, but Koch's script and Huston's direction depict him as a bloated capitalist, his large frame and pompous declamations, and his unhealthy interest in his niece, demonstrating the ultimate fatuousness and danger of the American inclination to honor financial achievement over public commitment.

Asa Timberlake's family is solidly middle class and can afford to hire a housekeeper, Minerva, yet their daughter Roy lives at home to help with expenses and to be with those she loves. Asa's original family home is seen at the film's opening being torn down: by comparison where they now live is modest. However, William's enormous house, empty but for his timid wife and black servants, represents the bulbous wealth of those who earn everything and give nothing in return. Comparing his grand plantation-style mansion to the Timberlakes' modest home demonstrates William's delight in asserting his superiority over Asa. His lack of children bespeaks his own moral sterility, and only Stanley benefits from his wealth, demonstrating capitalism at its most corrupt.

This is similarly evinced by his offer to give some business to Craig for some of his legal concerns. However, the offer is conditional on Peter's abandoning "certain persons I can't approve of." To Roy's delight, Craig refuses, the former asserting that "Perhaps he prefers his ideas to fees ... Craig has convictions — I like that." However, Craig's refusal will also keep his law practice a small concern and his own contributions to society limited; that nod of realism central to Huston's works appears through subtle implication.

Huston's movies often portrayed greed as one of the greatest sins. Consider for example the band of fortune hunters in *The Maltese Falcon*, the gold miners in *Treasure of the Sierra Madre* (1948), the con artists in *Beat the Devil* (1953), the mustang ropers in *The Misfits* (1961), or the power-hungry adventurers in *The Man Who Would Be King*. Even Huston's own performance as the corrupt Noah Cross, trading his daughter's life for expensive Los Angeles water rights in *Chinatown* (1974), reiterates this recurrent theme in his films. *In This Our Life* literally kills off those who would profit most from their selfish impulses, leaving the viewer with the implications that the Timberlake clan will be the stronger at the end and ultimately triumph over the sins of the uncles and sisters.

African American Experience

Without question, the most significant aspect of *In This Our Life* is the depiction of African Americans. John Huston was proud of this element of the film and noted in his autobiography, "It was the first time, I believe, that a black character was presented as anything other than a good and faithful servant or comic relief" (1981: 81). Ellen Glasgow's novel addressed the positions of blacks in southern society in detail. Bravely, Koch's screenplay posited that subplot centrally in the film's action, contravening previous decisions made by Joseph Breen and the Production Code Administration which rejected certain scripts dealing with "such an inflammatory subject" as "race prejudice" (Maltby 2003: 278).

Hattie McDaniel's character remained a maid, despite her best supporting actress Oscar two years before for *Gone with the Wind*. Yet McDaniel had tested for the role of Minerva Clay over some objections of studio advisors, who felt she "was suited only for comedy" (Watts 2005: 206). She knew that the role was serious and greatly wanted to demonstrate her acting abilities. Fortunately, Jack Warner supported her desires with producer Hal Wallis and "[a]t his insistence, McDaniel was hired. It was an encouraging sign" (*ibid.*). It should also be noted that throughout the 1930s and 1940s, Warners was consistently proactive in its employment of black actors, albeit in stereotypical roles, compared to other major studios.

Although McDaniel has only three scenes, her Minerva is clearly central to the Timberlake family, and her brief scenes with Olivia de Havilland demonstrate a mutual respect between the characters and the actresses — de Havilland had lost the 1939 Oscar to McDaniel. McDaniel uses the skills for both irony and sorrow she demonstrated in *Gone with the Wind* in her scenes with de Havilland, sometimes humorous, at other times poignantly dignified, but always a commanding screen presence.

Ernest Anderson offers an equally compelling portrayal of McDaniel's son. He is always respectful to the Timberlakes, but he is also quietly forceful. Parry's explanation to Roy about his ambitions is startling in a 1942 film, and as written by Koch and played by Anderson, it is a quiet and proud assertion of the way he sees the world:

> A white boy — he can take most any kind of job and improve himself. Well, like in this store. Maybe he can get to be a clerk or a manager. But a colored boy — he can't do that. He can keep a job or he can lose a job, but he can't get any higher up. So he's got to figure something he can do that no one can take away. And that's why I want to be a lawyer.

As directed by Huston, there is no disdain or overt sentimentality in this or any of Anderson's scenes.

When Parry is accused of the hit and run accident by Stanley, Roy immediately goes to Minerva, for "I couldn't have Minerva think we'd let her down when her boy's in trouble." Minerva in turn finds the courage to accuse Stanley — another major change in a film of the time:

> With a quiet dignity, the clearly worried yet proud Minerva confronts the white woman with the truth not only about her scheming sister but also about the fate of African Americans in the justice system [Watts 2005: 206].

Roy believes Minerva when she explains that the police "just come and took him off, and he tried to tell 'em, but they don't listen to no colored boy."

In the scene when Craig and Stanley interview Parry in jail, orchestrated by Craig to break down Stanley, Ernest Anderson's performance is heartbreaking. All of the calm confidence and desire of his character is lost behind bars. He looks beaten. But even here, he refuses to bend to Stanley's white-hot will, asserting, "Miss Stanley — she knows.... My telling the truth ain't gonna help me. There ain't nothin' gonna help me."

Although this is the last time we see Parry in the film, we learn later that he has been released from jail and exonerated. One must remember, however, that the film is set in Virginia, and the mere accusation of Parry will likely stay with him in this southern town. It's a happy ending with an unspoken Hustonian irony.

The efforts of the film to present the racism in American society did not go unnoticed. *In This Our Life* was not only Warner Bros.' biggest hit of 1942; it was recognized for its sympathetic treatment of blacks and led to Warner Bros. being named to the Honor Roll of Race maintained by the New York Public Library's Schomberg Collection of Negro Literature Relations.

Additionally, as Jill Watts notes in her biography of Hattie McDaniel, several critics recognized that the film addressed racial inequality in the United States. Bosley Crowther's contemporary review in the *New York Times* noted this was

> the one exceptional component of the film — this brief but frank allusion to racial discrimination. And it is presented in a realistic manner, uncommon to Hollywood, by the definition of the Negro as an educated and comprehending character.

Warner Bros. received fan letters which thanked the studio for the film, and black Private James Samuels wrote, "Thank God that you see the light" (Watts 2005: 221).

Walter White, the leader of the NAACP, wrote both to Harry Warner and Olivia de Havilland, thanking them for the film. In turn, de Havilland wrote to White:

> Several of us who were associated with the film felt that it would have been a much more interesting picture if it had been a less conventional story of romance and trouble ... and had dealt more deeply and extensively with the story of Parry and Minerva and their relationship to the principal characters.

Sadly, there were still unpleasant responses to the movie. When the film was shown in many Southern theatres, all mentions of racism were edited. While *In This Our Life* was run in its entirety in Manhattan theatres after its release in May 1942, many Harlem theatres showed edited versions as well. Despite her best-supporting Oscar, McDaniel was billed on the second page of the closing credits.

Additionally, Warner Bros. press releases demonstrated condescension towards both Ernest Anderson and Hattie McDaniel. Anderson had graduated from Northwestern University's theatre department, but the press releases stressed that he'd been a service attendant at the studio and a favorite of Bette Davis. Some releases also emphasized the stereotype of McDaniel as Mammy in *Gone with the Wind*. Still, "Hattie McDaniel had become the first black actress to voice direct criticism of American racism on the Hollywood screen" (Watts 2005: 222).

Conclusion

Despite John Huston's ambivalence about *In This Our Life*, it remains an important (and thoroughly enjoyable) film. From the excellence of the performances to the controversial subject matter, the film remains a classic representation of Huston's directorial style. He worked sensitively with his actors, explored the perverse motivations behind love, desire, and forgiveness and critiqued the American institutions of moneymaking and big business. He also presented black characters as humans rather than stereotypes and dared to criticize racial discrimination at a time when America's self-mythologizing on the screen was in full flower. Years after completing the film Huston remarked, "[W]hen I saw it on the screen I felt, I knew, that it was good" (Pratley 1997: 44). He was right. The melodramatic conscience of *In This Our Life* still provokes while it entertains its audience.

The Irish Accent of *The Dead*
Michael Patrick Gillespie

As is the case with many Americans, John Huston liked to think of himself as Irish, and in his endeavors to affirm that identity he did a great deal more than most who ascribe to [themselves] that designation. Huston had a home in Galway from the mid–1950s to the mid–1970s, where he reveled in fox hunting and other trappings of the Big House life. He became an Irish citizen in 1964 (though this may have been motivated as much by tax laws in the United States and Ireland as by nationalistic impulses). From *Moby Dick* (1956) to *The Macintosh Man* (1973), Huston made a concerted effort to film in Ireland. And in the late 1960s he took an active, if largely unsuccessful, part in fostering indigenous filmmaking. At the same time, there is little or no evidence of Huston having or even feeling the need to have a clear sense of what the designation Irish meant (Grobel 1989; Huston 1980; Carson 1990: 26–29).

One can understand and even excuse Huston's lack of concern for a precise articulation of Irishness. Generalizations grounded on indefinite meanings have traditionally characterized notions of national identity, and Ireland stands as no less susceptible to this condition than any other country. Eighty-five years ago James Joyce, in the Cyclops chapter of *Ulysses*, neatly summarized the slipperiness of the concept when barroom bullies, challenging the authenticity of Leopold Bloom's Irishness, highlight ambiguities surrounding the idea of nation and hence of a national identity.

— But do you know what a nation means? says John Wyse.
— Yes, says Bloom.
— What is it? says John Wyse.
— A nation? says Bloom. A nation is the same people living in the same place.
— By God, then, says Ned, laughing, if that's so I'm a nation for I'm living in the same place for the past five years.

So of course everyone had the laugh at Bloom and says he, trying to muck out of it:

— Or also living in different places.

— That covers my case, says Joe.
— What is your nation if I may ask? says the citizen.
— Ireland, says Bloom. I was born here. Ireland[1] [Joyce, 1986: 1419–1431].

Over the past decade and a half, as the Celtic Tiger accelerated Irish internationalization, the issue of identity has grown increasingly popular as a topic for inquiry among both academics and non-academics. However, contemporary studies have proven no more adept than Joyce's characters at reaching a consensus understanding of the term's meaning. Rather, they have succeeded only in reiterating the idea that a diversity of concepts all adhere to the term Irishness (Kornprobst 2005: 403–421; Donohue 1988; Peillon and Slater 1998; Logue 2000; McWilliams 2005). Problems of identity have raised specific interpretive questions relating to film in Ireland that remain at best only provisionally resolved.[2] How then, in an essay focusing on Huston's most overtly Irish themed work, *The Dead* (1987), does one judge the effect of Irish identity on interpretations without risking misprision in both biographic and critical assumptions?

The first step toward engagement involves acknowledging the mutability of the features contributing to one's sense of the Irishness within the motion picture. Specific elements — social, geographic, and cultural — within *The Dead* invite viewers to give primacy to its Irish environment. At the same time, as one endeavors to assign specific significance to these features, the inherent subjectivity of individual reactions leads to interpretive difficulties. For example, despite the film's elaborate celebration of Irish hospitality, instances of the conflicted way characters extend that hospitality to one another throughout the evening — Mr. Browne's treatment of Freddy, Molly Ivor's interaction with Gabriel, Lily's attitude toward the guests — call any single concept of the term into question. Obviously, the Irish markers that Huston incorporated into the creative milieu inform the structure of welcome within the work. Nonetheless even with these features in evidence, persistent questions remain as to how one should apply to interpretations of *The Dead* this subjective sense of the cultural context from which concepts like Irish hospitality emerged.

Elsewhere, I have explored the challenges presented by the multiplicity represented under the broad category of Irish themed films (Gillespie 2006: 44–64). In that essay, I expand upon the idea that employing a single perspective for viewing Irish themed films can no longer produce satisfactory interpretations. Instead, one needs to cultivate understanding based upon an awareness of numerous, co-existent states of Irishness. Each condition remains self-contained and distinct from the others, yet all develop from the same cultural context and all legitimately lay claim to the designation. Consequently, interpretations of *The Dead* need to identify the particular Irish features acting upon the narrative and to acknowledge the range of interpretive possibilities fostered by each of these elements.

Given the cultural markers that characterize *The Dead*, set in an environment that preceded the recent seismic changes in Irish society by nearly a century, the task may at first glance seem fairly straightforward. Clearly, the Irishness of the film is not in dispute, despite the fact that, when Huston finally came to an Irish themed motion picture as his last project, it was shot in a warehouse converted to a soundstage in Valencia, California. (Huston had wanted to film in Dublin, but his poor health made this impossible.)

Regardless of the production venue, Irishness stands as a central feature of *The Dead*. Huston drew inspiration for his film from James Joyce's magisterial Irish short story "The Dead" from his *Dubliners* collection. He cast his project with well known Irish actors — like Donal McCann, Dan O'Herlihy, and Cathleen Delany — or actors of Irish descent well-known for playing Irish roles — like Donal Donnelly. And he allowed his narrative to unfold with a sufficient number of markers — historic references to Parnell and O'Connell, nationalistic talk of the Celtic Revival, and social recollections of the nineteenth-century Irish musical scene — to convey the presumption that viewers would immerse themselves in its cultural context.

In each of these instances, however, signs of national identity disrupt rather than enforce causal comprehension. They emphatically call for the viewer's attention while at the same time they provoke discursive or subjective responses. The *mise en scène* (itself a term fraught with ambiguity and multiple delineations) reiterates the necessity of culturally contextualizing any interpretation. However, time and again the narrative in its assertions and its silences refuse to lay out prescriptive formulations for contextualization. Instead, by insinuating ambiguity into the most seemingly straightforward scenes — see, for example Gabriel's initial interaction with Lily — the film aggressively reiterates the need for individuals to acknowledge a subjective sense of the Irishness of the work.

Before engaging the options for individual responses to Irishness in *The Dead*, however, I think it important to make clear the delineation between it and that of the film's source, James Joyce's short story, "The Dead."[3] In no uncertain terms, the figure of Joyce, a presence always on the periphery of Huston's *The Dead*, enhances the imperative to see the film's Irishness. At the same time, to read Huston's motion picture as simply an illustrated version of the short story imposes an unfairly narrow analysis on the motion picture.

Of course, like so many of Huston's other projects, his last movie came to fruition as an adaptation of a literary work, but none of the others created the interest in the director's source material that this did. Even when Huston drew upon the works of authors as prominent as Herman Melville (*Moby Dick*) and Stephen Crane (*The Red Badge of Courage*), interpreters of earlier films by Huston could nod to the authors of the works upon which the motion pictures were based without drawing attention away from Huston's effort. This project, however, distinguished itself from its predecessors by turning for inspiration to the most critically acclaimed and widely anthologized English language short story of the twentieth century. Because of this renown and familiarity, many critics and countless ordinary viewers find impressions from Joyce's short story dominating their experiences of viewing Huston's movie, and, indeed, a number of scholars have made detailed comparisons between the two works, basing their assessments of the value of the film upon their perceptions of its fidelity to the details of the short story (Barry 2001; Hart 1988; Moylan Mills 1999: 120–127).

Initially such comparisons may have been necessary and even desirable given the proprietary interest that many scholars feel for the integrity of Joyce's canon.[4] However, the proliferation of so many assessments of Huston's film that reiterate critiques of its perceived response to Joyce's short story has created a body of work that diverts critical attention from the central issues of both. Too much has gone into such comparisons to allow one simply to dismiss this practice out of hand, so, for the next few paragraphs, I wish to elaborate on my grounds for asserting the danger that an emphasis on what Joyce accomplished in his short story poses to a full understanding of Huston's cinematic achievement.

The most obvious reason for insisting on separate analyses of Huston and Joyce's works rests on a fundamental interpretive assumption: any imaginative effort deserves the respect of consideration as independent artistic creators rather than enduring invidious and unproductive comparisons. Though such an observation seems indisputably obvious in the case of a renowned author, Huston's status as a filmmaker should not prohibit his meriting the same consideration. To judge a cinematic achievement on the basis of its ability to mimic its fictional source demeans the filmmaker's creative efforts. Kazuo Ishiguro summed up the difference very nicely, if less stridently, when commenting on the cinematic adaptation of one of his novels: "there is this other thing that is called James Ivory's *The Remains of the Day* which is a cousin of my *The Remains of the Day*, but it is a different work of art. It is one I have a lot of affection for" (Gallix 2000: 166).

Our reading of Joyce can certainly inform expectations that we bring to our viewing of Huston, but projecting that influence beyond a broad associative level to prescriptive protocols for apprehension leads only to reductive concepts. One sees this amply illustrated in the history of interpretive responses to Joyce's *Ulysses*. While initially (and with Joyce's encouragement) readers formed laborious analogies to *The Odyssey*, within a relatively short time critics saw this approach as far too narrow (Gilbert 1930). Similarly, the time has come to discard the short story as a yardstick for gauging the value of the motion picture.

The structures of film and literature further militate against this sort of alignment.[5] Literary works create broad impressions, often more suggestive than descriptive, giving the reader a great deal of latitude in the construction of images of individuals and their actions. The cinema, in contrast, produces a far more directed experience, with shots selected and framed to the inevitable exclusion of other elements on the set.[6] Detail becomes a key feature in any cinematic understanding and the elements, held in tension through the *mise en scene*, demand from viewers sharply different interpretive accomplishments than do the lines of exposition featured in fiction. If one accepts these fundamental epistemological differences, then comparisons between media become irrelevant.

That is not to say that interpretations of *The Dead* must unfold without an imaginative regard for provenance or context. Understanding the creative tradition from which the film emerged and the cultural milieu that it reflects as an Irish themed film stand as important challenges to anyone seeking a full sense of Huston's motion picture. However, the fullest interpretations of *The Dead* inevitably grow out of individualized responses to the images on the screen and a personalized sense of the cultural context from which they emerge. At the same time, acknowledging the subjectivity surrounding issues of identity does not negate interpretive efforts or preclude the ability of individuals to exchange impressions of the film in a productive fashion. Rather, in rejecting assumptions of causality fostered by an impulse toward closure, the approach that I advocate invites a toleration of multiplicity sustained by nonlinearity as a means of making accessible a range of cultural imperatives and hermeneutic alternatives into expressions of responses to the film (Gillespie 2006: 123–141). Fortunately, a familiar motion picture has articulated a fundamental approach to identity that no filmmaker can ignore and has established the wide ranging expectations that viewers have brought to any Irish themed film made within the last half century: John Ford's *The Quiet Man*.

I have already written on what I see as the paradigmatic impact of *The Quiet Man* on films devoted to Ireland and Irish identity, so allow me simply to summarize the key elements of my argument (Gillespie 2002: 18–32). Ford's ability to play off common stereotypes applied to native Irish and returning emigrants enables him to present a detailed and sophisticated examination of the complex elements that inform an Irish identity. At the same time, *The Quiet Man's* versatility leaves ample range for a variety of understandings. In particular, rather than attempting to offer a definitive representation of Irishness, Ford's film highlights how class, location, and sentiment evokes and authenticates multiple manifestations of diverse representations of identity.

In *The Quiet Man* Ford deftly plays upon concepts of community and more specifically upon the impulse for inclusion into the community as the animating force in the narrative. From the start of the film, Sean Thornton strives for acceptance into a society that he has idealized, and in the end he becomes incorporated into and molded by a much harsher version of that world, though in his sustained delusions Thornton does not seem aware of the change he has undergone or of the differences between the world he envisioned and the one he now inhabits. Perhaps most damning he does not ever realize how profoundly fragmented is this presumed community.

The Quiet Man has had a defining effect upon several generations of filmgoers and filmmakers. As a result, Huston, having the benefit of impressions of the multiplicity of Irishness created by Ford's hugely popular film, can dispense with the exposition on problems of identity that Ford has already provided. He inverts the process of communal exploration that Sean Thornton followed and instead takes up an examination of individual identity as it frees itself from societal prescriptions that culminates in the epiphany of Gabriel Conroy, confident in the preparation his audience has had for understanding this topic.

Huston opens the film with a seemingly unquestioned assumption of the unifying impact of communal bonds, depicting the gathering of friends and family at the Morkan's annual Christmas party, and then moves progressively to explore diverse and forceful manifestations of the intense individuality of various characters. Building on these impressions, Huston concludes with a paradigmatic representation of identity through his central character, Gabriel Conroy. By exploring the range of feelings associated with Conroy's profound emotional isolation, the film portrays a vivid sense of the consequences of his seclusion while leaving each viewer to decide what significance to give to that revelation.

In preparation for this cumulative scene Huston employs a number of thematic devices to forward his interpretations of isolation as the key element in various forms of Irishness. Music emerges as one of the most insistent and diverse. Huston uses it deftly, both as an overlay to dialogue and as a topic of conversation, to underscore marginality without stamping that condition as a positive or negative state. The central feature of this approach lies in Huston's trust that filmgoers can appreciate the function of suggestion over exposition. Music in *The Dead* does not underscore meaning in the fashion popular in many motion pictures. Rather it invites one to develop a sense of alternate possible interpretations, particularly relating to the way diverse representations of isolation exemplify an oscillating sense of Irishness inherent in the narrative.[7]

Performance presents the most overt and at the same time the most subjective application of music in the film. In the tradition of party pieces, three individuals — Aunt Julia, Mary Jane, and Bartel D'Arcy — give renditions of very different types of music. (Mr. Grace, with his recitation of a poem from the Irish, also performs, and there is impromptu singing after Gabriel's speech and of course the musical accompaniment to the dancing assumes an insistent ambient quality.) In each instance, representations by the singer and reactions from the audience highlight unique aspects of isolation without imposing a prescriptive response to these gestures.

Mary Jane's piano playing lays out the issues that music engages. Though uncredited, her selection stands out as a highly technical and not very melodic composition. It foregrounds Mary Jane's proficiency as a pianist, but from the expressions on the faces of her guests it fails to provoke a unified response. Several guests seem to be straining to understand what they are hearing. Others have looks suggesting bafflement or simply distraction. Two of the young men make no effort at engagement, and instead wander into the other room for a drink, coming back only at the conclusion to applaud loudly.

One might feel tempted to see the scene as little more than a demonstration of Mary Jane's solipsism. That may well be the case, but it would be a mistake to extrapolate from this to find fault with her attitude. Ingrid Craigie, the actor portraying Mary Jane, clearly conveys the self-absorption of an artist completely contained by her performance, to the point that she seems unconcerned or even unaware of its impact on anyone else (including Aunt Julia who is dutifully turning the pages of the sheet music). However, given her circumstances, supporting herself and her aunts with music lessons for young women who seem at best lukewarm to the project (one has earlier apologized for a missed lesson), finding comfort in one's art seems as noble and courageous as it might be self-absorbed. The point, however, is not that one must resolve Mary Jane's motivations one way or another. Rather, with deft images and little dialogue the narrative manages to sustain the complex and often contradictory range of feelings that delineate Mary Jane's withdrawal into a private emotional life while at the same time divorcing it from the contrasting attitudes of the other people in the room.

Aunt Julia's performance offers an equally assertive refusal to submit to causal interpretations. She sings "Arrayed for the Bridal"—an adaptation of a piece from the opera *I Puritani* by Vincenzo Bellini. Some commentators have interpreted this as a sardonic jab at the spinster performer while in fact in the context of the opera the song emphasizes the possibility for escape from captivity (Gifford 1982: 118). With this serving as a warning, if one comes to the concept of isolation with an uncommitted sense of its possibilities, the scene offers a much more complex vision of identity than the surface might suggest.

Of course, the act highlights a moment of extreme vulnerability. Cathleen Delany, the actor playing Aunt Julia, projects a physical fragility that makes each movement seem fraught. Though she undertakes the piece in an unselfconscious, straightforward fashion, Aunt Julia's voice proves to be no match for Bellini's music. Her notes are flat. Her singing is off-key. Her expression is wooden. Like the bored young men who left for a drink while Mary Jane played, the camera strays from the room in which the singing takes place to move to a survey of family mementoes that remind us of the singer's younger, more vibrant days. Nonetheless, the audience offers warm applause at its conclusion, and Aunt Julia seems touched by the reception.

Again, the narrative does not invite a linear response, for the possibilities already suggested by Mary Jane's performance caution against coming to a definitive sense of what has transpired. As emphasized by the camera's decision to wander from the room where Aunt Julia is singing to explore the mementoes of a life time collected in her bedroom, viewers stand at a remove from the scene. How then should the audience judge the dinner guests' enthusiastic response to what they have heard?

Certainly, a measure of kindness informs some of the listeners. Visual and audio representations strongly assert the harshness of Aunt Julia's voice and the frailness of her body. While reactions to Mary Jane's performance have already suggested a latent capacity for insensitivity, to have behaved in similar fashion toward one who seems as vulnerable as does Aunt Julia would have been inordinately cruel.

Nonetheless, at least one guest shows a willingness to offer a sardonic response when Mr. Browne proclaims: "Miss Julia Morkan. My latest discovery." At the same time, although the satirical tone of the statement comes across clearly to all, its significance stands open to interpretation. The fatuousness of Mr. Browne's proclamation almost, though not completely, draws any venom from the remark. More significantly, however, it reminds the viewer of the heterogeneity of the group assembled at the annual Christmas celebration. Mr. Browne, the lone acknowledged Protestant at the party, distinguishes himself as much by his need for recognition as by his hyperbolic encomium. Rather than participating in the warm feelings that seem to unite the company in its good natured acclaim of Aunt Julia, Mr. Browne introduces a note of fatuousness that calls attention to himself and insinuates the possibility of doubt for the genuineness of all other responses.

Perhaps even more troubling in terms of understanding the scene is Freddy Malin's unbridled enthusiasm. When he proclaims, twice for emphasis, that he has never heard Aunt Julia sing better, he produces for the viewer the most difficult interpretive challenge of all the responses. Freddy's sincerity seems all too genuine, yet the fact that he is clearly under the influence of alcohol has been reiterated from the start. How then does one take his remark? Does it sum up in its stumbling innocence the hypocrisy which has greeted Aunt Julia's performance? Does it remind us of the less verbose but equally kind efforts of others to shield her? Or does it suggest the broad lack of discrimination that infects everyone at the party?

The simplest answer to these questions would be yes. Freddy's muddled disquisition catches the range of impulses that Aunt Julia provokes, and it touches on the need to avoid easy resolution. No feeling sums up reaction to the performance because a unified perception does not animate the audience. Rather, individuality, even isolation, moves each character to a unique attitude, and the most perceptive impression of the scene holds this range of feelings in tension.

Aunt Julia's response remains the most striking of all. As a trained musician, she can hardly have failed to recognize the flaws in her own performance, yet the viewer's growing sense of the complexity of isolation makes her reaction consistent and plausible. Just as Mary Jane retreats into the technical triumph that dominates her moment of playing, Aunt Julia uses her singing to draw herself back to an earlier time of achievement and contentment. (As she accepts the audience's plaudits she recalls that she "had a good voice at one time.") In this community that defines itself through isolation, Aunt Julia repositions herself into a more congenial time, untroubled by the circumstances surrounding her.

If solipsism and retrospection personify isolation in the first two performances, rejection emerges as the dominating image of the last one. At the end of the evening, Bartel d'Arcy offers a solitary rendition of "The Lass of Aughram," a traditional Irish ballad and a tune sung by Michael Furey as well. The theme of d'Arcy's song — isolation through rejection — most powerfully prepares viewers for the film's conclusion. (It has been introduced by Mr. Grace's dramatic recitation of "Broken Vows," a poem from Irish, and Grace's recitation counterpoints Gabriel's final soliloquy which mediates on loss and love (de Cacqueray and Costa de Beuregard 2000: 188).

D'Arcy's beautiful tenor voice makes the piece the most accessible and agreeable of the three musical presentations of the evening. At the same time, the setting reminds viewers more forcefully than the others of the segregation of characters in the film. Throughout the performance, the singer remains off camera, a disembodied voice, and in his place viewers watch Gretta (Anjelica Huston) responding to the song and Gabriel (Donal McCann) transfixed by the image of Gretta's shifting emotions. The song itself focuses on the abandonment of a young mother and child by the woman's lover, completing the image of isolation.

As with the performances that preceded this one, a single perspective on the scene, literal or metaphoric, cannot offer sufficient scope for a fully engaged interpretation. Instead, the poignancy of feeling and the specificity of understanding in both Gretta and Gabriel, again unvoiced but powerfully conveyed by gesture and expression, expand the viewers' impressions of both characters, and provide sharp contrasts to the often awkward and even guarded exchanges that they had shared throughout the night. Isolation becomes a necessity for them to reveal themselves just as d'Arcy, so self-conscious about the quality of his voice because of a cold that he had refused to perform all night, now sings offstage with only Miss O'Callaghan for an audience.

Despite being the most evocative of the three presentations, at least as measured by the listeners' reactions, this last performance underscores the neutrality of isolation. Detachment dominates all of the characters involved, yet the narrative offers no judgment on the significance of their remoteness. Of course, the scene introduces the song as an absolutely necessary condition for provoking the strong emotions in Gretta that dominate the final scenes of the film. At the same time, it offers no gloss to those feelings or interpretation of the incident. While the starkness of the settings and sentiments remain unmistakable, their significance stands as very much the viewer's determination.

Taken together, these three scenes provide a richly complex sense of the world evoked by the film, and in that regard they form a tutorial for approaching the end of *The Dead*. For the first two thirds of the motion picture, Huston brilliantly develops the paradox that isolation and multiplicity stand as dominant features of Irish national identity. However, the narrative does not content itself simply with antinomies. It deftly employs a variety of images to invite attentiveness to the complexity of the disposition toward seclusion. Indeed, in a number of instances outside the performances already examined, it highlights variations on solipsism: the narcissism, the misanthropy, and the alienation as alternate manifestations of the communally shared feature shaping the natures of so many characters.

In a series of scenes from the start of the film, the narrative offers flashes of self-absorption, some comic some otherwise, that create a wonderful tension that both critiques and elaborates upon the nature of community at the party. Gabriel Conroy stands out as the most prominent example. His fussiness over galoshes, his awkward exchange with Lily, Molly Ivors, and Gretta, his repeated withdrawals to effect obsessive re-examinations of his after-dinner speech all mark the man designated to celebrate Irish hospitality as the one most uncomfortable when immersed in it.

Other characters, however, prove equally disposed to their own company over that of others, though they display their dispositions with greater subtlety. Mr. Browne effuses cordiality as he presents each of the Morkan sisters with a rather meager flower, yet he brushes aside the implicit invitation to respond to their concern for the possible inebriation of Freddy Malins in favor of moving immediately to the whiskey decanter where he will rapidly drink himself into a stupor. The mechanical, repetitive recital by Mrs. Malins of the domestic arrangements that she shares with her daughter and son-in-law serve to inhibit discourse and suppress any effort at conversation by a guest who would foolishly seek her company. Along similar lines, her son Freddy's drunken solicitousness to Gabriel, to his mother, to Browne, and to Aunt Julia, while seeming to effect a kind gregariousness, in fact shows no clear perception of the environment surrounding him. Rather, those he encounters simply provide the excuse for his own rambling disquisitions. Even the hyper-Irish Molly Ivors advocates only a smug and dismissive nationalism that shows itself intolerant of difference and reveals an unwillingness to submit to the company of her fellow Irish long enough for dinner with them. Indeed, the very make-up of the party displays a sinuous elasticity, for, as Tony Huston has noted, to accommodate cinematic concerns a number of the male guests simply disappear on the way into dinner.[8]

At the same time, a paradoxical need for community asserts itself. The Morkan Christmas party establishes a sense of a society that tolerates and even thrives on such determined separateness. Theses characters do not so much seek seclusion as separation from the world around them. In this fashion, conventional Irish hospitality emerges as a facet for displaying the complexity of Irish character. If isolation highlights individuality, social intercourse reminds viewers of the contradictions in their natures that these characters readily embrace. There is sincerity in the way the company honors the Morkans, yet the gossiping, heavy drinking, and patronizing tone of some of the guests continually calls any straightforward interpretation of this inclination into question.

Though elaborate and even digressive, this representation of variations of Irishness dominating most of the film's running time plays a crucial interpretive role. It outlines the milieu from which the action emerges. It prepares views for the complexities presented in the final scene. And, in the process, it makes filmgoers aware of the range of possible ways for understanding both Gretta and Gabriel.

Gretta's virtuoso performance at the close of the film deftly mixes ruthlessness and vulnerability. Throughout the film in a skillful combination of gesture and expression Anjelica Huston has imbued a profound emotional depth into Gretta's character without circumscribing it with single-minded sentimentality. Quite the contrary, the juxtaposition of her dismissive response to Gabriel's complaint over the time it takes her to dress, the unbounded enthusiasm for the idea of a trip to the West, and the deep emotional response on the stairs to "The Lass of Aughrim" suggest a woman with a complicated emotional range. Even these images, however, do not prepare one for the profound self-absorption evident in Gretta's offhanded revelation to Gabriel of a lover whose memory she continues to cherish. (Indeed, self-absorption stands as the kindest interpretation of a gesture that, if it were at all calculated, could only be seen as profoundly cruel.) The very moving description of the last time she saw Michael Furey is capped by the unapologetic egotism of the statement: "I think he died for love of me." After her passionate recollections of Michael Furey, Gretta falls into a postcoital-like slumber, oblivious to the presence of her wounded husband and presumably no longer engaged by recollections of her former lover.

Gabriel in his own right demonstrates no less isolation throughout the process. During Gretta's account, he stands as a mute audience, in a role similar to the one he took during the performance of "The Lass of Aughrim." Later he remains pensively awake dissecting his feelings.

As with Gretta, though his language seems straightforward, its meaning remains ambiguous. We see him castigating himself as a lackey to his aunts. We follow his dour reflections on the inevitability of death. And we overhear his ruminations on the lack he feels over the disparity between his own emotional experiences and those of Michael Furey.

In this final scene Gabriel and Gretta make overt the dominant impulse toward solitary reflection, whether introspective or bombastic, manifest in nearly everyone who has attended the party. An emotional and spiritual isolation is a *donné* in their environment, an element inherent in their natures. What we have come to see, however, over the course of the film is the remarkable ability of each individual to adapt that trait to his or her life. Isolation becomes a powerful protective force, blunting the impact of powerful feelings. It also stands as a preservative, ensuring that gratifying experiences are protected from the eroding features of passing time and subsequent activity. Most significantly isolation rebuffs the scrutiny of others and allows one the luxury of conflicting feelings without the need for resolution.

In the end, the isolation dominating Huston's representation of the Irish identity prohibits viewers from conclusive judgments of the central characters. Instead it encourages us to come to the same accommodation that they have. We understand the world of *The Dead* most fully when we embrace the contradictions that the isolation of the central characters enable.

Notes

1. Later in the chapter Bloom has the satisfaction of playing upon the concept of identity when he reminds the virulent anti–Semite, the Citizen, "Your god was a Jew. Christ was a Jew like me" (1808–1809).

2. For a summary of the problems created by the subjectivity of concepts of nationalism, see my *The Myth of an Irish Cinema* (Syracuse, NY: Syracuse University Press, 2008).

3. To avoid any confusion between the film and the short story, whenever I reference Huston's work I identify it in italics, *The Dead*. When I mention Joyce's short story, I use quotation marks, "The Dead."

4. One finds instances of this in two early scholarly reviews of the film, the first written by A. Walton Litz and Lea Baechelor and the second by Richard Gerber, each comparing it minutely to the short story, appeared in *James Joyce Quarterly* 52.4 (Summer 1988): 521–533.

5. At least one critic has argued for attentiveness to cinematic qualities in Joyce's short story. See Paul Dean, "Motion Picture Techniques in James Joyce's 'The Dead.'" *James Joyce Quarterly* 6 (1968/69): 231–36. That observation, however, does not warrant many of the subsequent associations of it with Huston's film that have followed.

6. This is summed up, though not with the same meaning that I intend, by Frank Pilipp when he says: "the essence of understanding the work lies not exclusively in discovering its meaning, but also in recognizing the means or devices by which the work achieves meaning" ("Narrative Devices and Aesthetic Perception in Joyce's and Huston's 'The Dead'" *Literature Film Quarterly* 21.1 [1993]: 61). Pilipp goes on to compare the works without giving sufficient attention to his own perceptive opening statement. The radically different media of film and literature themselves assert strikingly different perceptive demands upon their audiences and by extension produce strikingly different interpretive responses. Irving Singer takes a different approach, exploring similarities in epiphanic experiences, in his essay "The Dead: Story and Film" (*The Hudson Review* 56.4 [Winter 2004]: 655–665). While Singer makes a very perceptive point about the broad epiphanic nature of film, I think that his approach works best when the comparison remains general. However, using epiphanies in Joyce's work to judge specific aspects of Huston's creative expression leads to prescriptive responses.

7. Huston's inclination to develop viewers' interpretive skills by challenging narratives is by no means unique to *The Dead*. Norman Hollander, in an essay on *Freud*, has commented on its recurrence. See "How to See Huston's *Freud*." In *Perspectives on John Huston*, Ed. Stephen Cooper (New York: G.K. Hall 1994) 179.

8. Huston mentions this in a talk on the film given at the Philadelphia James Joyce Conference in 1989. I am grateful to Professor Tim Martin for providing me a copy of this address.

A Walk with Love and Death
From the Jacquerie of 1358 to the Turbulence of 1968

PETER G. CHRISTENSEN

If *A Walk with Love and Death* is a difficult film in the John Huston canon to evaluate, it may well be because it is rarely seen and those viewers who have, will almost certainly not know what it is about. Temporally set during Hundred Years' War (1337–1453) between England And France, the narrative follows the exploits of Heron of Foix (Assaf Dayan) a Parisian university student who absents himself on a quest to go to the sea which he has never seen (and which it turns out he never will see). On his journey he encounters signs of civil strife between the nobility and the peasantry: bodies float down-river, peasants are summarily (and randomly) executed by noble-backed militia. Heron seeks refuge in the castle of St Jean, home to the king's intendant and therefore theoretically "inviolate" from peasant attack. There he encounters the intendant's daughter Claudia (Anjelica Huston) with whom he falls in love. When the castle is sacked by peasants (who murder the intendant), Heron brings Claudia to the protection of Ermenonville, the castle occupied by her uncle, Robert de Lorris (referred to in the film as Robert the Elder and played by John Huston). On their arrival, however, Robert expresses the view that the peasants have right on their side and announces that he has renounced his nobility to lead a peasant army. A disgusted Claudia flees the castle with Heron and they fall in with Sir Meles of Bohemia who leads a group of knights who travel the country crushing the rebellion. Heron inadvertently becomes involved in combat against the peasants at Rheims but both he and Claudia are horrified by the zeal which the knights pursue their objective and they part company with Meles. The two lovers now find themselves caught between the two sides: regarded as nobles by the peasantry, the noble militias associate them with the "traitor" Robert the Elder. They finally find safe haven in a Cistercian abbey at Châalis but even this sanctuary proves short-lived: as the film draws to a close, the lovers awake to find the monastery abandoned and unspecified forces massing outside. Facing certain death, they perform a marriage ceremony and await their fate.

The first question to consider in looking at *A Walk with Love and Death* is whether to look at it as an ahistorical fable or as a film suggesting a parallel between the Hundred Years' War and our own day with a few specific points to make about the fourteenth century? As it turns out, there was a peasant uprising in northern France during this period, the Jacquerie, or peasant revolt of 1358. However, although *We Were Strangers* (1949), *Moulin Rouge* (1952), *The Barbarian and the Geisha* (1958), and *The Life and Times of Judge Roy Bean* (1972), are all historical films, they are so different that they do not offer much of an entry into thinking about history in *A Walk with Love and Death*. These films are not set in the Middle Ages and only *We Were Strangers* deals with the morality of violence, although under vastly different social conditions.

Film scholars have spent little time on *A Walk with Love and Death* in part because until a recent BFI re-issue it has not been easy to get a copy of the film. Allen Cohen and Harry Lawton's *John Huston: A Guide to References and Resources* (1997) lists no articles or book chapters about the film. What brief critical references do exist on the film are generally positive, however. A first group of group critics is not much interested in the fourteenth century setting. For example, Morandino Morandini (1980: 103) claims that Heron is a student in revolt similar to today's students and sees the film entirely as a story about 1968. Carlos Hernández Heredero (1984: 163) also praises it as a parable about 1968, while John McCarty calls the protagonists "flower children" (1987: 172). For Axel Madsen it is a kind of *Romeo and Juliet* story (1978: 226). Robert Benayoun, referring approvingly to Norman O. Brown and George Bataille, considers it a fable that exalts the eroticism of death (1985: 100–03). A second group of critics connects the film to other themes in Huston's films. Like Lesley Brill (1997: 67) Stuart Kaminsky (1978: 182) points out its strong criticism of conventional Christianity. Relating it to *The Asphalt Jungle*, Patrick Brion (2003) finds Heron to be a character with a deathwish akin to Dix Handley (Sterling Hayden). A third group feels that the film does evoke the Middle Ages. Gerald Pratley describes the style of the film as a "saga" (1977: 172). Louis Seguin (1988: 135) suggests that the historical backdrop comes from the chronicles of Froissart and Jean le Bel. Scott Hammen, who devotes only five paragraphs to it, is unusual in that he unproblematically considers the film to be about the peasants' uprising of 1358 (1985: 118–19). His claim is true to a larger extent than has been recognized.[1]

In this paper I will argue that knowledge about the Jacquerie of 1358 is more important to interpreting the film than has previously been recognized since our historical understanding guides our sense of (1) what sympathy if any Claudia and Heron should have toward the peasants, (2) what action they should take—participation or withdrawal, and (3) what fate they should anticipate at the end of the film. Current historical understanding shows the Jacquerie of 1358 to have been:

> (a) a spontaneous revolt of the peasants not of the bourgeoisie,
> (b) undertaken by the peasants against their own lords for failing to offer protection from the English, brigands, and natural disaster,
> (c) carried out with almost no aggression aimed toward the Church or its property,
> (d) short in duration, lasting only two weeks, and
> (e) succeeded by far more extensive and bloodier reprisals from the nobility.

In Huston's film, which follows Hans Koningsberger's eponymous novel, items (a) and (b) can be assumed, but not (c), (d), and (e).

First, if one comes to the film as a historical film not as a fable, one will have more sympathy for the peasants, since historians have shown that they did not always kill those they attacked or robbed, whereas the nobility killed everyone brutally in their reprisals. Such sympathy for the peasants may be suggested by the film if one considers the character of Robert, the Elder the master of Ermenonville (and defender of the peasants), to be the voice of reason. Furthermore, the film is deliberately set up so that we do not see the peasants on an attack. We hear about such attacks (on Saint-Leu and Dammartin), but the only violence actually *depicted* is that visited upon the peasants by nobles seeking to crush the rebellion. Second, in a historical film rather than a fable, we can accept better why Heron (briefly) allowed himself to be used by the nobles to fight the peasants. Historically, the revolt was just about over, and success for the peasants was impossible. The third issue is more complicated. If we stress the fact that there was almost no attack on Church property, then we will necessarily *not* presume that it is the peasants who are going to kill Heron and Claudia at the end of the film. At this point after the end of the revolt and the beginning of the repression, there would be no peasants still in a position to hunt down two insignificant young people. Thus, the possibility is raised those approaching the abbey are nobles, seeking revenge on Claudia and Heron either for her uncle's pro-peasant actions or for Heron's desertion of the nobles' cause. In this scenario, one might conclude that the monks and nuns have departed not because the monastery is going to be pillaged by the nobles but to evade complicity in the deaths of the two lovers. If so, it would be the film's final attack on Church's hypocrisy.

In contrast, if the audience knows nothing about medieval peasant revolts, it will more likely assume that *A Walk with Love and Death* is a film about the turbulence of 1968. It certainly has the credentials for it. It was originally intended to film in northern France in spring 1968, but the student and labor protests of 6 May to 16 June 1968 intervened. There was a general strike, with a million people marching in protest through Paris on 13 May. So production moved to Austria with shooting planned just beyond the border in Czechoslovakia. However, the Russians invaded that country to stamp out Alexander Dubček's reforms on 20 August. Finally, the film crew moved to Italy where the magnificent Cistercian abbey of Fossanova (64 miles southeast of Rome) could be used for the Cistercian abbey of Châalis in the Valois region. The film's protagonists, even more peripatetic than the film crew, are caught up in a revolt and repression in a world they never made, ultimately facing death bravely, not even knowing which side their attackers will be on. Unfortunately, treating *A Walk with Love and Death* as a film about 1968 is only partially useful. The phrase, "Make love not war," which characterized American protest against the Vietnam War in that year is not useful when we think about Huston's film, since the young people in flight are unlikely to be understood as representing Vietnamese escaping from the Americans and the Viet Cong. In addition, in France and Czechoslovakia, peasants were not at the forefront of the protests, so events in those countries in 1968 are not very relevant.

Huston himself never drew attention to the Jacquerie of 1358 when talking about *A Walk with Love and Death*. He stated his dissatisfaction with the film in an interview with Bernard Drew in 1979. He claims of *Roots of Heaven*, *A Walk with Love and Death*, and *The Kremlin Letter*, "I chose these stories, helped write them, directed them, and virtually produced them, and they didn't turn out well" (Drew 2001: 97). Huston himself allows the film only a paragraph in his autobiography, *An Open Book* (1980). He writes, "I only wish [it] had been received everywhere as it was in Paris, where it played in three houses simultaneously and was praised to the skies It may be that a French audience was the one most interested in a French Jacquerie" (337).

The description of the unpleasantness of the film's shooting, presented by Lawrence Grobel in *The Hustons*, suggests that, when Huston brought in the novel's author Hans Koningsberger to the set in Italy, and Dale Wasserman, the original screenwriter abandoned the shoot, protesting that the novelist's presence violated his screenwriting contract, the end product suffered from a case of too many cooks spoiling the broth (1987: 596–610). Grobel claims, "Wasserman attempted to make *Love and Death* 'as contemporaneous in feeling as I could.' But, he said, 'John felt it was strictly a period picture and should adhere to period mores'" (599). Grobel states that Huston "contended that keeping it a period piece would demonstrate that history repeated itself, thus making the film universal. 'The setting seems to be Europe, [Huston] said, 'but actually it's anyplace and everyplace'" (599). Whereas Wasserman was so unhappy with the experience that he apparently never returned to film adaptation, Koningsberger was so thrilled with his experience that he wrote a short article in praise of Huston's work on the film in the Spring 1969 issue of *Film Quarterly*, a piece later reprinted in *John Huston*, the book produced to accompany the 1983 American Film Institute tribute to Huston.[2]

Grobel also comments at length on the difficulties engendered by the fact that Anjelica was being directed by her father. Anjelica had wanted to land the part of Juliet in Franco Zeffirelli's famous film. For some reviewers *A Walk with Love and Death* seemed to be a kind of *Romeo and Juliet* story itself, and in the 1 October 1968 issue of *Vogue*, Richard Goldstein in a four-page spread, "In the Face of Beauty" juxtaposed Anjelica Huston and Assaf Dayan to Olivia Hussey and Leonard Whiting (170–71), before presenting Anjelica and her mother Ricki as two women whose timeless beauty closes up the generation gap.[3]

Unfortunately, any comparison between Huston's film and *Romeo and Juliet* will only mislead viewers since the Capulet and Montague families are for all intents the same, and Shakespeare offers no reason for their feud. In contrast, Claudia (Anjelica Huston) and Heron (Assaf Dayan) are members of the nobility and the bourgeoisie, respectively, and they are caught up in a peasant's revolt against the nobility. Whereas Romeo and Juliet seek only to escape the contention of the warring families, Claudia wants revenge on the peasants who killed her father, and Heron, pressured into joining the nobles' savage reprisal against the peasants, becomes all too enthusiastic in killing a young peasant lad. They have "les mains sales." Furthermore, although Shakespeare's Friar Laurence can be portrayed as anything from a bumbling fool to a well-meaning *raisonneur*, Shakespeare's play is hardly a challenge to the Roman Catholic Church or the Franciscans. In contrast, several critics have noticed the intense unpleasantness of the Christian characters in Huston's film. This attack on the Church is already present in Koningsberger's novel, but Huston's film magnifies it, particularly by including a sequence in which Heron encounters a group of dishonest, life-denying mendicants.

Koningsberger himself had just been radicalized by 1968. His novel, first published in 1961 by Macmillan was reprinted in 1969 by Penguin Books at the time of the film's release. It was the third of his fourteen novels issued between 1958 and 2001. Koningsberger has also published ten books of non-fiction, including an account of 1968, called *Nineteen Sixty-Eight: A Personal Report* (1987). Here he tells how the events of 1968 in the United States had just changed his political beliefs before he met up with John Huston on the film set.

The essence of 1968 was a clarity of perception. It was as if a curtain had been raised, a veil lifted. The clichés, platitudes, and myths of our public life, what may politely be called our Fourth of July rhetoric, were suddenly seen as such, and not just by a handful of lefties in small magazines, but by the people at large, many of them [13].

Koningsberger strongly opposed the Vietnamese War and continues to publish magazine articles against the American invasion of Iraq. He believes, according to an article from 2005, "Spike Helmets for the Youths of America," that with the opposition to the Vietnam war, the gung-ho militaristic aspect of American life was at last attacked: "Americans felt a righteous contempt for this brand of militarism as a left-over from the middle ages." However, in invading Iraq, Americans now honor this sinister jingoism again (Koningsberger 2005 para 7). In his novel *A Walk with Love and Death* the repression of the peasants led by Charles of Navarre is an example of this militarism.[4]

When Huston's *A Walk with Love and Death* was first released, the scholarly debate about the possibility of portraying the Middle Ages on film was not an academic issue. Today there are at least two journals devoted to the academic discipline of medievalism, *The Years' Work in Medievalism* and *Studies in Medievalism* in the United Kingdom. In 2006 Kevin J. Harty published a revised second edition of his groundbreaking 1999 book, *The Reel Middle Ages,* which appeared almost coterminously with a special double issue of *Film & History* (No. 29, Nos. 1–4), edited by Peter C. Rollins, devoted to films about the medieval period.

Since so many films set in the Middle Ages have distorted historical details in major ways, a debate has developed as to whether a film about the Middle Ages can be anything but a projection of current concerns onto a medieval backdrop. The debates strike even a well researched film as Liv Ullmann's 1995 adaptation of Sigrid Undset's *The Wreath* (1920), the first volume of *Kristin Lavransdatter,* set in the early fourteenth century in southern Norway. Ellen Rees and Gunnar Iversen are highly dubious of recapturing the Middle Ages on film. Rees writes that Ullmann's film:

> not only uses the Middle Ages as a pretext in which to place its primary concern with the psychology of modern romantic love, but it also exemplifies what Eco calls the "Middle Ages of national identities" in which "the medieval model was taken as a political utopia, a celebration of past grandeur, to be opposed to the miseries of national enslavements and foreign domination" [Eco 70 quoted in Rees 2003: 409].

Rees is much impressed by Umberto Eco's essay "The Return of the Middle Ages" in his *Travels in Hyperreality.* Here Eco presents ten quite distinct ways in which it is possible to construct the Middle Ages, concluding that an authentic representation of the period must always elude us. Given this impossibility, Rees argues that "using historicity as a tool for determining the relative quality of a film is not particularly constructive" (408). Iversen, who also cites Eco, claims that both Undset and Ullmann were successful because they chose a timeless main theme — love, a "theme so powerful that it drowns out everything else, and consequently, it also drowns out the representation of the medieval period" (2000: 19). One suspects that Iversen would say the same thing about Koningsberger and Huston, who also tell a love story. Representing a different point of view is Arthur Lindley, who in "The Ahistoricism of Medieval Film" regrets that films about the Middle Ages have more difficulty in creating an understandable causal nexus for events than films about, say, the Victorian period. One suspects that Lindley would find next to no credible causal nexus in Huston's film, since the average viewer will have such trouble identifying something "specifically historical" about it.

There seems to be something too essentializing in this discussion of whether a film with a medieval setting can tell us something about the medieval period or not. If, as Eco says, all versions of the Middle Ages, are our own projections, then analyzing the degree of medieval authenticity of a film seems next to pointless. Consequently, I think that a different approach to the problem should be made. Critics can analyze to a greater extent than they usually do the nature of the audience's possible knowledge about the medieval events depicted in the film and then assess whether the removal of authentic medieval detail makes any sense given potential expectations. *A Walk with Love and Death* serves as a good test case since all the primary materials in chronicles and documents, if placed together, would, by my estimate, fill up only about two hundred pages.

The question of whether to make *A Walk with Love and Death* as a historical film or as a timeless parable must have included a discussion on how much the audience could possibly know about the Jacquerie of 1358. If they were expected to know nothing about it, a parable would be the more probable choice. So let us review the sources for the Jacquerie, beginning with the fact that hardly anyone other than an expert on the Middle Ages would have known much about it in 1969.

For the most part references to the Jacquerie in mainstream histories are brief: Robin Neillands' *The Hundred Years War*, published in 2001 devotes about a page to the subject as does the Duc de Castries in his 1979 book on kings and queens of France. There are also references to the Jacquerie in a number of biographies of Etienne Marcel, the leader of the Parisian bourgeoisie who lead the opposition against the then Dauphin of France (and later

Charles V). These include books by Claude Poulain (1994), Jacques d'Avout (1960) and Anne-Marie Cazalis (1977). Poulain's book is particularly interesting in the light of Huston's film since, in contrast to the fictional representation, Poulain notes that the family of Robert de Lorris (i.e., Robert the Elder, the one historical character in Huston's film) was not killed, when he changed sides and joined the peasants under coercion (not voluntarily as in the film). Nonetheless both Poulain's and Cazalis's books post-date Huston's film and thus cannot have shaped public understanding of the backdrop against which the events of the film are set.

There were contemporary primary and secondary materials on the Jacquerie of 1358 which predated both the film and Konigsberger's novel although they were not extensive. Anyone in 1969 who knew about the Jacquerie most likely had first found it mentioned in Jean Froissart's (c. 1327–c. 1405) famous four-volume chronicle of the reigns of Edward II, Edward III, and Richard II. Froissart's account presented the peasants as contemptible, violent butchers (as one would expect in the work of this courtly writer). Froissart had been translated in full from French into English by Lord Berners in the mid–sixteenth century and by Thomas Johnes at the beginning of the nineteenth century. In the 1960s, between 1961 and 1969, between film and movie, three volumes of newly translated excerpts were made by Peter Edmund Thompson in 1966 for the Folio Society, Jean Joliffe in 1968 for the Modern Library, and Geoffrey Brereton in 1968 for Penguin books. In addition, AMS Press reprinted Lord Berners' edition in 1967.[5]

The second most important chronicle for study of the Jacquerie, that of the eyewitness cleric of peasant origin, Jean Fillon de Venette (c. 1308–c. 1369), was also accessible to English readers in a scholarly translation from the Latin by Jean Birdsall made in 1953 for Columbia University Press, and featuring an introduction by Richard A. Newhall, who points out that Jean de Venette was the chronicler of his time most sympathetic to the peasants.

There is also the official *Chronique des quatre premiers Valois (1327–1393)*, edited by M. Siméon Luce in 1862, who concluded that the anonymous author was a Norman. Luce went on in 1894 to publish the first book-length volume on the Jacquerie, an edition which also included passages from relevant chronicles and documents.

However, of all the contemporary chronicles, only the anonymous *Chronique normande du XIVe siècle*, edited by Auguste Molinier and Émile Molinier in 1882, contains material that could have served as a spur for Koningsberger's novel and Huston's film, which mentions de Lorris as lord of Ermenonville. In this chronicle of events from 1294 to 1370 by an anonymous Norman we find the following detail excerpted by Madeiros:

> At that time those in Paris went to Ermenonville and assaulted the castle and gained control of it. Within was Lorris, a knight, but out of fear he acted in a gracious manner and swore that he preferred the bourgeoisie and the commune of Paris to the nobles. He was thus saved, along with his wife and children but his goods within the castle were all taken away and stolen. Then the men returned to Paris [Molinier and Molinier 1882: 127–32 quoted in Madeiros 197].

The first name of "Robert" (Medeiros 1979: 198) for the knight of the castle of Lorris is given in a later chronicle which has essentially the same information: *Istoire et chronique de Flandre*, edited by Kevyn de Lettnhove's (2: 55–88). As we can see, Koningsberger made several changes to this account. Lorris is given a son, not a wife and children. They are both sympathetic to the revolt. In the novel they are sympathetic to the peasants; the bourgeoisie of Paris never makes an appearance.

Huston follows these two changes, and in addition gives himself the role of Robert's father, who speaks about the degeneracy of the knights, and who is killed by them, as we realize when the ring from his finger is thrown back to Robert, who, separated from him, returns to the castle. As a Dutchman, Koningsberger could have availed himself of the chapter on the Jacquerie in *Drie Boerenopstanden uit de veertiende eeuw* (1949: 35–53) by F.W.N. Hugenholtz, who agrees (49) with the *Chronique normande* view that Robert de Lorris was allowed to live by changing sides.

Sadly, there are no personal accounts of the Jacquerie. The point of view of the peasants has to be inferred from the chronicles and documents. Given this situation, it seems much less of an intrusive star-turn cameo for Huston himself to speak on behalf of the peasants. Luce believed that the peasants had been prompted to rebel with some help from the bourgeoisie of Paris from the very beginning. However, other historians (Dommanget 1971) have offered compelling evidence to suggest that the peasant revolt was spontaneous, and not prompted by the contemporary political struggle on the part of the Dauphin (the son of the captured Jean II), with the Estates General and the Parisian bourgeoisie. Thus, the Koningsberger-Huston view of a spontaneous peasant revolt is likely to be correct, even if it runs against a speculation in Luce's 1894 book on the Jacquerie.

Koningsberger did not bring in any information on Etienne Marcel, the leader of the Parisian opposition to royal power, in his novel, although he does mention several times Charles the Bad, King of Navarre (1332–1387), who, as a son of the daughter of Louis X, had his own claims to the throne. Charles, originally sympathetic to the bourgeoisie in Paris because of his opposition to his rival, the Dauphin, turned against the Jacquerie and repressed it savagely. Huston made no mention of either Charles of Navarre. Koningsberger had thrice mentioned the French King's imprisonment, never calling him Jean II directly, and Huston omits any mention of the king up-for-ransom. These were reasonable decisions. An audience without easy access to historical materials would most likely only have been confused by the French dynastic struggle and the Dauphin's quarrel with the Estates General.

In sum, it made great sense for Huston to avoid specific historical references in his film. An English-language audience had no books on the Jacquerie to consult. Next to no Anglophone viewers could have found the few anti-peasant pages in Froissart. Only a historian would know of the pro-peasant sentences in Jean de Venette. A French-speaking audience would only have been slightly more informed.

In Koningsberger's novel, we are told the year in the first sentence: "In the spring of that year, 1358, the peasants of northern France did not sow their fields any more" (1969: 5). There are only a few historical personages mentioned: the King of Navarre, the French King [Jean II] imprisoned in England, Jean Vaillant and Edward III (137). In the novel, there are many more place names of towns and geographic features in Northern France than one finds in the film. At the end of the novel Koningsberger offers all the information that the reader needs to understand the details of the Jacquerie in late May and early June:

> The soldiers who had killed Robert were part of Navarre's men. Other French, and English, knights had descended on Ile de France from all directions. The town of Senlis, sheltering peasant soldiers just like Meaux, had escaped the fate of that place and beaten off the attacking nobles. Yet the massacres of Clermont and Meaulx must have broken the back of the people's rising. There had been talk of having each village give up the four "most guilty men" and pay a fine; but with the rising tide of battle against the peasant that was forgotten and the knights wanted what they called total revenge [136].

As one motivation for the revolt Koningsberger suggests that the peasants believed that that Jean II had left England and was somehow coming to their aid (47, 138). Robert de Lorris makes it clear to Heron and Claudia in the middle of the novel that this is a false rumor (110–11). In Huston's film no character is able to arrive at an overview of events. Heron and Claudia are caught up in a conflict whose dimensions are clearly unknown to them and thus to us. Koningsberger (138) makes the point that French knights defeated by the English had become brigands, although the film is not clear about it. Thus although at the beginning of the film Heron encounters a floating body in a river and some dead cows, it is unclear as to whether they died of some disease or were killed by someone.

Whereas Koningsberger has Heron express hope in the peasant cause, Heron never has enough information in Huston's film to even conceive of such a statement. In the novel Heron states:

> There is a giving up when all seem in vain, but it is no real giving up, for some untapped strength remains. Such was the giving up in northern France in the spring of that year, 1358, ten years after the great plague, two years after the battle of Poitiers where the king was taken and the defeated French knights became brigands. It only took the very small miracle of Saint-Leu, nine knights in mail slain by men in rags, to create an awakening [138].

In Huston's film we do not see this awakening of the peasants, who are kept offstage except when slaughtered by the nobles.

Huston is more interested in attacking the Church than in portraying the peasant revolt. The film adds to the plot a whole sequence in which Heron, after leaving Claudia in Dammartin, seeks the sea and encounters on the river the crazed monks who mortify the flesh. In the film, after Heron and Claudia have married themselves, which would be a sacrilege to the Church, and made love in their makeshift bedroom in the monastery, they await an attack that leads to their death. Heron in voice-over says, "Death came in like a great tide. Death came on forever." This line echoes his statement at the very beginning of the film that "Spring came in like a great tide." After the final voice-over, the camera leaves Heron and Claudia in medium shot and moves to a panorama of the clouds. The ending is ambiguous, since the clouds suggest heaven, while the idea of earth as a vale of tears before the happiness of heaven has been shown to be life-denying. The clouds could suggest Heron's goal of happiness, which is in part seeing the sea (which he actually does see in the book unlike the film) and in part being with Claudia. Only as a voice from beyond the grave can Heron speak to us of death's arrival. In effect, we find that the whole story has been told by a dead man. Thus there is dramatic irony in the spiritual ending. Koningsberger simply closes his novel with the lines, "I put my arms around her hips and kissed her" (144).

With this closing line (and many others throughout the novel) Koningsberger stresses the sexual awakening of Claudia. Although it has not been noticed, Huston had to play down the sexual element of the story since he was filming his own daughter. Although in *Excalibur* (1981) John Boorman would film his daughter playing a character being raped, his action was unusual. Huston has one extreme long shot of Anjelica and Assaf Dayan romping in the nude and lying near each other. He does not include the scene in which Koningsberger writes, "There was a soft late light around us, and she looked at me with wide-open clear eyes, while I was in her" (76).

In conclusion, Huston, diminishing the sexual element as well as the specific historical references, turned a good novel into a better film. As Koningsberger noted in his article about the production, Huston simplified matters and he got good results. This practice, however, is not the same as turning the film into a fable. As Huston stated, he saw a similarity between events in the fourteenth century and in our own time. Audience response to the film will vary depending on how much a person knows about the length of the Jacquerie, numbers killed, and the general absence of attacks on the Church. Thus historical understanding does color audience response to the story and the characters. If the film had been an historical fable, chances are it would have allowed less scope for different personal reactions.[6]

Notes

1. There are no essays on *A Walk with Love and Death* in the three previous collections of essays on Huston edited by Costanzo (1990), Studlar and Desser (1993) and Cooper (1994).

2. Dale Wasserman (b. 1917), had adapted several novels for television and film: *The Vikings* (1958), *The Citadel* (1960), *The Power and the Glory* (1961), *Quick Before It Melts* (1964), and *Mr. Buddwing* (1965), before creating the libretto for *Man of La Mancha* on Broadway (1966).

3. Of course, despite the stinging reviews of the performances of Anjelica Huston and Assaf Dayan, some critics did appreciate the film, particularly the work of those crew members concerned with the film's visual beauty and recreation of northern France in the fourteenth century: Edward Scaife (cinematographer), Stephen B. Grimes (production designer), Josie MacAvin (set decoration), and Leonora Fini (costume design). Although surprisingly little was said in praise of the beautiful overture and incidental music by Georges Delerue as well as his seven short songs and song fragments for which Gladys Hill was the lyricist, they too contributed significantly to the medieval "aura" of the film.

4. Oddly enough two novels in French on the Jacquerie were published in 1966, perhaps prompted by the success of Koningsberger's book: Robin Carvel, *Les Orgues du diable* (Paris : Éditeurs Français Réunis, 1966) ; Yves Gandon, *Jacquette des effrois* (Paris: Laffont, 1966). For other novels of the 1358 Jacquerie see G. P. R. James, *The Jacquerie; or, The lady and the Page; An Historical Romance* (London: London, Longman, Brown, Green & Longmans, 1841); George Perkins, *Before the Dawn: A Story of Paris and the Jacquerie* (New York: G. P. Putnam's Sons, 1887).

5. Selections from Froissart's lengthy Chronicles are available in several modern one-volume English versions. Peter Edmund Thompson's 1966 Folio Society edition of chronicles of the Hundred Years War only summarizes the Jacquerie (131–32) in its section by Froissart (85–257). John Joliffe's 1968 Modern Library edition includes Book 1, Chapters 182–184 on the Jacquerie on pp. 177–81. Geoffrey Brereton's 1968 Penguin edition, slightly revised in 1978, includes the Jacquerie (1978: 151–55), but he does not use a book and chapter numbering system. For all the related events of 1358 see the complete translations by Jean Bouchier Berners (1967) 1: 401–15 and by Thomas Johnes (1806) 2: 387–421. Berners was first published in 1523–1525 in London by Pynson and later in 1545 in London by Wyllam Myddylton. Johnes was first published in London in 4 volumes by Hafod Press in 1803–1805. The three main chapters on the Jacquerie are number Book 1, Chapters 182–84 by Berners but they are number 179, 181, 182 by Johnes for reasons that are not clear to me. H. P. Dunster (1906) in his one-volume abridgement of Johnes's edition does not

include the Jacquerie at all (see Dunster 68–69). For a useful scholarly French edition of Froissart, see that of Peter F. Ainsworth and George Diller, Chroniques, tome 3, covering 1346–1369 (1992).

    6. The mention in the film of only a few places — Dammartin, Ermenonville, and Châalis — connects it to Gérard de Nerval's great love story, "Sylvie" from Les Filles du Feu. Key events take place in all these locations in Nerval's story.

The Western, *The Westerner*, The Westernest
William Wyler, Menippean Satire and John Huston's The Life and Times of Judge Roy Bean

LESLEY BRILL

Thanks to his own considerable literary talent, John Huston may well have been the most adroit adapter of great novels and stories in the history of the cinema to date. From the initial triumph of *The Maltese Falcon* (1941), a book that had been twice before brought to the screen without much success, to the close of his career with the magnificent, intense *The Dead* (1987), Huston made into films some of the most revered fiction of the nineteenth and twentieth centuries. In prospect, many of his chosen sources might have seemed so difficult to translate into visual terms as to be downright perverse. *The Treasure of the Sierra Madre* (1948) lacks a single female character of consequence; *The Man Who Would Be King* (1975) is based on a Kipling story so short that it could be called, in modern terms, an "idea" more than a narrative. Need one add *Wise Blood* (1979), or *Freud* (1962), with no story at all beyond Freud's psychoanalytic essays, or *Under the Volcano* (1984), an avant-garde novel difficult to follow in the reading but perfectly clear in Huston's redaction? And there are many others.

Unique among Huston's adaptations, however, is *The Life and Times of Judge Roy Bean* (hereafter *Roy Bean*, 1972), which derives to a great extent from one movie, William Wyler's *The Westerner* (1940), and imitates another, *Butch Cassidy and the Sundance Kid* (1969), for a crucial sequence. Wyler, one should note, was Huston's good friend; and the producer of *Roy Bean*, John Forman, also produced *Butch Cassidy*. The latter film and *Roy Bean* share a star as well, Paul Newman.

Beyond these specific sources lies the vast cinematic terrain of the western movie in general, a genre that *Roy Bean* pays tribute to, explores, extends, and makes fun of. The French critic Frédéric Vitoux recalls the centrality of that genre in his discussion of Huston's film:

> There is much talk of the myths that find in the western their vehicle. And yet, isn't the western itself one of the most prodigious and persistent (as an illusion persists) myths in the history of cinema? [1974: 47].

Huston's invocation of this *uber*-myth and his freewheeling, ludic approach signal the membership of *Roy Bean* in yet another, mostly bookish, tradition. Northrop Frye proposed renaming this genre the "anatomy" and Mikhail Bakhtin strongly associated it with the carnivalesque. It is perhaps best known — by those who know that they know it — as Menippean satire. In addition to invoking the sprawling filmic genre of the western, then, *Roy Bean* also adapts to film an exotic species that is primarily literary; one that includes such works as Rabelais's *Gargantua and Pantagruel*, Swift's *Gulliver's Travels*, Cervantes's *Don Quixote*, Voltaire's *Candide*, Carroll's *Alice in Wonderland*, and Joyce's *Finnegans Wake* and *Ulysses* — the last a novel that greatly impressed young John Huston. Some notable examples of Menippean satire do exist in cinema — among them are the first version of *Bedazzled* (Donen, 1967), Godard's *Weekend* (1967), *Monty Python's The Meaning of Life* (Terry Jones, 1983), and *The Big Lebowski* (Joel and Ethan Coen, 1998). With a drawling cowboy (Sam Elliot) as its framing narrator, its tumbling tumbleweeds, and its thematic concentration on the collision of traditional American folkways with contemporary realities, the Coens' movie shares much with Huston's Menippean predecessor. Elliot Silverstein's *Cat Ballou* (1965) anticipates some of Huston's parodying of the western — though such burlesques go almost as far back in the history of the genre as does the genre itself. The film contemporary with *Roy Bean* that is closest to it as a Menippean satire may be René Goscinny's animated Lucky Luke adventure, *Daisy Town* (1971), a movie little known, as far as I can tell, outside of France.

Huston said, "I made deliberate use of a technique that has since become much more popular, letting all sorts of events occur without logical justification. Things appear, things happen, funny, sad, comic, dramatic. Ludicrous one minute and sober the next" (Huston 1980: 340). In a word, a Bakhtinian might assert, "carnivalesque." I shall have more to say later about the importance of recognizing *Roy Bean*'s membership in the unruly fellowship of the Menippean satire; but for the moment let us turn to the relation between Huston's film and its most direct forebear, *The Westerner*.

The Westernest Westerner

What *Roy Bean* takes from *The Westerner* it persistently exaggerates, intensifies, and enlarges. *Roy Bean*'s transformations of the earlier film discover in Wyler's movie tendencies that are manifest but mostly unemphatic. By giving them centrality and blowing them up (literally, sometimes), *Roy Bean* refines and purifies elements already present in the rich ore of Wyler's eccentric western.

From their first sequences, the kinship of Wyler's and Huston's films is marked. In both, the opening titles and credits run over the image of a rider moving through the dusk and include a map of Texas and a written exposition of the setting and story. The allusion to its predecessor of Huston's movie thus seems pointed, and remarkably explicit, from its first frames. As elsewhere, *Roy Bean* strengthens and expands the imagery and the mythological quality of its parent. In *The Westerner*, Cole Hardin (Gary Cooper) appears for only a few seconds; the rest of the credit sequence pictures empty desert. In Huston's reprise of Wyler's credit sequence, the rider who will be revealed to be Roy Bean (Newman) fords the Pecos and trots through the gathering darkness throughout the opening credits, which run nearly three minutes. The beginning of *The Westerner* ends with a modest disclaimer: "This story is legend founded on fact." That of *Roy Bean* is more emphatic and self-conscious about its mythic orientation: "Near the turn of the last century the Pecos River marked the boundaries of civilization in western Texas. West of the Pecos there was no law, no order, and only bad men and rattlesnakes lived there. ... [ellipsis in original] Maybe this isn't the way it was ... [ellipsis in original] it's the way it should have been."

Historical background follows the credits and precedes the action in *The Westerner*; scrolling text pays tribute to Judge Roy Bean's lasting legacy in Texas and sets the stage for a familiar cowboy-versus-farmer conflict. Those texts disappear entirely from the more mythopoetic opening of *Roy Bean*, as does that conventional conflict from its plot. (Missing too from Huston's film — though perhaps not entirely from the screenplay that John Milius provided the director — is a referent of another kind, especially relevant to the time of Wyler's work: the suggestion that the "so-called Judge Roy Bean" can be taken as an image of a fascist autocrat, like those who had come to power in Europe preceding World War II. In this regard, Wyler's film is timely in a way quite different from Huston's, whose subtexts are overwhelmingly aesthetic and generic rather than political and historical.)

The sets of Judge Roy Bean's compound are virtually identical in Wyler's and Huston's films; but this fact can perhaps be ascribed to the existence of a number of photos of the actual structures left by Roy Bean and to the survival of the buildings themselves. Indeed, several have been restored and today make up a State of Texas historical site and "tourist destination." Inside the main building in both films — the "Jersey Lilly" bar and courtroom — posters of Lillie Langtree paper the walls; and for both Wyler's and Huston's Roy Bean, unqualified veneration of that personage is essential for those who wish to be counted among the Judge's friends and allies.

Wyler's Roy Bean was played by Walter Brennan, who received an Oscar as best supporting actor for his efforts. He tells Cooper, "I was hung once, but my friends cut me down in time." Consistent with its tendency to intensify the details of its predecessor, Huston's movie does not tell but shows the hanging of its hero when he is dragged behind a speeding horse by a noose around his neck. The earlier work's opportune friends are replaced in the later one by the miraculous riflery of Maria Elena (Victoria Principal, in her introductory role), whose bullet cuts the rope that connects Bean's neck to the saddle horn.

A subtle detail in *The Westerner* suggests the extent of Roy Bean's lethal justice: when Cole Hardin rides out of Bean's domain, we glimpse briefly behind him an abundantly stocked graveyard. *Roy Bean*'s subtlety — and it does have subtlety of a kind — hides behind the blindingly obvious; a series of shots as the narrative progresses traces the rapidly growing plantation of crosses in the cemetery of Vinegarroon (which Bean will later rename "Langtree"). Huston's Judge brags at one point that he has "a graveyard full of previous cases." (The reputation of the historical Roy Bean as a hanging judge, incidentally, appears to be almost entirely legendary; according to his biographers, he sentenced one or two defendants to death, but they escaped — perhaps with the Judge's collusion — before they could be hung (Skiles, 1996)).

Like *Roy Bean*, *The Westerner* is also self-consciously aware of its use of the standard vocabulary of western movies — a kind of film that Wyler knew well, having begun his career by making a series of them. Wyler's movie too is frequently playful — but with a somewhat skeptical edge — in its invocation of standard motifs of the western. The most obvious manifestation of its ambiguous antic muse occurs early in the film when an unlucky farm hand is hung for accidentally killing a steer while shooting at Bean's marauding cowboys. "That's the trouble with you sodbusters," the Judge says as he prepares to kick the horse on which the unlucky man sits with a noose around his neck, "you can't shoot straight."

A familiar set-piece for westerns — especially those in which farmers have their often beleaguered role — finds a protagonist declaring that civilization will come to the frontier, that the wilderness will be transformed into a garden. *The Westerner* renders its version of this *topos* with a touch of light comedy, combining it with the climax of what has been a hesitant courtship between Cole and Jane (Doris Davenport), a farmer's daughter. Huston follows Wyler's lead pretty much step for step through this action; but, as we would expect, his treatment is broad where Wyler's is subtle, openly sexual where the considerable erotic energy of Wyler's rendition is restrained and sublimated. Nonetheless, Huston's satire, even in its self-conscious absurdity, retains much of the real emotion of Wyler's original. This combination of the absurd and the moving, one might add, is entirely typical of *The Life and Times of Judge Roy Bean* as a whole.

Between the festivity of the farmers' harvest celebration and its sudden, tragic termination by Bean's men setting fire to the settlers' crops and buildings, Jane takes Cole to see "the best piece of homestead land in the entire country." Cole has noticed "a strip along the bottom ... just fine for wheat or corn," and Jane points out "a little knoll right there. It's just beggin' for a house." (Bean's plans are more grandiose. He has a "dream about this land, and what I'm gonna make of it. Someday it's gonna be covered with farms and towns. There's gonna be a railroad.") After Cole has sketched a rough floor plan, Jane fills in the homey and poetic details: "fires, lamplight, warm beds, the smell of coffee in the morning, the sound of rain on the roof." Cole is enchanted, "That's a nice house, Jane." He kisses her, and her acceptance of his embrace implicitly declares their engagement.

Alone together, Cole and Jane gaze at grassland studded with scattered trees and backed up by distant mountains; similarly, Bean and Maria-Elena stand on a grassy plain studded with clumps of brush and also backed up by distant mountains. The following sequence in *Roy Bean* is bracketed by contrasting actions, as it is in *The Westerner*. But the frames in *Roy Bean* are comic, whereas those of *The Westerner* go from joy to a desperate evacuation. The episode in *The Westerner* begins when Jane and Cole, hand in hand, slip away from the jamboree. In *Roy Bean*, Maria-Elena bustles off in fury after firing a shotgun at Bean and the whore whose rump he was embracing as he declared her to be "a ward of the court."

The conclusion of the action in *Roy Bean* is twice framed, the first time by the arrival of Grizzly Adams (played by the director) and his "son" (played by "Bruno"). The second frame concludes the other function of this taming-of-the-west sequence, which is also, as in *The Westerner*, the culmination of an awkward courtship. Where the scene between Cole and Jane ends with an implicit proposal and acceptance, that between Maria-Elena and Bean ends with an explicit liaison — illogically rationalized, but still focused on the idea of a home. Having established that the shack in which Maria-Elena has been dwelling is cold in the winter, leaks in the rain, and lets the wind blow through, Bean reasons, "It is summer, the sky is clear, and there's no wind; so I think you ought to spend the night with me in the court house, so I can protect you from the elements." His proposition eventually brings us to the ultimate conclusion of the episode. After Bean and Maria-Elena have gone into the Jersey Lilly, the bear that Grizzly Adams has abandoned creeps in behind them. From the dark bar, we hear Bean's voice, "Get in there now, go on. Go to bed and lie down." Then we hear a voice-over from one of his deputies, Tector Crites (Ned Beatty), "I don't know which one he was talkin' to, but either way it must have been one helluva night."

Late in the film, Wyler brings out a well-traveled western movie cliché — again, I think, with some self-conscious playfulness, though without the comedy-killing violence and pathos of the hanging scene. Having decided to come to Fort Davis, where Lillie Langtree is performing and where, also, the recently deputized Cole Harden awaits him with a warrant, Bean sets out protectively surrounded by his men. When the Judge rides into town with his ruffians — whom he has designated his "guard o' honor" — a cry goes up: "Bean and his men are comin'! Get off the streets!" As in numberless other westerns, horses rear and drag carriages hastily away while panicked pedestrians scurry out of sight, leaving deserted dirt thoroughfares for the dreaded interlopers.

Roy Bean appropriates this action, but once again Huston hyperbolizes and mythologizes it, transforming it into an action Tector introduces in voice-over, "The only real attempt to question the authority of the Judge's court occurred the time Bad Bob came to town — not Dirty Bad Bob, the Mexican, but the original Bad Bob, the mean one, the albino." The expected cry again sweeps through town, "Bad Bob is comin'!" The reaction, predictably, is over the top. Men flee two to a horse; the barber deserts his supine, lathered client; the undertaker and his helper seek refuge by hopping into empty coffins and slamming the lids on themselves. Rendered with manic enthusiasm by Stacy Keach, Bad Bob gratuitously shoots off the same toe on each foot of one hapless man, kills the horse of another, and demands that its owner cook it for his breakfast, smothered in onions and done "bleu." He hoists a coffee pot from a fire, pours its contents into his mouth, and belches loudly as he goes off to challenge "Beano" with a volley of gruesome threats and — much worse — slanders of the "pig-face, whore, bitch, dog" Lillie Langtree. Huston's hero responds by shooting the obscene renegade in the back, from ambush. As the albino falls, Huston heightens the tall tale by zooming in to shoot the desert landscape through the immense hole that Bean has blasted in his challenger's torso. The episode ends with the inversion of another western movie cliché. "He never had a chance," protests one of Bean's deputies. "Not at all," the Judge replies complacently, "Never did. Never would have. Didn't ask him to come here. Don't abide givin' killers a chance. Wants a chance, let 'm go someplace else."

The turning point in the narrative of *The Westerner* arrives when Bean has his men set fire to the crops and buildings of the settlers. Once again, *Roy Bean* appropriates this element of Wyler's movie and, once again, enlarges and intensifies it. Huston moves the fire to the penultimate sequence of the film — the climax of its action — in which Judge Bean reappears after twenty years "down the pike." Before he "cashes in his chips" — a death we neither see nor are offered any information about — he will resurrect his disgraced deputies, reunite with his daughter, and create an inferno that destroys the oil-fueled empire of his hated successor, the Lawyer Gass (Roddy McDowall).

The Judge's departure and return in Huston's film are explicitly mythologized. After the death of Maria Elena and the betrayal of Bean by his deputies, Tector tells us in another voice-over, "The Judge left everything he owned, or built, rode off into the desert just like he came. Time and the country just swallowed him up. Some say he never did return. Like the historians, they call it a romantic fabrication. Hell, what do they know?" The Judge does return, as he must in this movie of "how things should have been." When Rose, who has never seen her father, glimpses him first, back-lit by a setting sun, she sees a "man on horseback, [who] looks like somethin' out of an old picture book" — a reappearance that recalls his arrival in Vinegarroon County, mounted and riding back-lit through the desert.

The fire in *The Westerner* is destructive of life and property; and it is truly appalling. In *Roy Bean* it is ratcheted up to the genuinely apocalyptic, destroying everything in Langtree except the original Jersey Lilly and leaving only ruins that are eventually effaced and reclaimed by the desert. But for Huston's version, the fire is not appalling; in its manifest exuberance and Hollywood fakery, it is beautiful, joyous and comic. It answers to what Bakhtin called the "Festive folk laughter [that] presents an element of victory not only over supernatural awe, over the sacred, over death; it also means the defeat of power, of earthly kings [like Gass and his "brown-shirted" private army], of all that oppresses and restricts" (Bakhtin 1984: 92). It also celebrates the return of the rightful regime to power, or at least the downfall of the usurpers. The obliteration of Gass Gulch is constructive for nature and humanity alike. As Elias Canetti wrote, crowds (here the audience of the film) can hear the crashing of destruction as "the robust sounds of fresh life, ... the cries of something new-born" (Canetti 1962: 19). Or, in the case of *Roy Bean*, of something re-born.

Roy Bean strikingly borrows its final shot from *The Westerner*. The central story of the earlier film, the acutely ambivalent relation between Cole

Hardin and Roy Bean, ends with the dying Judge carried into the presence of Lillie Langtree by Hardin, who has fatally wounded him. Just before entering the star's dressing room, Judge Bean insists that Hardin put him down. A moment later, Wyler renders Bean's death with a subjective shot; through the Judge's eyes we see Lillie Langtree darken and diminish via a track-out of the camera, which simultaneously goes out of focus. The final shot of *Roy Bean* is also of Lillie Langtree (Ava Gardner), who has come to visit the Jersey Lilly, now the Judge Roy Bean Museum. As Huston's film concludes and the closing credits begin to scroll up the screen, her image goes slowly and radically out of focus. (Huston reverses Wyler's camera movement; he precedes the defocusing of the lens with a slow zoom-in.) The point of view in Wyler's film is that of Roy Bean, "the legend founded on fact." The point of view in Huston's version of this shot is unassigned or, more accurately, is that of the film and its genre as a whole, the western movie as "one of the most prodigious myths in the history of cinema."

In the published screenplay of *The Life and Times of Judge Roy Bean*, one finds modest evidence that John Milius was aware of Wyler's earlier version, but only a few instances of direct borrowing. (Since the screenplay was published after the movie was filmed, one cannot be certain which, if any, of Huston's changes made it into the publication; references to Wyler's film may have followed, rather than preceded, Huston's modifications of Milius's work.) Milius does partly appropriate the mixed comic-ironic tone of *The Westerner*; but Huston, in his direction and consistent alteration of his screenwriter's work, greatly heightens the comic side of the story, deliberately sentimentalizes it, and largely rids it of Milius's dark ironies and cynicism. In Milius's screenplay, the Judge is much less sympathetic, amusing, or mythically configured than he became in Huston's collaboration with Paul Newman.

Besides the opening "full shot — man and horse," Milius transfers a few specific details from *The Westerner*. When he has Lillie Langtree visit Bean's saloon, near the end of the screenplay, she notices "a bullet hole in my teeth" on one of the posters. A poster with the same bullet hole hangs on the wall of the Jersey Lilly in *The Westerner*. In filming, however, Huston moved the bullet hole to the image's heart and shows it being made; he also slightly expanded the sequence as Milius wrote it.

Milius also has his own version of Wyler's concluding fading, tracking-out, and defocusing image of Lilly Langtree. At the end of his screenplay, the aging but still beautiful actress arrives to visit the Judge's compound and is given his pistol and a letter that he has left for her. As she leaves in the train that is also bearing Bean's coffin to Fort Worth, Milius specifies that we are to see her, reading the letter, through the window of the train; "she folded the letter — the train whistle blew — clouds of steam obscured her" (Milius 1973: 179). Huston's filming retains Lillie Langtree's disappearance but removes the apparatus that Milius invented to give it a diegetic basis — Lillie's aging and the steam. As a result, Huston invokes much more directly Wyler's shot from *The Westerner*, while at the same time emphasizing the fabulous over the realistic.

Huston's conversion of Milius's intermittently naturalistic script into a more mythic mode is evident when we compare dialogue from the screenplay with the director's revisions in the completed film. Reflecting on his idealized love in Milius's version, for example, Roy Bean muses, "A man has two kinds of women — wanting women and having women" — he appreciates the having women by wanting Lillie Langtree (*ibid.*, 70).

Although Huston retained a reference to Aphrodite that Milius included in his version, the director removed this slightly precious, folksy business about "wanting women" and "having women." He changed the speech into something more pointedly pretentious, comic, and (paradoxically) profounder: "The ancient Greeks worshipped at the feet of Aphrodite; they loved mortal women as well.... A man has two loves, an unattainable goddess, a mortal woman; and he loves the mortal woman twice as much for having worshipped Lillie Langtree." As Huston said, "I think we put the Judge into the legendary class" (Grobel 1989: 646).

Milius was less than pleased with the results of the director's work on his screenplay. He "felt that Huston 'ruined it.... It should have been a very gritty kind of Sergio Leone–looking film. Instead it became a caricature'" (Grobel 1989: 640). Had Milius understood that Huston was transposing his "gritty Sergio-Leone–looking" western into the polytonal register of the Menippean satire, he might have been less outraged.

The Life and Times of Judge Roy Bean
and Menippean Satire

What is Menippean satire? Generally speaking, as Northrop Frye wrote, "Satire is ... a combination of fantasy and morality" (Frye 1957: 310). More specifically, "The Menippean satire deals less with people as such than with mental attitudes. Pedants, bigots, cranks, parvenus, virtuosi, enthusiasts, rapacious and incompetent professional men of all kinds are handled in terms of their occupational approach to life" (*ibid.*, 309). Huston's Judge Roy Bean pretty much qualifies in every one of these categories. Characterization in Menippean satire, again according to Frye, "is stylized rather than naturalistic, presents people as mouthpieces of the ideas they represent" (*ibid.*, 309). Judge Bean qualifies on this account also; so do Bad Bob, Grizzly Adams, The Reverend Mr. LaSalle (Anthony Perkins), and Lawyer Gass (Roddy McDowall)—as their names promise, the last doubly or triply. Characterization in *The Westerner* presents an illuminating contrast to that in *Roy Bean*. Wyler's film has its heart in the enormously complex relation between Brennan's Bean and Cooper's Hardin, a relationship made up in shifting proportions of homo-eroticism, father-son affections and rivalries, cowhand-farmer conflicts, and violent, ultimately fatal clashes of principle. No label or brief summary can begin to do justice to the variable energies generated between Wyler's remarkable protagonists.

Menippean satire, Frye also noted, is primarily "a prose form, though one of its recurrent features ... is the use of incidental verse" (*ibid.*, 309). The two-and-a-quarter minute idyll portraying the pastoral recreations of the Judge, his now-lover Maria-Elena, and the Watchbear constitute a cinematic equivalent of such "incidental verse." Additionally, the whole episode and — especially — its wonderfully saccharine song, "Marmalade, Molasses, and Honey," parodies by exaggerating to ridiculousness the insertion of a similar idyll in *Butch Cassidy and the Sundance Kid*, with its Bacharach-David contribution of musical sentimentality, "Raindrops Keep Fallin' on My Head."

If Milius didn't fully understand what Huston was doing to his screenplay, Huston himself clearly did: "*Roy Bean* was in the fine old American tradition of the Tall Tale, the Whopper, the yarn peopled with outrageous characters capable of prodigious and highly improbable deeds" (Huston 1980: 339). One example of such an outrageous character in *Roy Bean* is embodied in Neil Summers's virtuoso performance as Snake River Rufus Krile — a portrayal, as usual for this movie, that is also a parody. This "blood kin to a Gila monster" who makes "violent love to mountain lions" is a frail, enervated, whining figure. When he turns his gun on the helpless poster of Lillie Langtree, the entire clientele of the bar, joining the Judge, fells him in a thunderstorm of bullets.

"In nearly every period ... there are many romances, confessions, and anatomies that are neglected only because the categories to which they belong are unrecognized" (Frye 1959: 312). Although Huston's contribution to the small group of cinematic Menippean satires has not gone wholly unnoticed, it is rarely mentioned in the same paragraphs with such of his major works as, say, *The Misfits* (1961) or *Reflections in a Golden Eye* (1967). Nor has its close, suggestive relation to *The Westerner* been considered in any detail. Huston's shrewd comprehension of his friend's movie and his amplification of its wacky comedy into full-blooded Menippean satire may represent a unique "remake" in the history of commercial film. For that reason alone, *The Life and Times of Judge Roy Bean* deserves attention.

But Huston's loony western has much to offer besides its relation to its predecessor. It expresses what, in a relevant context, Bakhtin called "a universal spirit, ... a special condition of the world's revival and renewal, in which all take part" (Bakhtin 1984: 7). In this regard, one recalls most vividly the destruction of Gass's hideous oil city and the return of the desert. More generally, death in *Roy Bean* is persistently associated with rebirth and return. In its first action, its hero comes back from his hanging to vanquish his persecutors and establish "law and order west of the Pecos." The Reverend Mr. LaSalle and others — among them Tab Hunter in a brief appearance — provide post-mortem voice-overs. Grizzly Adams arrives announcing, "This here's my dyin' ground." But Bean will allow "no illegal dyin'," and Grizzly Adams is sent grumbling on his way, leaving behind him his literally ursine son, "Zachary Taylor," evidently the result of his having "cohabitated with the Bars." Maria-Elena announces immediately after the Watchbear's funeral and the Judge's melancholy meditations on the mortality of humanity that she expects his baby "in the spring." After her mother's death and the disappearance of her father, that baby, Rose Bean, "grew like a young colt." Death and disappearance have no power in the eternal, eternally renewing world of *Roy Bean*, her world and that of her father and his legendary companions and adversaries. When the Judge miraculously reappears and apologizes to Rose — in a considerable understatement — for having been "no kind of a father," she replies, "You're always here, Pa. You 'n' Ma, an' the Watchbear, Miss Lillie."

For those of us who admire Huston's filmmaking career as a whole, *Roy Bean* exemplifies much that is characteristic of his work: his wit and eloquence, his sympathetic amusement at the simultaneous glory and folly of human aspirations, his painter's eye for striking composition and apt camera movements, and his refusal to remove himself from the human comedy he portrays with the artist's passionate detachment. Like Roy Bean, John Huston appears to have been a 480 volt character in his 120 volt world, a moviemaking law unto himself. And like Roy Bean, his vices and defects seem to have been as high-charged as his remarkable virtues. Neither the hero of Huston's Menippean western nor what we know of its director ever hints at meanness or deviousness. Nor did either have much use for Prudence, that rich, ugly old maid — as William Blake wrote — courted by Incapacity (Blake, 1965: 35). If few of us can ever achieve the sheer size and exuberance of Roy Bean or that of his chronicler, equally few of us will fail to admire such grandeur and even the glorious silliness that seems inevitably to accompany it. Bakhtin could have been writing with *Roy Bean* and John Huston in mind — though he surely was not — when he contrasted "The satirist whose laughter is negative, [who] places himself above the object of his mockery" against a Hustonian "ambivalent laughter [that] expresses the point of view of the whole world; he who is laughing also belongs to it" (Bakhtin 1984: 12).

John Huston and an Irish Film Industry

RODDY FLYNN *and*
DIOG O'CONNELL

> *Mr. Gregory Peck has been assigned the role, which is my obvious due. We had to send to America for a person of heroistic aspect, although this country contains none else.... Will nobody ever give us a chance? Will the Americans cynically exploit us as ceaselessly as we ourselves exploit the police force of Chicago?* — Myles na gCopaleen, Irish humourist, on the casting of Gregory Peck as Ahab in John Huston's *Moby Dick* (1954). *Irish Times*, July 31 1954.

John Huston's commitment to Ireland has been acknowledged principally through his almost two-decade domicile there dating from the mid 1950s until the early 1970s. Having first rented Courtown House in Kilcock, County Kildare, he purchased St. Cleran's, a Georgian Manor located just outside Craughwell, in County Galway in Autumn 1955. In a 1967 newspaper interview he described Ireland as a good place to go and "lick my wounds" (a phrase repeated in his 1980 biography). His claims on Irish identity were made official when he took out Irish citizenship in January 1964 and he subsequently took the opportunity to make an official contribution to Irish cinematic culture through contributions to film policy culminating in the 1968 "Huston Report" (officially titled "The Report of the Film Industry Committee"). But he was also to demonstrate a practical commitment to Irish film through his decision to base a series of feature productions — from *Moby Dick* in 1954 through to *The Mackintosh Man* in 1973 — in his adopted homeland.

Indeed, until the 1980s, what film activity there was in Ireland was dominated by foreign productions, as a series of mainly Hollywood films were drawn by the combination of the extensive Irish diaspora and the status of Ireland as an English-speaking nation. As early as 1910 the Kalem Company traveled across the Atlantic to film around the lakes of Killarney (Rockett

Gibbons, Hill, 1987: 7–12; Condon 2008: 125–177). This practice continued throughout the twentieth century with lasting consequences. The filming in 1951 and 1968/9 of, respectively, *The Quiet Man* and *Ryan's Daughter* in Cong, County Galway and Dingle, County Kerry, for instance, had social, cultural and economic effects which endured long after the cast and crews left these locations. Micheal de Mordha's description of the production of *Ryan's Daughter* as "An rialtas ab Fhearr" ("the best government ever") points to the potentially positive — that is, financial — contribution these productions could make to rural communities (de Mordha, 1993).

The five films shot in Ireland by Huston between 1954 and 1973 (six if one includes the exterior scenes for his final film *The Dead* in 1986) suggest a particular loyalty to the country given that the majority of them employed Ireland as a stand-in for another location. Youghal (County Cork) doubled for Connecticut in *Moby Dick* (1956) whilst Glencree and Sally Gap in Wicklow stood in for Scotland in *Casino Royal* in 1967 and again in *Sinful Davey* (1969). These decisions may have been driven by pragmatism: despite owning St. Cleran's for nearly two decades, Huston was frequently absent due to filming commitments. Where possible, he adjusted his films to suit his domicile. Thus Huston transposed the setting of his 1963 production *The List of Adrian Messenger* from London (as in the original Philip MacDonald novel) to Ireland "so he could get in a bit of fox-hunting and work at the same time" (Grobel 1989: 521). Similarly, it is tempting to ponder whether Huston's decision to film an adaptation of Desmond Bagley's novel *The Freedom Trap* as *The Mackintosh Man* (1973) was at least in part motivated by the fact that elements of the source material were set in Ireland, thus permitting him to film an extended car chase sequence along the Cliffs of Moher. Of his nearly fifty films only *The Dead* (1987) had a specific Irish theme and connection. Ironically, this production was shot mainly in California and those scenes that were shot in Ireland weren't in fact directed by Huston who was too ill to travel.

This chapter sets out to examine the nature and intention of Huston's relationship with the Irish film industry. The first part of the chapter is a case study of *Moby Dick* (1954) which explores Huston's decision to film in Ireland and the contributions made to the local community arising from this decision. Our analysis suggests that this kind of film activity ultimately did little to stimulate local and indigenous productions. While there are indeed benefits from offshore productions, they operate in parallel to whatever indigenous activity is taking place rather than having a synchronous relationship that can be mutually beneficial.

The second part of the chapter considers the extent to which Huston's formal engagement with Irish Film Policy in the late 1960s was successful in creating an environment in which both Irish filmmakers and international directors like Huston himself could work.

In the Picture: Moby Dick *in Ireland*

Huston had hoped to set a film in Ireland as early as 1953 when he announced that he was working on a script about the eighteenth century blind itinerant poet Anthony Raftery (to have been played by American singer Burl Ives). However, when this came to nothing ("Film Planned about Irish Poet" 1953: 4), Huston moved on to an adaptation of *Moby Dick*, which he later described as "the most difficult picture I ever made" (Huston 1980: 251). Initially budgeted at $3 million and scheduled for six months, the production mushroomed to a $4.5 million, nine-month shoot which moved from Portugal to Ireland, to Wales and ultimately the Canaries. The difficulties associated with the film began before shooting commenced and in part explained why elements of the film were eventually shot in Ireland.

The source material, Herman Melville's 1851 novel, is set in the New England town of New Bedford in the 1840s but by the 1950s the real New Bedford had become heavily industrialized. Thus Huston sought an alternative location, "a port that hadn't changed materially for the last hundred years," as production manager Cecil Ford put it. The quest brought Huston first to the Scilly Isles and a series of small ports in England and Wales. When these proved equally unsuitable, Huston's eye came to rest on Ireland. As Cecil Ford noted in an *Irish Times* interview:

> He has a soft spot for Ireland anyway, and when the search shifted over here the possibilities were finally reduced to four—Wicklow, Arklow, Kinsale and Youghal. The others were eliminated for various technical reasons, and Youghal won [Quidnunc 1954: 5].

Once Youghal was selected the production enjoyed a smooth relationship with the local authorities. The pre-production phase, which ought to have involved extensive official correspondence given the scale of the film, appears to have made little or no impact on Irish government officials. On May 13 1954, Cecil Ford wrote from Elstree Studios (where the film's production office was located) to the Secretary of the Irish Department of External Affairs outlining a proposal to shoot in Powerscourt, County Wicklow for one day, followed by two weeks of filming in Youghal in early July. Ford concluded the letter by seeking "the blessing of your Department on the project." The Secretary replied (May 22) stating that the Department would be glad "to furnish any assistance possible in this matter."

The tone of all such correspondence was courteous, polite and conspicuously unbureaucratic. Later on of course, Huston would become intimately involved in Irish film policy at an official level, but the absence of evidence for red tape around the filming of *Moby Dick* suggests that he had already become well acquainted with the unofficial routes for doing business in Ireland.

The New Bedford sequences in the finished film amounted to just over 10 minutes of screen time (although 25,000 foot of film stock would ultimately be shot in Ireland). Nonetheless the *Moby Dick* production spent about three months in Youghal in the summer of 1954 transforming the lives of the locals on many levels. Set construction began in mid-June with the main production unit arriving on July 8. Scarcely a month later — on August 4 — the departure of the schooner used as the Captain Ahab's vessel the *Pequod* from Youghal harbor marked the completion of shooting there. This did not represent the end of film-related activity in the town, however, as the extensive sets took many weeks to disassemble.

On a financial level, the shooting was a huge economic benefit to the local economy. At its high point, the production brought 120 cast and crew to Youghal, plus the largest peacetime gathering of American and British journalists (35 in all) ever to arrive in Ireland. Unofficial estimates suggested that during the three-week shooting phase, the production spent in the region of 8,000 Irish pounds a day ("Moby Dick Schooner Leaves Youghal" 1954: 7). Much of this was expended on the very involved process of transforming the town into New Bedford circa 1840. Youghal was the location for the shore scenes of the film, set principally in the early part of the narrative, which required mock timber facades to be placed on traditional storefronts. A local construction businessman, Mick Murray, was charged with set construction. Murray describes how:

> the Market Quay was first dredged and then dug by hand where the dredger could not reach. Meanwhile, [my] firm was putting up timber house-fronts everywhere one looked. "Widows walks" too were erected on rooftops — they were small platforms where the women would wait and watch for the return of their husbands from sea voyages [Hackett 2004: 19].

Local historian Mike Hackett describes locals remembering how:

> telegraph poles were stuck in the ground and fitted out with the sails to resemble masts and there was a church doorway through which extras walked, only to find themselves out in the open Market square with crowds of onlookers awestruck at the simplicity of it all. With all those masts sticking out of the ground, the whole sea-front seemed to be swamped in tall ships and yet there were only four real tall ships at the quays!' [*ibid.*].

Hackett suggests how the experience, while exciting and enlightening, must have had

> "some serious film fans ... questioning their belief in, and enrapture with, many great films they had enjoyed, when they now saw the pretence that went into setting up mock scenes to look genuine" (*ibid.*).

Local fishermen, boat owners, hoteliers, food suppliers and especially painters and carpenters all benefited from the production. Paddy Linehan's pub, now known as "The Moby Dick," rented out two rooms at a cost of £5 a week for the duration. The press noted how social life in the town was

> stepped up to an almost trans–Atlantic pace.... Public houses keep almost continental hours. For the duration of the film-making they are open from 7 A.M. until midnight [Shaw 1954: 3].

Takings in Linehan's bar shot up from an average of £7 or £8 a day to £100 a day during the shoot, the pub's "early-house" license being extensively availed of. The local undertaker was called on to make a coffin to fit Friedrich Ledebur who played Queequeg while local nylon manufacturer, Seafield Fabrics, re-engineered their equipment to produce the skin-tight masks used to create the effect of tattoos on Queequeg's face [Tobin 1954: 4].

Others got parts as extras, with the retired sailors of Youghal simply playing themselves. According to Mike Hackett:

> the men on the quayside seats had grey beards and sailor caps as normal wear ever before the film crew arrived. The color navy and sailor garb was a proud part of their lives in retirement. The older sailors were overjoyed at re-enacting their sea days in tall ships and getting paid for it as well! [Hackett 2004: 7].

Exactly how well paid can be gleaned from the story of Dick White, a 78-year-old, British navy veteran who received 188 shillings a week (37 shillings 6 pence a day) at a point when the average weekly industrial wage in Ireland was 138 shillings, 6 pence (Shaw 1954: 3). Even children were employed in the huge support services that were required to make the production process roll. A young boy called Billy Butler was taken on to be friends with Tamba Alleney, a young actor from London who played Pip. Part of Billy's duties was to hang out with Tamba, including accompanying him each evening to one of the two local cinemas, the Regal or Horgans.

The people of Youghal were clearly delighted with the presence of the production. On August 1, the local Urban District Council admitted Huston as a freeman of town, an honor they would later extend to American Ambassador William Howard Taft, merely for arranging a local screening of a film of present day New Bedford ("*Moby Dick* Town on Screen" 1954: 1). Huston, in turn, was effusive in his praise for the town. In an open letter published in *The Irish Times* he extended his thanks for the welcome afforded to the filmmakers:

> Our thanks are especially due to the townspeople of Youghal, who have gone out of their way to make our stay a happy one. This is by no means an easy picture to make, and so much depends on the first weeks of production. If it is, as we hope and think it will be, a successful picture, this will be in no small measure due to the kindness and consideration which have been shown to us at all times and on all sides since we first selected this very lovely harbor for our location [Huston 1954: 5].

The Bigger Picture: Huston and the Irish Film Industry

Although Gregory Peck expressed the hope at a luncheon during filming that *Moby Dick* "would show other film directors, and producers, that Ireland was a place in which films could be made" ("No Ship but the Film Must Go On" 1954: 1), there was little to suggest that this was directed at anyone other than American directors and producers. Although the cast included several Irish-born actors including Noel Purcell and journalist Seamus Kelly (as Flask), Irish involvement in the crew was limited, despite contemporary attempts to imply a more substantial indigenous representation on the production. Aside from Cecil Ford (Dublin born but an employee of Elstree Studios) and Mick Murray's set construction crew, Irish crew involvement was limited to a single assistant director in the person of Kevin McClory.

Thus although *Moby Dick*—and later—Hollywood productions created spin-off economic activity, for the most part, those who benefited most directly from these productions were the film crews, interlopers who would return to their respective home countries with their spending power once filming in Ireland was complete. One journalist reviewing Youghal town in the weeks after filming wrapped, asked:

> What does Youghal need most now? Another visit from an America film unit. And I'm told that if it would not be considered improper, the Youghal Chamber of Commerce would pray for it [Shaw 1954b: 2].

Despite this reality there was a popular perception throughout his time in Ireland that Huston's dual identity—at once a part of Hollywood and Ireland—could bridge the gap between the use of Ireland as a location and as a site for an indigenous film industry. An April 13, 1967, *Irish Times* editorial lauding the work of Irish film maker Vincent Corcoran ended by asking, "When someone will have the pluck to call on John Huston to gather all this talent together and make the film that would give Ireland a new industry." But this never happened. However, it was through his contributions to official film policy that Huston offered better prospects for tangible progress.

By the late 1960s, John Huston had been resident in the Republic of Ireland for nearly 15 years and, in January 1964, he became an Irish citizen. His reasons for doing so seem to have been based on a genuine sense of connection with his domicile. Dismissing the suggestion that the renunciation of U.S. citizenship was based on tax reasons—"The tax is more or less the same for me on either side of the Atlantic"[1] ("John Huston Enjoys Becoming a Full-Fledged Irishman" 1964: 5)—he pointed out that:

> I find that I now have more connections here than in the United States and I regard Ireland as my home ... I always like to spend as much time as possible here. In fact after filming abroad it is a wonderful place to come back to and lick one's wounds [*ibid.*].

At the time of acquiring citizenship he had also expressed the hope that he could "play some role in the future of the film industry in this country" (*ibid.*). Four years later, in an interview for Peter Lennon's 1968 documentary film *The Rocky Road to Dublin*, Huston outlined his understanding of the responsibilities which came with citizenship:

> Since becoming an Irish citizen I've naturally given some thoughts to the best way I could serve my country, and as the only thing I know about is film-making, why my speculations naturally took that direction.

By the mid–1960s, Irish film policy, (to the extent that it was explicitly stated at all) comprised of subsidizing the notionally privately-owned Ardmore Studios in Bray County Wicklow and the related but less defined policy of facilitating the activities of incoming foreign production crews filming in Ireland. As we've noted, Huston's own contribution to such activity continued after *Moby Dick* and the 1967 production of *Sinful Davey* provided a backdrop against which Huston's most overt intervention in Irish domestic film policy occurred.

This intervention followed the publication, between March 27 and April 1 1967, of a series of articles in the *Irish Times* by local film-maker Louis Marcus as part of a larger series exploring how various aspects of Ireland might be developed. Marcus' articles stressed the importance of developing an indigenous film industry, painstakingly outlining how initiatives such as Ardmore Studios and the state-funded Irish Film Finance Corporation had consistently failed to act as a motor for such development. Instead Marcus called for state-support of small-scale short film and documentary production with a view to ultimately supporting arthouse scale feature production (the only sector of the local exhibition market Marcus identified as lying outside control of UK–based film distributors).

After reading the articles, Huston invited Marcus to his chambers at the Gresham Hotel in Dublin. In Marcus' account, Huston expressed his admiration for the views expressed and left Marcus with the impression that he intended to throw whatever weight he had behind the ongoing effort being made by Marcus (and other Irish filmmakers) to develop an indigenous Irish film industry. This found expression in Huston's carefully choreographed 3 July 1967 invitation to Taoiseach Jack Lynch to visit him on the County Wicklow set of *Sinful Davey*. Having shown Lynch around, Huston invited Lynch to join the crew for lunch at the close of which he delivered an extensive and detailed speech — scripted by Ernie Anderson, his long-time publicist — about an Irish film industry which began by drawing attention to his own considerable efforts:

> This set at Glencree, for example, was built by 180 Irish workers in ten weeks. 81 Irish players have speaking parts in our picture and before *Sinful Davey* is finished we will have employed through Irish Actors Equity more than 2,000 Irish extras. All told, *Sinful Davey* will plough something more than $1,000,000 into the Irish economy ["Plea for Film Industry" 1967].

All this was in the way of a lead-in to his key point however:

> But my view is that an Irish picture costing a fraction of what this film will cost might in the long run be of considerably greater benefit to Ireland. There is no reason why Ireland can't make her own native films and have foreign companies making films here as well.... But it is another aspect entirely of Irish films that compels my own deep interest. The creative aspect. There is a great natural resource in Ireland: it flows like an underground river. Tap it and foundations will leap forth. The name of that resource is talent ... Ireland is one of the few countries in the world today without her own film industry. That is neither fitting nor proper. Israel, Denmark, Finland, Rumania — even Ceylon — all have thriving native film industries. Each of these have found solutions to problems as complicated as those now facing Ireland [*ibid.*].

In effect, Huston was conceding the inherently short-term and limited impact of large-scale Hollywood productions in Ireland in terms outlined in our discussion of *Moby Dick*. He went on to suggest state support for the production of six Irish films per year aimed at Irish communities in the United States, United Kingdom and other centers. He further suggested establishing a film school "to which recognized masters from outside the country would be invited to come and give lectures and demonstrations" before concluding:

> I suggest as a first step the creation of a small committee whose initial function would be to discover the right formula. There should be elements repre-

senting the financial community both within and outside the Government. The Departments of Education and Labour should be represented and on an artistic level so should artists, writers, players and directors. Finally there must be someone with a thorough knowledge of the economic workings of the motion picture industry.... Such a council's recommendations would provide a basis for the beginning of a motion picture industry here that would properly reflect Ireland's image to the world [*ibid.*].

In a response which made clear that Jack Lynch had prior warning of the content of Huston's speech, the Taoiseach opined that his experience at the Department of Industry and Commerce and at Finance, as well as his time as the nation's leader had "convinced him" that Ireland should have a film industry. He conceded that Ardmore had not properly addressed the question of a native industry, adding that the lack of private capital and climatic conditions had also militated against the spontaneous emergence of such an industry. These obstacles notwithstanding, Lynch concluded by stating that

There is a future for film making here, but it is not going to be easy. We must have acting ability which we have in abundance; technical skill, which I feel we can create; finance, which I think should be provided, and above all the good will of people like Mr. Huston [*ibid.*].

Although Lynch's willingness to go out on a limb, if only rhetorically, suggests that some lines of communications had been opened between himself and Huston prior to the set visit, it is difficult to assess the nature or extent of these. Nonetheless, three weeks after the trip to Glencree (at the launch of a short film by Louis Marcus), Lynch would refer to "blueprints for an Irish film industry" (Quidnunc 1967: 5) which had been submitted to him by both Huston and Marcus adding that they were "under examination in a number of Government Departments." One journalist in attendance noted that "Mr. Lynch spoke with an air of purpose that left nobody in much doubt that at last there will be serious Government interest and support for Irish filmmakers." While it is unclear as to the level of detail contained within these "blueprints," Lynch did move to establish the "small committee" suggested by Huston. Unfortunately, the group who would ultimately constitute this group were from far from being of one mind as to how to develop an Irish film industry. In fact, Huston found himself chairing a committee on which almost all the participants disagreed with his proposals.

When the final membership of what would become known as "The Huston Committee" was announced in November 1967 it included 24 people. Six were civil or public servants from the Industrial Credit Corporation (which had indirectly funded the establishment of Ardmore Studios in 1957) and the

Departments of Finance, Industry and Commerce, External Affairs and Education. They were joined by six film-makers including Huston himself and Louis Marcus, a further nine individuals from film-related institutions including Donal O'Morain of Gael Linn and representatives from bodies like the Cork Film Festival, RTE and the Censorship of Film Appeals Board, and three individuals representing exhibition and distribution interests in Ireland.

The committee's first meeting commenced with a lunch at Dublin's Shelbourne Hotel and then moved to the Department of Industry and Commerce around the corner on Kildare St. In the absence of published minutes, the only surviving account of what transpired at the committee derives from Louis Marcus' recollections. Marcus suggests that Huston's initial address to the committee echoed the language of his July 3 speech to Lynch: it assumed that hitherto untapped cinematic creativity lay just beneath the surface of the Irish mind. Furthermore, in contrast to the status quo prevailing at the beginning of his own career, Huston said that the major studios were no longer the dominant forces on the international film landscape. Instead the pendulum had swung to favor the creativity of small scale independent production companies which the "majors" relied upon to provide a flow of material for release. Given this, all that was required to kickstart an Irish industry was for the Irish state to underwrite the cost of developing a number of films per annum to a stage where they could be presented to the major studios for production funding.

Huston's rationale reflected the manner in which the bulk of his own activity had been funded since he "escaped" the studio system with *The African Queen* in 1951. Huston and producers like Sam Spiegel and Darryl Zanuck packaged a story with their own finances and presented them to a production company. However, those finances were often substantial and relied more on Hollywood sources than Huston's own vision for an Irish industry implied. In his biography, *An Open Book*, Huston recalls how producer Sam Spiegel convinced a sound equipment company to stump up $50,000 to acquire the film rights to C.S Forester's novel *The African Queen*. A few years later, Huston convinced Humphrey Bogart to shell out $10,000 of his own money simply to acquire the rights to Claude Cockburn's novel *Beat the Devil* which the pair later filmed (Huston 1980: 245). Although such resources were relatively accessible within a Hollywood context they were extremely difficult to come by in a country such as Ireland. Thus, for Marcus and others, Huston's model simply didn't fit the Irish context — no Irish producer would have the financial wherewithal to develop the kind of films that could secure Hollywood backing: presold properties with casts which could be marketed to a global market.

Having delivered his vision, with the coda that the solutions were so self-evident as to require no more than a week or two's work from the committee, Huston was absent from the next meeting. It was at that meeting that Louis Marcus submitted a paper noting that the cost of developing for Hollywood could range anywhere from $250,000 to $1m, a figure far in excess of the level of resources being contemplated by the Irish state. Though absent, Huston clearly read the minutes for, at the next meeting, he expressed his unhappiness with this discussion of development costs. He was countered by an official from the Department of Finance, C.J. Byrnes who noted that although the state was interested in developing Irish abilities in this area, it could not contemplate spending unlimited sums of money on development which would essentially assist the film industries of other countries. Clearly there was diverse thinking and perception of what an Irish film industry might look like.

Perhaps more surprisingly, given his warm response to Louis Marcus' articles the previous Spring, Huston was uncomfortable with the assumption made by other committee members that their report should promote short film and documentary production. He reportedly stated that if this report was to cover documentaries then he would resign. Here, however, he was entirely outnumbered by the other committee members. Donal O'Morain, the head of *Gael Linn*, the Irish cultural group, countered that if the report *didn't* cover documentary then Huston could take it that several other members would resign.

Facing this impasse, Huston proposed that rather than continuing with a full meeting that a sub-committee comprising himself and William Eades of Ardmore Studios (who it may be surmised was more sympathetic to Huston's position than other members) on the one hand and Marcus and O'Morain on the other should continue to see if the points of dispute could be thrashed out. In Marcus' account, with Conor Maguire of the Censorship of Films Appeals Board acting as referee, the five men sat down for a number of hours with a bottle of whiskey Huston had sent over from the Shelbourne hotel. Although the meeting appears to have ended amicably, it is apparent that the views of Marcus and O'Morain prevailed. Realizing he was outnumbered, Huston took the pragmatic course of action, wished the remaining committee members the best of luck and absented himself from all the subsequent committee meetings, concentrating instead on preproduction work for *A Walk with Love and Death* in Spain. To his credit, however, when the report was completed in June 1968 after eight months' work, he came along to the launch lunch, posed for photos with the Minister George Colley, and formally endorsed the report's conclusions.

This was not a trivial act on Huston's part for the report which bore his name would undermine all of the assumptions which had informed Irish film policy since the 1940s: namely, that state support for the development of the sector could not be justified and that the development of a film industry was best served by encouraging Foreign Direct Investment (i.e. creating conditions conducive for foreign production companies to film in Ireland). Instead, it advanced a cultural rationale for developing a native film industry which created the conditions whereby the idea of an ongoing state subsidy for such an industry could at least be entertained:

> The cinema is among the most powerful communications media of the age, exerting as it does a deep influence on the habits, attitudes, motivations and aspirations of its audiences. But, Irish life is represented only very rarely on Irish cinema screens, and this dearth of native material is not conducive to a sense of community awareness and identity. Some regular display of Irish life on Irish screens is highly desirable to take advantage of the cinema's potential or social, cultural and economic good [FIC 30].

In this regard, it is impossible to overstate the significance of Huston's connection with the committee, regardless of his private views on its recommendations. Huston's imprimatur was vital in getting the state and George Colley to take film seriously. Certainly, the state moved relatively swiftly to act upon the recommendations. The report was delivered in October 1968. On January 6, 1969, George Colley circulated a memo to his cabinet colleagues rehearsing the conclusions of the Huston Committee, adding his agreement and proposing to legislate accordingly. He subsequently oversaw the drafting of a bill which transposed the report's recommendations almost word for word and which was submitted for cabinet approval on 28 May 1970.

However, although the Film Board Bill was read before the Dail in July 1970, it became less of a political priority as events connected with the contemporaneous explosion of violence in the North saw it pushed down the legislative agenda. Thus, despite ongoing reassurances from figures like Jack Lynch that the bill was still "live," when the Dail was dissolved before the general election of 1973, the bill was one of ten which automatically lapsed.

Huston's own feelings on the collapse of the bill are not on record. In a cable sent to a symposium on "The Future of the Irish Film Industry" at the September 1970 Cork Film Festival, Huston had welcomed the fact that the recommendations of the Huston Committee were "being acted upon" whilst reaffirming his faith in the viability of an Irish industry drawing upon the "writing, acting, musical and technical talents of the country." Interviewed by Lawrence Grobel in the early 1980s for the latter's book on the Huston dynasty, Huston was more cynical, stating that as a result of his July Speech, "the prime minister had me be chairman of an Irish Film Board, which was never formed. Just a lot of publicity."

However, Huston's own actions suggest that he had long lost faith in the bona fides of the state well before the Bill finally officially lapsed. By August 1972 Huston, along with Bing Crosby and Robert Altman had become a non-executive directors of Ardmore Studios, International (1972), a company formed in January that year to buy out the Ardmore facility which had been placed in receivership in July 1971. Arguably Huston's interest in the single most important piece of film-making infrastructure in the Republic pointed to a reluctance to rely on the government development of the industry.

However, by this stage, Huston's broader engagement with Ireland had already begun to wane. In January 1971, estate agents Osbourne King announced the sale by private treaty of St. Cleran's and although Huston was at pains to emphasize that this did not mean he was leaving Ireland, the eventual sale of the house in January 1973 clearly signalled a diminished commitment to the country. Although he maintained a smaller property in Connemara from 1974 onwards, and retained his Irish citizenship, he moved to Puerto Vallarta in Mexico, which remained his home until his death in 1987.

What then was Huston's ultimate legacy was to film-making in Ireland? Huston's own words on the subject are ambiguous. His Glencree suggestion that an Irish picture with a considerably smaller budget than *Sinful Davey* might be of considerably greater benefit to Ireland in the long run hints at some conception of a national cinema (a still nascent theoretical concept in the late 1960s). His suggestion that it was the creative aspect of the question that compelled his own deep interest in film policy appears to confirm this.

Yet, for the most part, Huston himself didn't produce Irish films as such but made films in Ireland, with the contributions to Irish society appearing in the form of direct economic benefit and less quantifiable provision of access to new social and cultural experiences. These films clearly didn't advance the cause of a national cinema and may even have hindered indigenous production by allowing officials of the state to focus on the economic benefits of inward investment instead of encouraging film as an indigenous form of cultural self-expression. Huston believed these types of offshore productions could advance the infrastructural development of a national cinema, facilitating training and employment in particular. He saw a "creative pool of talent" existing in Ireland but argued that these people must have training. Such training could happen on the big feature productions which Huston himself was willing to take on. He argued that an Irish film industry could be based on six films a year (*Sunday Press*, 16 July 1967) initially, but he failed to distinguish between indigenous and offshore productions. The gap between Huston's model and the Committee's vision was reflected in the Irish state's vacillation over film policy throughout the 1970s: in 1973 the state opted to pursue an indigenous industry throughout the 1970s. While the Huston Committee made recommendations that may have served the cultural project of film well, without the political will another decade of film inactivity lay in waiting.

Note

1. In 1969, the Minister for Finance Charles J. Haughey introduced an exemption from income tax for artists resident in Ireland. Perhaps not coincidentally the same Charles J. Haughey, as then Minister for Justice, had handed Huston his citizenship papers in 1964.

Recollections of Huston
A Conversation with Wieland Schulz-Keil
Tony Tracy

I first met John Huston late in his life — in 1982 — when, after quite a bit of work my partner Moritz Borman and I had acquired the rights of *Under the Volcano* and were hoping that he would direct the movie adaptation. He just seemed right for the project in every way: he had been living in Mexico for some time and it was the sort of subject matter I felt he would like and understand. So I went to meet him during the shooting of *Annie*. I had very long hair and a long beard at the time and he immediately hired me as a "bomb-throwing anarchist" in the film — a casting that was supposed to be for an afternoon ... an afternoon which lasted two weeks.

[Albert] Finney was playing Daddy Warbucks, and we talked a lot about how to do *Under the Volcano* and wouldn't it be great and it was sort of agreed that the project would happen with Huston and Finney. With Huston working at the top of his game — *Annie* had a huge budget for the time and was central to the take over of Columbia by Coca-Cola — and the involvement of Finney, we were able to put together some financing for the picture. Then I went to find a writer. This turned out to be more difficult than it sounds.

First of all, there were already many screenplays based on the *Under the Volcano* knocking around. I remember we counted over 60 and lots of them were pretty poor stuff, written by film students or by college professors. But there were also some very good ones because quite a number of important directors had been thinking of making this picture since the novel was first published in 1947. Jean-Claude Carrière, for example, had written a screenplay for Luis Buñuel, and the Cuban writer Guillermo Cabrera-Infante had written one for Joseph Losey. Most of the screenplays were using complicated montage and voiceover techniques, trying to imitate the literary form of the novel, and we didn't like that. Even though the novel uses a sort of interior monologue, a stream of consciousness, we decided early on that we'd try to do a "hard surface" movie: we would show the outside of our characters and their actions, and people could then figure out for themselves what was going on in their minds and souls.

In the meantime Moritz Borman and I had been joined by Michael Fitzgerald who later became the executive producer of the picture. He had come upon a screenplay by somebody who was then a student at Harvard that we liked, a fellow by the name of Guy Gallo. Guy and I then moved to Mexico and worked for several months with John on the screenplay and that's when I got to know him very well. We stayed at his compound near Puerto Vallarta where he had been given a piece of land by an Indian tribe on their reservation after he had made *Night of the Iguana* and made the place something of a tourist attraction. There was no electricity except for a small generator and I remember we had a refrigerator operated by gas. The place was very nice, very simple, consisting of four or five little cabins. One of those was the "office" where we worked. It was, overall, a very stimulating and convivial working process. I've always been very interested in Herman Melville and we talked a lot about how his stories should be made into movies and how nobody understood them and what we would need to make them into a movie. John loved writing, particularly about certain types of men; the sort of loser-heroes, a specialty of American writers belonging to his generation. But like other American artists and intellectuals from the 1920s John also was very influenced by the European avant-garde, particularly literature. His mother had smuggled a copy of *Ulysses* for him to the United States — the second printing of the Shakespeare Company edition — and he still had that copy with him in Mexico. His great idol H.L. Mencken published a couple of John's stories in *American Mercury* at the height of the 1920s and it was something which he was very proud of. Whenever you saw John, he was either engaged in conversation, or he was putting a book away to mix a martini and after the martini, he would go right back to the book, or to the conversation. Whenever you met him, he was reading, and he talked constantly about literature.

Huston was wonderful to work with on screenplays. He knew what he wanted, what he didn't want, what should be done, what should not be done, and at the same time he was willing to listen to others and be surprised by their suggestions and ideas. We had a very good system that I learned from him: we would always assemble in the morning and discuss what would be done and then during the day, everybody would work on certain pages or scenes allocated to him. In the evening we would exchange what everybody had done. I remember he was always working with these yellow legal pads and everybody would exchange notes and then we would put it all together again and again and again and after several months we were done with it.

After the film was finished, we got an award in Cannes and we were constantly thinking about what to do next and how to do it. *Wise Blood* and *Annie* and *Under the Volcano* ignited the last phase of his career. Before *Wise Blood*, John hadn't directed much for some time, he'd mostly acted for a number of years. And so one day we decided to do a screenplay for *The Dead*.

I first had talked with John about making a movie based on *The Dead* while preparing *Under the Volcano*. It was All Saints Day, the Mexican Day of the Dead — the one day on which the story of *Under the Volcano* unfolds, Malcolm Lowry's "Bloomsday" so to speak. After nightfall John, the screenwriter Guy Gallo and I took a walk through a cemetery in Puerto Vallarta in Mexico. There was a sea of yellow flowers and lighted candles. Children dressed as skeletons, carrying skeleton toys and eating skeleton cookies, were everywhere. Families had set up the graves of their ancestors as tables, dining on black beans and other dark colored food. There was music and a festive atmosphere. We talked about the seeming contradiction displayed by these rituals, the mixture of remembrance of the dead, and fear of their possible return. Apparently, the Mexicans with their graveyard meals felt they succeeded in placating the dead, and in keeping them at bay — so very different from the carving of the goose at Aunt Kate and Aunt Julia's dinner table in Joyce's story.

Joyce's ambiguous relationship with religion was congenial to John's. John was the first to declare himself an agnostic. He only reluctantly set foot in a church, and then only if there were some paintings, or some architectural details worth seeing. Still, little seemed to intrigue him as much as themes rooted in religion. His adaptation of Flannery O'Connor's *Wise Blood* is a theological reflection on the Christian notion of love and its destruction. And in other films of his, revelations and miracles abound, even miracles that follow prayers: in *The African Queen* and in *Under the Volcano*, for example, the stories take sudden turns for the better after the heroes pray. "The Dead," finally, is the story of a revelation. But, like Joyce, John cherished revelations not as religious, but as profane manifestations. John had no ambition whatsoever to become religious before or after death. At the same time, he was very interested in the profane manifestations of what you might consider religious experiences. A surprisingly large number of John's films deals with metaphysical issues as they manifest themselves in ordinary life, and these manifestations are then shown from the outside. This is realism in the strict sense of the term: the sublime as it reveals itself in everyday life.

From the beginning, we thought *The Dead* would lend itself to a particular type of storytelling and photography. We both felt that Joyce's story was showing something that didn't exist anymore: people talking and thinking of their past, and their dead, in a very different way from how we relate to our own past. And there was the most intriguing aspect of this project: right after its invention in the 1830s, people were fascinated by photography's mysterious ability to capture and preserve moments in the lives of people, and the same fascination characterizes the earliest film experiments by the Lumière brothers: they filmed the trembling leaves on a tree, and the arrival of a locomotive in a station as if to preserve these moments for eternity. Already long before the Victorian period this profane mystery of photography had been sensed, but the Victorians began to systematically produce photographic records designed to end up as part of a gallery of dead friends and relatives on a chest of drawers, or even in the center of a tombstone. Looking at Victorian studio photographs we feel that the subject's glance at the small lens with the almost invisible man behind it betrays a melancholy knowledge of the secret purpose of the studio session, to immortalize a man or a woman or a child for a time when they will be no longer around. The dinner at Aunt Kate and Aunt Julia's house reminded us of such sessions. We hoped retelling Joyce's story on celluloid would allow us to reveal photography's peculiar play with the foreseeable death of its subjects, and to reveal a hidden dimension of the cinematic experience, which you might call an art condemned to show the not-yet-dead.

We talked about this for a long time and then John suggested we employ his son Tony as a screenwriter. Could we do this, should we do that, back and forth. Working on the screenplay was a long and laborious process, and I think Tony suffered a bit, but in the end he produced a screenplay that was marvelous because it was amazingly close to Joyce's text. Then began the equally long process of choosing the actors and technicians, the casting and crewing, which was very important. John believed that once you've written the screenplay, the train has left the station. You shouldn't change anything. You should be open to what happens in front of the camera with the people you hired, and with the screenplay you approved. So, he kind of took off the hat of screenwriter and put on the entirely different hat of the person trying to achieve as much as he possibly could with the available elements.

After the script was finished, I went to Dublin to begin the pre-production process. We had hoped to shoot the film entirely in Ireland, but the very serious deterioration in John's health made it impossible for him to fly. John called me from Los Angeles to tell me that he wouldn't be able to come and he was very saddened. He liked Ireland so much and he thought it would be so wonderful to be doing this in Dublin where he had all these friends and such happy memories.

At this point he had sort of given up hope of making the movie at all. But my partner Chris Sievernich and I got together with Stephen Grimes, who was an old friend of John's, a very good production designer, who had worked with him on several films.[1] Stephen went by the nickname "Stephen Why-Rent-It-If-You-Can-Buy-It Grimes" and we figured we would shoot the picture in California, in Los Angeles, but of course we had no money. We had no money because it was considered a nutty project, and also because nobody would insure the production. John was in the final stages of emphysema and he was sitting in a wheelchair with an oxygen bottle on the back which made insurance companies very nervous indeed, so we had to finance it through a video company—Vestron Video—that at the time had started producing and theatrically distributing in America. Vestron was joined by another financier, a U.K. company, Zenith productions. My partner and I also put up some money and we had to cash-flow the picture ourselves.

Chris Sievernich and I cast the picture in Dublin with Nuala Moiselle. We interviewed well over one hundred actors and actresses and then we prepared reports and sent them to John and discussed everyone in great detail with him. Then others came to see us in Los Angeles like Donal Donnelly and Marie Kean and Donal McCann. While we completed the casting, Stephen Grimes started building the set in a very miserable, extremely bare hangar north of Los Angeles, a kind of warehouse which we made into a make-shift studio. The place had been found by Tom Shaw who then served as production manager and first assistant director on *The Dead* as he had on *Under the Volcano* and on many earlier films of John's.

In a kind of ironic contrast to the atmosphere of extravagance and plenty in the film, it was all very low budget and everybody always went to this awful restaurant for lunch and dinner and we all stayed in a very cheap motel. But John, like a Boy Scout leader keeping everybody in good spirits, would make speeches about this incredible steak he had eaten at the awful restaurant, where thought the food was "superb."

In order to obtain insurance we needed another director who would be on standby and that was Karel Reisz (*The French Lieutenant's Woman*)—one of the nicest people ever in motion pictures. He was staying at the Chateau Marmont—which was very down-market in those days—and occasionally came to visit the set. He was fascinated by John's style of directing which appeared to him as a kind of directing by mere presence—John said very little, if anything. I remember Karel kept telling people afterwards it was the strangest thing he'd ever seen. He came in and there's this guy sitting in a corner reading a book and having amusing conversations with all sorts of people, and meanwhile all the technicians and the actors were running around seemingly knowing exactly what he wanted.

John not only cast his actors very rigorously, he also cast his crew with great care. Lots of them had worked with him many times before and they understood exactly what he wanted. For instance Tommy Shaw, a wonderful guy. Tommy was an Irish-American, the absolute opposite of John in temperament and outlook. He was a very practical production man but incredibly good and very pleasant to work with. There was Stephen Grimes and a world-famous wardrobe designer Dorothy Jeakins, who at that time had won more Oscars than anyone — she was the one who had somehow made Marilyn Monroe work on *The Misfits*. All these people made John's job much easier and meant that he didn't have to intervene in every aspect of the production; they instinctively knew that he wanted. And as I said before, John felt an obligation to work with the people he had chosen. He took the full responsibility for all casting decisions and was very reluctant to fire people. For example on *Under the Volcano* we had this wonderful director of photography, Gaby Figueroa, who brought in this operator who was an older guy. Already on the first day we noticed that he didn't operate very well. Under any other circumstances, one would have fired this operator and hired another one, but John wouldn't — he was absolutely loyal to his crew. We used a lot of steadi-cam work in the picture so the operator didn't have to do much anymore. But he wouldn't fire him.

It was the same with actors. If he had made a mistake hiring somebody, he would never ever fire the actor and hire another one, but you would notice doing the shoot how the part of this actor was shrinking. On the other hand, if he had hired someone more interesting, that person's part would increase. Sean McClory is a case in point. He was supposed to play the small part of Mr. Grace, basically to say "hello," read a poem and go, but in the course of the shoot, he became an important character.

I don't want to suggest for one moment that John was not very active during the shoot, he just worked primarily through his presence. He would come to the set in the morning and Tommy Shaw had already prepared something, such as two people on the stairs, and between Tommy Shaw and the DP, they had worked it out that one should place the camera at the bottom of the stairs, the people would look above the banister and we would shoot up. This was kind of already more or less set up, and Tommy Shaw would ask John what he thought and John would say something like "what an absolutely fabulous idea." He occasionally added a comment like "a bit more to the right perhaps," or, after the actors had rehearsed, "a bit slower."

Working with John was a model of economy, in every respect. Generally he didn't like telling actors what to do, or talking at length with them about their part, and some actors very much enjoyed this and liked working with him and others did not. Most of the time he only did two takes. Three takes was seen as a gross over-indulgence — partly because there was not enough film stock in the budget. But he knew, completely in his head, what he was shooting and why. He would cut in the middle of the sentence because he knew that's where the cut would be. On *The Dead*, we never worked more than eight or nine hours. He wasn't one of those people who would work sixteen hours; he thought that was utter nonsense. And we always finished ahead of schedule. Although, he was constantly concerned about two things; that we would go over budget and that the picture would get too short. Of course *The Dead* is short. But it's a jewel. And we came in under budget because we finished three days early.

A striking aspect of his direction was how good he was at continuity; he was extremely good at keeping his eye on detail. It was fairly complicated to shoot the dinner scene in *The Dead* for instance, because you have many different angles and many things are happening — a plate with a goose being passed around from one person to the next, people are eating and drinking and so on. And if you do a different set up, the goose always has to be in the same place. Very quickly the continuity person gave up because we didn't know where we were but Huston had it all down. The goose is here, the sauce is there, the potatoes are here — he noticed everything.

When it came to post-production I don't think John actually liked music very much, but rather saw it as a sort of necessary evil. Both *The Dead* and *Under the Volcano* were done by the same excellent composer, Alex North. He would get the finished film but John would barely talk with him. They would talk about other things, but not the score. Then Alex went away and composed and wondered if he was on the right track. This was before computers. At the time we didn't have the digital temp scores for the cut which you would orchestrate later. Alex came in and explained the score, perhaps humming a few sections, and predictably John thought it was too much. Alex was miffed, but after a bit of discussion we kind of agreed that it was okay and we got this orchestra together and Alex conducted the orchestra and then the recordings were edited by the music editor. John came and saw it again and said it was way too much, do we really need all of this music? Alex was even more miffed, but finally John accepted that a score was necessary, and in the end he even very much liked the music. And he and Alex remained the friends they had been for many years.

When we were making *The Dead* it was generally assumed this would be his last film; he was very sick by then. And a few journalists came to the set and tentatively put this mortality issue to him: did he see a connection between his own impending death and the story. He thought there was none. He would say, "I don't know the experience of dying any more than I did when I was 20 years old." What he was interested in was the theme of the dead and how they relate to the living and what role they play, how various social formations are dealing with their dead and how these certain attitudes and methods would change over time. This all interested him enormously. What was remarkable was this kind of indifference to his own condition.

My prevailing memory was that John was an absolute delight to work with. He understood the production process from top to bottom. He was constantly concerned; he would ask me twice a day, can we do this? Is this too expensive? He was enormously inventive and concerned about everyone on the set. In a way, he kind of spoiled us all. Later on, making movies was never the same.

Note

1. No one collaborated with Huston as much as the English-born Stephen Grimes. He began working with Huston on *Moby Dick* (1956) and thereafter worked as art director/production designer on *Heaven Knows, Mr. Allison* (1957); *The Unforgiven* (1960); *The Misfits* (1961); *Freud* (1962); *The List of Adrian Messenger* (1963); *The Night of the Iguana* (1964); *Reflections in a Golden Eye* (1967); *Sinful Davy* (1969); *A Walk With Love and Death* (1969); and *The Dead* (1987).

Bibliography

Agee, James. 1969. *Agee on Film*, Vol. 1. New York: Grosset & Dunlap.

Ainsworth, Peter F., and George Diller, eds. 1992. *Chroniques, Tome 3, Depuis la bataille de Crécy jusqu'au mariage du duc de Bourgogne avec Marguerite de Flandre (1346–1369)/Livre II, Le Manuscrit d'Amiens, Bibliothèque municipale no. 486*. Geneva: Droz.

Alarcón, Daniel Cooper. 1997. *The Aztec Palimpsest*. Tucson: University of Arizona Press.

Almond, Ian. 2002. "Lessons from Kipling and Rao: How to Re-Appropriate Another Culture." *Orbis Litterarum* 57: 275–87.

Andrews, Geoff. 1999. *The Director's Vision: A Concise Guide to the Art of 250 Great Filmmakers*. Chicago: Chicago Review Press.

Avout, Jacques, comte d.' 1960. *Le Meurtre d'Etienne Marcel, 31 juillet 1358*. Paris: Gallimard.

Bacall, Lauren. 1979. *By Myself*. New York: Alfred A. Knopf.

Bakhtin, Mikhail. 1984. *Rabelais and His World*, trans. Helene Iswolsky. Bloomington: Indiana University Press.

Barry, Kevin. 2001. *The Dead*. Cork: Cork University Press.

Bataillard, Pascal, and Dominique Sipière, eds. 2000. *Dubliners, James Joyce; The Dead, John Huston*. Paris: Ellipses Édition.

Bell, Jeffrey. 1997. "Thinking with Cinema: Deleuze and Film Theory." *Film Philosophy* 1, no. 8 (September 1997). www.film-philosophy.com/vol1-1997/n8bell, accessed 22 July 2009.

Benayoun, Robert. 1985. *John Huston: La grande ombre de l'aventure*. Paris: Editions Pierre L'Herminie.

Bessie, Alvah. 1967. *Inquisition in Eden*. Berlin: Seven Seas.

Bhabha, Homi. 1994. *The Location of Culture*. London: Routledge.

Boyum, Joy Gould. 1985. *Double Exposure: Fiction into Film*. New York: Universe.

Bradbury, Malcolm. 1997. "Arthur Miller's Fiction." In *The Cambridge Companion to Arthur Miller*, Christopher Bigsby, ed. Cambridge: Cambridge University Press.

Bradbury, Ray. 2002. *Green Shadows, White Whale*. New York: Perennial.

Brill, Lesley. 1988. *The Hitchcock Romance*. Princeton, NJ: Princeton University Press.

———. 1995. "The African Queen and John Huston's Filmmaking." *Cinema Journal* 34, no. 2 (Winter): 3–21.

———. 1997. *John Huston's Filmmaking*. Cambridge: Cambridge University Press.

Brion, Patrick. 2003. *John Huston: Biographie, filmographie illustrée, analyse critique*. Paris: La Martinière.

Brouwers, Anke, and Tom Paulus. 2006. "The Mortgage the Merrier: Hollywood Comedies of Remarriage in the Age of Domesticity." *Film International* 4, no. 4: 21–34.

Bruce-Novoa, Juan. 2005. "Pancho Villa: Post-Colonial Colonialism, Or the Return of the Americano." Presented at the 30th Annual Conference on Literature and Film, Florida State University, January 27–29.

Busch, Niven. 1955. *The Actor*, New York: Simon and Schuster.

Cacqueray, Elizabeth de, and Raphaëlle Costa de Beauregard. 2000. "Polyphony in *The Dead* by John Huston." In *The ubliners, James Joyce; The Dead, John Huston*, ed. Pascal Bataillard and Dominique Sipière. Paris: Ellipses.

Canby, Vincent. 1975. "Connery and Caine Flee Kipling India." *New York Times*, 18 December, p. 62.

Canetti, Elias. 1962. *Crowds and Power*, trans. Carol Stewart. New York: Farrar, Straus and Giroux.

Carson, John F. 1990. "John Huston's The Dead: An Irish Encomium." *Proteus* 7, no. 2: 26–29.

Castries, duc de [René de la Croix]. 1979. *The Lives of the Kings and Queens of France*, trans. Anne Dobell. New York: Knopf.

Caute, David. 1978. *The Great Fear. The Anti-Communist Purge under Truman and Eisenhower*. New York: Simon and Schuster.

Cavell, Stanley. 1981. *Pursuits of Happiness: The Hollywood Comedy of Remarriage*. Cambridge, MA: Harvard University Press.

Cazalis, Anne-Marie. 1977. *La Jacquerie de Paris, 1358: Le destin tragique du "maire" Etienne Marcel*. Paris: Société de Production Littéraire.

Ceplair, Larry. 1989. "A Communist Labor Organizer in Hollywood: Jeff Kibre Challenges the IATSE, 1937-1939." *The Velvet Light Trap* 23 (Spring): 64–74.

———, and Steven Englund. 1980. *The Inquisition in Hollywood: Politics in the Film Community, 1930–1960*. Garden City, NY: Anchor Press/Doubleday.

Champlin, Charles. 1981. "Huston Wartime Films on KCET." *Los Angeles Times*, April 30.

Chowdhry, Prem. 2000. *Colonial India and the Making of Empire Cinema*. Manchester, UK: Manchester University Press.

Cohen, Allen, and Harry Lawton, eds. 1997. *John Huston: A Guide to References and Resources*. New York: G.K. Hall.

Cooper, Stephen. 1993. "The Undeclared War: Political Reflections in a Golden Eye." In *Reflections in a Male Eye: John Huston and the American Experience*, ed. Gayle Studlar and David Desser. Washington, DC: Smithsonian Institution.

———, ed. 1994. *Perspectives on John Huston*. New York: G.K. Hall.

Coopey, Richard, and Nicholas Woodward. 1996. *Britain in the 1970s: The Troubled Economy*. London: Palgrave.

Cortés, Carlos E. 1997. "Chicanas in Film: History of an Image." In *Latina Looks*, ed. Clara E. Rodríguez, 121–141. Bolder, CO: Westview.

Costanzo, Angelo ed. 1990. "The Film Career of John Huston." *Proteus* 7, no. 2 (Fall).

Crane, Stephen. 1917. *The Red Badge of Courage*, New York: D. Appleton.

Crowther, Bosley. 9 May 1942. "The Screen: 'In This Our Life,' Film Version of Ellen Glasgow Prize Novel, With Bette Davis and Olivia de Havilland, Opens at Strand." *The New York Times Online*, http://movies2.nytimes.com/mem/movies/review.html?_r=1&titlel=In%20This%20our%20Lifetitle2, accessed 26 October 2006.

Deane, Paul. 1969. "Motion Picture Techniques in James Joyce's 'The Dead.'" *James Joyce Quarterly* 6 (Spring): 231–36.

Deleuze, Gilles. 1986. *The Movement Image*, trans. Hugh Tomlinson and Barbara Habberjam, Minneapolis: University of Minnesota Press.

Delpar, Helen. 1992. *The Enormous Vogue of Things Mexican: Cultural Relations Between the United States and Mexico, 1920–1935*. Tuscaloosa and London: University of Alabama Press.

de Mordha, Michael. 1993. *An rialtas ab fhearr!: Scannán David Lean — Ryan's Daughter*. Baile Atha Cliath: Coisceim.

Denby, David. 1981. Review. *New York Magazine*, January 19, 1981, p. 44.

Desser, David. 1993. "The Wartime Films of John Huston: Film Noir and the Emergence of the Therapeutic." In *Reflections in a Male Eye: John Huston and The American Experience*, ed. Gaylyn Studlar and David Desser. Washington, DC: Smithsonian Institution.

De Usabel, Gaizka S. 1982. *The High Noon of American Films in Latin America*. Ann Arbor, MI: UMI Research Press.

Doherty, Thomas. 1993. Projections of War: Hollywood, American Culture, and World War II. New York: Columbia University Press.

Dommanget, Maurice. 1971. *La Jacquerie*. Paris: Maspero.

Donohue, Dennis. 1988. *We Irish*. Berkley: University of California Press.

Drew, Bernard. 2001. "John Huston: At 74 No Formula." In *John Huston: Interviews*, ed. Robert Emmet Long. Jackson: University of Mississippi Press.

Dyer MacCann, Richard. 1973. *The People's Films: A Political History of U.S. Government Motion Pictures*, New York: Hastings House.

Ebert, Roger. 1975. "The Man Who Would Be King." *Chicago Sun-Times*, 1 January, p. 56.

Echart, Pablo. 2005. *La comedia romántica del Hollywood de los años 30 y 40*. Madrid: Cátedra.

Edgerton, Gary. 1993. "Revisiting the Recordings of Wars Past: Remembering the Documentary Trilogy of John Huston." In *Reflections in a Male Eye: John Huston and the American Experience*, ed. Gaylyn Studlar and David Desser. Washington, D.C.: Smithsonian Institute.

Engell, John. 1993. "Traven, Huston, and the Textual Treasures of the Sierra Madre." In *Reflections in a Male Eye: John Huston and the American Experience*, ed. Gaylyn Studlar and David Desser, 79–95. Washington: Smithsonian Institution.

Erdman, David V., ed. 1965. *The Marriage of Heaven and Hell: The Poetry and Prose of William Blake*. Garden City, NY: Doubleday.

Fariello, Griffin. 1995. *Red Scare. Memories of the American Inquisition*. New York: Avon.

Fein, Seth. 2001. "Myths of Cultural Imperialism and Nationalism in Golden Age Mexican Cinema." In *Fragments of a Golden Age: The Politics of Culture in Mexico Since 1940*, ed. Gilbert Joseph, Anne Rubgenstein and Eric Zolov, 159–198. Durham, NC, and London: Duke University Press.

"Film Planned about Irish Poet." *Irish Times*, 18 September 1953, p. 4.

French, Brandon. 1977. "Lost at Sea." In *The Classic American Novel and the Movies*, ed. Gerald Peary and Roger Shatzkin. New York: Unger.

Froissart, Jean. 1806. *Chronicles of England, France, Spain, and the Adjoining Countries, from the Latter Part of the Reign of Edward II to the Coronation of Henry IV*, trans. Thomas Johnes. London: Longman, Hurst, Rees and Orme.

———. 1968. *Froissart's Chronicles*, trans. and ed. Jean Joliffe. New York: Modern Library.

Frye, Northrop. 1957. *Anatomy of Criticism*. Princeton, NJ: Princeton University Press.

Frye, Northrop. 1965. *A Natural Perspective: The Development of Shakespearian Comedy and Romance*. New York: Columbia University Press.

Frye, Northrop. 1976. *The Secular Scripture: A Study of the Structure of Romance*. Cambridge, MA: Harvard University Press.

Fultz, James. 1982. "A Classic Case of Collaboration ... The African Queen." *Film Literature Quarterly* 10, no. 1: 13–24.

Fussell, Paul, Jr. 1958. "Irony, Freemasonry, and Human Ethics in Kipling's 'The Man Who Would Be King.'" *ELH* 25, no. 3 (September): 216–33.

Gabler, Neal. 1988. *An Empire of Their Own: How the Jews Invented Hollywood*. New York: Crown Publishers, Inc.

Gallix, François. 2000. "Silence! On tourne! À l'écoute des non-dits de John Huston dans *The Dead*," Bataillard, Pascal and Sipière, Dominique (eds.) *Dubliners, James Joyce; The Dead, John Huston*, Paris: Ellipses.

García Riera, Emilio. 1987. *Mexico visto por el cine extranjero, Vol. 1, 1894/1940*. México, D.F. Ediciones Era.

Gardner, Ava (1990). *Ava: My Story*. New York: Bantam.

Gerber, David A. 2000. "Heroes and Misfits: The Troubled Social Reintegration of Disabled Veterans in *The Best Years of Our Lives*." In *Disabled Veterans in History*, ed. David A. Gerber. Ann Arbor: University of Michigan Press.

Gibbons, Luke. 2000. *The Quiet Man*. Cork: Cork University Press.

Gifford, Don. 1982. *Joyce Annotated: Notes for Dubliners and A Portrait of the Artist as a Young Man*, 2nd ed. Berkeley: University of California Press.

Gilbert, Stuart. 1930. *Joyce's Ulysses: a Study*. London: Faber.

Gillespie, Michael Patrick. 2002. "The Myth of Hidden Ireland: The Corrosive

Effect of *The Quiet Man*." *New Hibernia Review* 6 (Summer): 18–32.

_____. 2006a. "The Chaos and Complexity of Classic Hollywood Cinema." *Nonlinear Dynamics, Psychology, and Life Science* 10, no. 1 (January): 123–141.

_____. 2006b. "The Myth of an Irish Cinema." *An Sionnach* 2, nos. 1 and 2 (Spring and Fall): 44–64.

_____, 2008. *The Myth of an Irish Cinema: Approaching Irish-Themed Films*. Syracuse, NY: Syracuse University Press.

Ginna, Robert Emmett, Jr. 2002. "In Search of *The Treasure of Sierra Madre*." *American Scholar* (Autumn): 75–89.

Glasgow, Ellen. 1941. *In This Our Life*, New York: Grosset and Dunlap.

_____. 2003. *Becoming a New Virginia: The Story of Virginia, An American Experience*. www.vahistorical.org/sva2003/glasgow.htm, accessed 26 October 2006.

Goldstein, Richard. 1968. "In the Face of Beauty." *Vogue* 152, no. 6 (No. 3006), 1 October, pp. 170–73.

Graebner, William. 2004. "Fathers and Sons: An Exploration of *The Treasure of the Sierra Madre*." *Literature Film Quarterly* 32, no, 1: 30–38.

Greenberg, Peter S. 2001. "Saints and Stinkers: The *Rolling Stone* Interview." In *John Huston: Interviews*, ed. Robert Emmet Long. Jackson: University Press of Mississippi.

Grobel, Lawrence. 1989. *The Hustons*. New York: Charles Scribner's Sons.

Hagen, W.M. 1991. "Under Huston's *Volcano*." *Literature Film Quarterly* 19, no 3: 138–147

Hamblett, Charles. 1956. *Crazy Kill*. London: Sidgwick and Jackson.

Hammen, Scott. 1985. *John Huston*. Boston: Twayne.

Hart, Clive. 1988. *Joyce, Huston, and the Making of The Dead*. Gerrards Cross: Colin Smythe.

Harty, Kevin J. 2006. *The Reel Middle Ages: American, Western and Eastern European, Middle Eastern and Asian Films about Medieval Europe*, 2d ed. Jefferson, NC: McFarland.

Henderson, Sanya. 2003. *Alex North, Film Composer: A Biography, with Musical Analyses of* A Streetcar Named Desire, Spartacus, The Misfits, Under the Volcano, *and* Prizzi's Honor. Jefferson, NC: McFarland.

Hepburn, Katherine. 1988. *The Making of the African Queen or How I Went to Africa with Bogart, Bacall and Huston and Almost Lost My Mind*. New York: New American Library.

Heredero, Carlos Fernande. 1984. *John Huston*, Madrid: Ediciones JC.

Higham, Charles. 1986. *Olivia and Joan*. London: New English Library.

Horne, Gerald. 2001. *Class Struggles in Hollywood, 1930–1950: Moguls, Mobsters, Stars, Reds, and Trade Unionists*. Austin: University of Texas Press.

_____. 2006. *The Final Victim of the Blacklist: John Howard Lawson, Dean of the Hollywood Ten*. Berkeley, Los Angeles, London: University of California Press.

Hugenholtz, F.W.N. 1949. *Drie Boerenopstanden uit de veertiende eeuw; Vlaanderen, 1323–1328; Frankrijk,1358; Engeland, 1381.* Haarlem: H.D. Tjeenk Willink & Zoon.

Hughes, Robert, ed. 1965. *Film: Book 2, Films of Peace and War*. New York: Grove.

Humphries, Reynold. 2004. "The Politics of Crime and the Crime of Politics: Post-War *Noir*, the Liberal Consensus and the Hollywood Left." In *Film Noir Reader 4*, ed. Alain Silver and James Ursini, pp. 227–45. Pompton Plains, NJ: Limelight.

_____. 2006. "Documenting Communist Subversion: The Case of *I Was a Communist for the FBI* (1951)." In *Docufictions: Essays on the Intersection of Documentary and Fictional Filmmaking*, ed. Gary D. Rhodes and John Parris Springer, pp. 102–23. Jefferson, NC: McFarland.

Huston, John. 1954. "Moby Dick" (letter to the editor). *Irish Times*, 5 August, p. 5.

_____. 1980. *An Open Book*. New York: Knopf.

Insausti, Gabriel. 2004. *Tras las huellas de Huston: La jungla de asfalto*. Ediciones Internacionales Universitarias.

Iversen, Gunnar. 2000. "Clear, from a Distance: The Image of the Mediaeval Period in Recent Norwegian Films." *Scandinavica* 39, no. 1: 7–23.

Jaffrey, Saeed. 1998. *An Actor's Journey*. London: Constable.

Jaikumar, Priya. 2006. *Cinema at the End of Empire*. Durham, NC: Duke University Press.

Jameson, Richard T. 1980. "John Huston." *Film Comment* 16, no. 3 (May–June): 25–56.

_____. 1994. "John Huston." In *Perspectives on John Huston*, ed. Stephen Cooper. New York: G.K. Hall.

"John Huston Enjoys Becoming a Full-Fledged Irishman." *Irish Times*, 4 January, 1964, p. 5.

Joyce, James. 1986. *Ulysses*, New York: Random House.

Kael, Pauline. 1985. "Under the Volcano." *State of the Art*. New York: E. P. Dutton.

Kagle, Steven E. 1992. "Homage to Melville: Ray Bradbury and the Nineteenth-Century American Romance." The Celebration of the Fantastic: Selected Papers from the Tenth Anniversary International Conference on the Fantastic in the Arts. *Contributions to the Study of Science Fiction and Fantasy* 49: 279–289.

Kaminsky, Stuart. 1978. *John Huston: Maker of Magic*. Boston: Houghton Mifflin.

Kaplan, E.A. 2000. "Classical Hollywood Film and Melodrama." In *American Cinema and Hollywood: Critical Approaches*, ed. John Hill and Pamela Church Gibson. Oxford: Oxford University Press.

Kaplan, Louise J. 1993. "Fits and Misfits: The Body of a Woman." *American Imago* 50, no. 4: 457–480.

Kardiner, Abram. 1941. *The Traumatic Neuroses of War*. New York: Paul B. Hoeber.

Kauffman, Stanley. 1961. "Across the Great Divide" (review of *The Misfits*). *New Republic*, 20 February, p. 26.

Keatinge, Richard. 1973. "Ardmore Studios to be Sold Because of Financial Row." *Irish Times*, 11 July, p.15.

Keyes, Evelyn. 1977. *Scarlett O'Hara's Younger Sister: My Lively Life In and Out of Hollywood*. Secaucus, NJ: L. Stuart.

Koning, Hans. 1987. *Nineteen Sixty-Eight: A Personal Report*. New York: Norton.

_____. 2005. "Spike Helmets for the Youths of America." www.hanskoning.net/misc, para. 8, accessed 28 October 2006.

Koningsberger, Hans. 1961. *A Walk with Love and Death*. London: Macmillan.

_____. 1969. "From Book to Film — Via John Huston." *Film Quarterly* 22, no. 3 (Spring): 2–4. Reprinted in *John Huston: The Eleventh Annual American Institute Life Achievement Award, March 3, 1983*. Los Angeles: Michael McCormick, 1983, pp. 16–18.

Kornprobst, Markus. 2005. "Episteme, Nation-Builders and National Identity: The Re-Construction of Irishness." *Nations and Nationalism* 11, no. 3 (June): 403–421.

Kozloff, Sarah. 1994. "Taking Us Along on *The Man Who Would Be King*." In *Perspectives on John Huston*, ed. Stephen Cooper. New York: Macmillan.

Kupfer, Joseph H. 1999. *Visions of Virtue in Popular Film*. Boulder, CO: Westview.

Laurents, Arthur. 1973. *The Way We Were*. New York: Harper & Row.

Laurot, Eduard. 2001. "An Encounter with John Huston (Excerpts from a Conversation)." In *John Huston Interviews*, ed. Robert Emmet Long. Jackson: University Press of Mississippi.

Lewis Herman, Judith. 1992. *Trauma and Recovery: The Aftermath of Violence, from Domestic Abuse to Political Terror*. New York: Basic/HarperCollins.

Lindley, Arthur. 1998. "The Ahistoricism of Medieval Film." *Screening the Past* 3. www.latrobe.au/screeningthepast, accessed 26 August 2006.

Logue, Paddy, ed. 2000. *Being Irish: Personal Reflections on Irish Identity Today*. Dublin: Oak Tree.

Long, Robert Emmet. 2001. *John Huston Interviews*. Jackson: University Press of Mississippi.

López, Ana. 1993. "Are All Latins from Manhattan? Hollywood, Ethnography and Cultural Colonialism." In *Mediating Two Worlds: Cinematic Encounters in the Americas*, ed. John King, Ana M. López and Manuel Alvarado, 67–80. London: British Film Institute.

Lora, Ronald. 1970. "A View from the Right: Conservative Intellectuals, the Cold War and McCarthyism." In *The Specter: Original Essays on the Cold War and the Origins of McCarthyism*, ed. Robert Griffith and Athan Theoharis. New York: New Viewpoints.

Lowry, Malcolm. 1971. *Under the Volcano*. New York: New American Library.

Luce, M. Siméon, ed. 1862. *Chronique des quatre premiers Valois (1327–1393); publ. pour la première fois pour la Société de l'histoire de France*. Paris: Renouard. Reprinted, New York: Johnson, 1965.

———. 1894. *Histoire de la Jacquerie d'après des documents inédits*. Paris: Honoré Champion. Reprinted, Geneva: Slatkine, 1978.

MacCannell, Dean. 1999. *The Tourist: A New Theory of the Leisure Class*. Berkeley and Los Angeles: University of California Press.

Macintyre, Ben. 2004. *Josiah the Great*. London: Harper Perennial.

MacKillop, James, ed. 1999. *Contemporary Irish Cinema: From The Quiet Man to Dancing at Lughnasa*. Syracuse, NY: Syracuse University Press.

Madsen, Axel. 1978. *John Huston: A Biography*. New York: Doubleday.

Mailer, Norman. 1973. *Marilyn: A Biography*. New York: Grosset and Dunlap.

Maltby, R. 2003. *Hollywood Cinema*, 2nd ed. Oxford: Blackwell.

Mast, Gerald. 1982. *Howard Hawks, Storyteller*. New York: Oxford University Press.

McBride, Joseph. 1992. *Frank Capra: The Catastrophe of Success*. New York: Simon and Schuster.

———. 2001. *Searching for John Ford*. New York: St. Martin's.

McCarthy, Todd. 1984. "Cracking the Volcano." *Film Comment* (July–August): 59–63.

McCarty, John. 1987. *The Films of John Huston*. Secaucus, NJ: Citadel.

McCullers, Carson. 1941. *Reflections in a Golden Eye*. Boston: Houghton Mifflin.

McGilligan, Patrick. 1999. *Clint: The Life and Legend*. New York: St. Martin's.

——— and Paul Buhle. 1999. *Tender Comrades: A Backstory of the Hollywood Blacklist*. New York: St. Martin's.

McWilliams, David. 2005. *The Pope's Children: Ireland's New Elite*. Dublin: Gill and Macmillan.

Medeiros, Marie-Thérèse de. 1979. *Jacques et Chroniquers*, Paris: Honoré Champion.

Melville, Herman. 1996. *Moby Dick*, New York: Tor.

Metz, Walter C. 2004. "The Cold War's 'Undigested Apple Dumpling': Imaging *Moby-Dick* in 1956 and 2001. *Literature/Film Quarterly* 32, no. 3: 222.

Meyers, Jeffrey. 1968. "The Idea of Moral Authority in The Man Who Would Be King." *Studies in English Literature, 1500–1900* 8, no. 4 (Autumn): 711–23.

Milius, John. 1973. *The Life and Times of Judge Roy Bean*. New York: Bantam.

Miller, Arthur. 1981. *Collected Plays*, Vol. II. New York: Viking.

———. 1987. *Timebends: A Life*. London: Methuen.

"Moby Dick." Town on Screen, *Irish Times*, 5 October 1954, p. 1.

"Moby Dick Schooner Leaves Youghal." *Irish Times*, 5 August 1954, p. 7.

Morandini, Morandino. 1980. *John Huston*. Florence: La Nuova Italia.

Moylan Mills, C. 1999. "Huston and Joyce: Bringing 'The Dead' to the Screen." In *Contemporary Irish Cinema: From The Quiet Man to Dancing at Lughnasa*, ed. James MacKillop. Syracuse, NY: Syracuse University Press.

Mulvey, Laura. 1989. "Visual Pleasure and Narrative Cinema." In *Visual and Other Pleasures*, Laura Mulvey. New York: Palgrave.

Munby, Jonathan. 1999. *Public Enemies, Public Heroes: Screening the Gangster from Little Caesar to Touch of Evil*. Chicago and London: University of Chicago Press.

Murray, Edward. 1972. *The Cinematic Imagination: Writers and the Motion Pictures*. New York: Frederick Ungar.

Naremore, James. 1979. *The Treasure of Sierra Madre*. Madison: University of Wisconsin Press.

———. 1998. *More than Night. Film Noir in Its Contexts*. Berkeley, Los Angeles, London: University of California Press.

Neillands, Robin. 2001. *The Hundred Years War*, 2nd ed. London: Routledge.

Nerval, Gérard de. 1999. *Selected Writings*, trans. Richard Siebureth. London: Penguin.

"The New Pictures." *Time* Magazine, 14 May 1942. www.time.com/time/Magazine/printout/0,8816,790443,00.html, accessed 26 October 2006.

Nielsen, Mike, and Gene Mailes. 1996. *Hollywood's Other Blacklist: Union Struggles in the Studio System*. London: BFI.

"No Ship but the Film Must go on." *Irish Times*, 17 July 1954, p. 1.

Nolan, William F. 1965. *John Huston: King Rebel*. Los Angeles: Sherbourne.

O'Connor, Flannery. 1952. *Wise Blood*, New York: Harcourt, Brace.

Ovid. 1916. *Metamorphoses*, trans. and ed. Frank Justus Miler. London: Heinemann.

Owens, Louis. 1998. *Mixedblood Message: Literature, Film, Family, Place*. Norman: University of Oklahoma Press.

Palmer, Barton R. 1997. "Arthur Miller and the Cinema." In *The Cambridge Companion to Arthur Miller*, ed. Christopher Bigsby, 184–210. Cambridge: Cambridge University Press.

Peillon, Michel, and Eamonn Slater, eds. 1998. *Encounters with Modern Ireland*. Dublin: Institution of Public Administration.

Pettit, Arthur G. 1980. *Images of the Mexican American in Fiction and Film*. College Station: Texas A&M University Press.

Phillips, Gene D. 2001. "Talking with John Huston." In *John Huston Interviews*, ed. Robert Emmet Long. Jackson: University Press of Mississippi.

Pike, Fredrick B. 1995. *FDR's Good Neighbor Policy: Sixty Years of Generally Gentle Chaos*. Austin: University of Texas Press.

Pilipp, Frank. 1993. "Narrative Devices and Aesthetic Perception in Joyce's and Huston's 'The Dead.'" *Literature/Film Quarterly* 21, no. 1: 61.

"Plea for Film Industry." *Irish Times*, 4 July 1967, p. 12.

Pomerantz, Charlotte, ed. 1963. *A Quarter-Century of Un-Americana: A Tragico-Comical Memorabilia of HUAC*. New York: Marzani and Munsell.

Poulain, Claude. 1994. *Etienne Marcel*. Paris: Denoël.

Prately, Gerard. 1997. *The Cinema of John Huston*. Cranbury, NJ: A.S. Barnes.

Pratt, Mary Louise. 1992. *Imperial Eyes: Travel Writing and Transculturation*. London and New York: Routledge.

Press, David P. 1980. "Arthur Miller's *The Misfits*: The Western Gunned Down." *Studies in the Humanities* 8, no. 1: 41–44.

Quidnunc. 1954. "An Irishman's Diary." *Irish Times*, 5 July, p. 5.

———. 1967. "An Irishman's Diary." *Irish Times*, 25 July, p 7.

Quintana, Àngel. 2005. Huston: "¿Cineasta del fracaso o cineasta de la voluntad?" *Dirigido por ... Revista de Cine* 345 (mayo): 70–71.

Reed, William. 2004. *Escape to Paradise: A Mexican Odyssey*. Puerto Vallarta, Jalisco: Garces.

Rees, Ellen. 2003. "Dreaming of the Mediaeval in Kristin Lavransdatter and Trollsyn." *Scandinavian Studies* 75.3 (2003): 399–416.

Riviere, Joan. 1929. "Womanliness as a Masquerade." *International Journal of Psychoanalysis* 10: 303–13.

Rollins, Peter C., ed. 1999. "Special Focus: Medieval Period in Film." *Film & History* 29, nos. 1–4.

Roszak, Theodore. 1991. *Flicker*. New York: Summit.

Rubin, Martin. 1993. "Heroic, Antiheroic, Aheroic: John Huston and the Problematical Protagonist." In *Reflections in a Male Eye*, ed. Gaylyn Studlar and David Desser. Washington: Smithsonian Institution.

Ruiz, Ramón Eduardo. 1992. *Triumphs and Tragedy: A History of the Mexican People*. New York and London: W.W. Norton.

Savran, David. 1992. *Communists, Cowboys, and Queers: The Politics of Masculinity in the Work of Arthur Miller and Tennessee Williams*. Minneapolis, London: University of Minnesota Press.

Seguin, Louis. 1970. "Nulle part ailleurs" *Positif* 118 (July–August). Reprinted in *John Huston*, ed. Gilles Ciment. Marseille: Positif-Rivages, 1988.

Server, Lee. 2006. *Ava Gardner "Love is Nothing."* New York: St. Martin's.

"Shadowboxing: *Fat City* and the Malaise of Masculinity." In *Reflections in a Male Eye: John Huston and the American Experience*, ed. Gaylyn Studlar and David

Desser. Washington: Smithsonian Institution.

Shaw, Kenneth. 1954a. "Ten Minute Boom Town." *The Irish Times*, July 24, p. 3.

Shaw, Kenneth. 1954b. "Hang-Over." *Irish Times*, 14 August, p. 2.

Singer, Irving. 2004. "The Dead: Story and Film." *The Hudson Review* 56, no. 4 (Winter): 655–665.

Skiles, Jack. 1996. *Judge Roy Bean Country*. Lubbock: Texas Tech University Press.

Sklar, Robert. 1993. "Havana Episode: The Revolutionary Situation of *We Were Strangers*." In *Reflections in a Male Eye: John Huston and the American Experience*, ed. Gaylyn Studlar and David Desser. Washington: Smithsonian Institution.

Slotkin, Richard. 1990. "The Continuity of Forms: Myth and Genre in Warner Brothers' *The Charge of the Light Brigade*." *Representations* 29 (Winter): 1–23.

Sobchack, Vivian C. 1980. "Beyond Visual Aids: American Film as American Culture." *American Quarterly* 32, no. 3: 280–300.

Spada, James. 1993. *More Than a Woman*. London: Time Warner.

Steinem, Gloria. 1986. *Marilyn*. New York: Henry Holt.

Stern, Milton R. 1956. "The Whale and the Minnow: *Moby Dick* and the Movies." *College English* 17, no. 8 (May): 470–473.

Strasberg, Lee. 1987. *A Dream of Passion: The Development of the Method*. Boston, Toronto: Little, Brown

Studlar, Gaylyn, and David Desser, eds. 1993. *Reflections in a Male Eye: John Huston and The American Experience*. Washington, DC: Smithsonian Institution.

Thomson, David. 2002. *The New Biographical Dictionary of Film*, 4th ed. London: Little Brown.

———. 1985. *Suspects.*, New York: Knopf.

Thompson, Peter Edmund, ed. 1966. *Contemporary Chronicles of the Hundred Years War: From the Works of Jean le Bel, Jean Froissart and Enguerrand de Monstrelet*. London: Folio Society.

Tobin, Tom. 1954. "Queequeg's Tatoo: A Youghal Factory's Part in 'Moby Dick.'" *Irish Times*, 7 August, p. 4.

Traven, B. 1963. *The Treasure of the Sierra Madre*. New York: Hill and Wang.

Vanderwood, Paul J. 1983. *Juárez*. Madison: University of Wisconsin Press.

Venette, Jean [Fillon] de. 1953. *Chronicle*, trans. Jean Birdsall, ed. Richard A. Newhall. New York: Columbia University Press, 1953

Viertel, Peter. 1953. *White Hunter, Black Heart*. New York: Dell.

———. 1992. *Dangerous Friends*. New York: Doubleday.

Vitoux, Frédéric. 1974. "The Life and Times of Director John Huston." *Positif* 155 (January): 46–48.

Walker, Alexander. 1995. *Bette Davis: A Celebration*, London: Claremont.

———. 2005. *National Heroes: British Cinema in the 70s and 80s*. London: Orion.

Watts, Jill. 2005. *Hattie McDaniel: Black Ambition, White Hollywood*. New York: Amistad.

Weatherby, William J. 1976. *Conversations with Marilyn*. London: Robson.

Wexman, Wright. 1993. "Mastery Through Masterpieces: American Culture, the Male Body, and Huston's Moulin Rouge." In *Reflections in a Male Eye*, ed. Gaylyn Studlar and David Desser. Washington: Smithsonian Institution.

Williams, Tennessee. 1998. *The Night of the Iguana*. New York: Dramatists Play Service.

About the Contributors

Victoria Amador teaches for Heriot Watt University and the Open University in Edinburgh, Scotland, as well as for the New School for General Studies in New York City. Her research interests include gothic and vampire film and literature, Hollywood actresses, and American popular culture. She was formerly a professor of English in New Mexico, with a Ph.D. in creative writing and American literature from the University of Denver.

Georgiana Banita is associate professor of literature and media studies at the University of Bamberg, Germany. Her research in North American film includes essays on post–9/11 New York cinema and on the Armenian genocide in Atom Egoyan's *Ararat*. She is currently at work on a project about globalization and the aesthetics of trauma in international film.

Lesley Brill is the author of *John Huston's Filmmaking* (1997). He has published 30 essays and two other books, *The Hitchcock Romance* (1988) and *Crowds, Power and Transformation in Cinema* (2006). He teaches film studies at Wayne State University in Detroit.

Peter G. Christensen taught English at Cardinal Stritch University in Milwaukee from 1995 to 2007. He published over more than 130 articles on twentieth-century literature and film, including essays on John Cowper Powys, D. H. Lawrence, Marguerite Yourcenar, Simone De Beauvoir, and Jean Cocteau. He died in September 2007.

Julie F. Codell is an art history professor in the Herberger College School of Art at Arizona State University. She wrote *The Victorian Artist* (2003) and edited *Photography and the Imperial Durbars of British India* (2010), *The Political Economy of Art* (2008), *Genre, Gender, Race, and World Cinema* (2007), and *Imperial Co-Histories* (2003), among other works, and was guest editor of special issues of *Victorian Periodicals Review* (1991 and 2004).

Pablo Echart is assistant director of the Department of Culture and Audiovisual Communication at the University of Navarra, Spain, and a regular film reviewer. In 2005 he published *La Comedia Romántica del Hollywood de los Años 30 y 40*. He is editor of a series of single film studies, with volumes on *Asphalt Jungle* by John Huston, *Autumn Tales* by Eric Rohmer and *The Spirit of the Beehive* by Victor Erice.

Roddy Flynn is a lecturer in communications at Dublin City University. He has contributed articles and delivered conference papers on multiple aspects of broadcasting history and policy and is working on a book-length history of Irish government film policy. He is co-author of *Historical Dictionary of Irish Cinema* (2006).

Michael Patrick Gillespie is a professor of English at Florida International University. He has written books on the works of James Joyce, Oscar Wilde, and William Kennedy. His most recent book is *The Myth of an Irish Cinema: Approaching Irish Themed Films* (2009). He is working on a book-length study of contemporary Irish filmmakers.

Reynold Humphries is a professor of film studies at the University of Lille III and has contributed to many journals and collections on a variety of film-related topics. Among his books are *Fritz Lang: Genre and Representation in his American Films* (1989), *The American Horror Film* (2002), *The Hollywood Horror Film 1931–1941* (2006), and *Hollywood's Blacklists* (2009).

Page Laws is a professor of English and director of the honors program at Norfolk State University in Virginia where she has taught since 1987. She served as Fulbright Distinguished Chair for Cultural Studies at Karl-Franzens Universität in 2001. She has had three NEH-funded fellowships. An avid film and theater critic, she received her Ph.D. and M.Phil. in comparative literature from Yale University.

Patrick McGilligan has written biographies of George Cukor and Fritz Lang, both of which were named New York Times Notable Books. His life story of Alfred Hitchcock was nominated for an Edgar Award, and his book about the pioneering African American novelist and filmmaker Oscar Micheaux was named by the New York Public Library as one of the "25 Books to Remember" of 2007. He has edited five volumes of "Backstory" interviews with Hollywood screenwriters for the University of California Press. He lives in Milwaukee, Wisconsin.

Diog O'Connell is a lecturer in film and media studies at the Institute of Art, Design & Technology, Dún Laoghaire, Ireland. Her book *New Irish Storytellers: Narrative Strategies in Film* is forthcoming in 2010.

Gary D. Rhodes is a lecturer at the Queen's University in Belfast, Northern Ireland. He is the author of such books as *Lugosi* (1997), *White Zombie* (2002), and *Alma Rubens, Silent Snowbird* (2006), and editor of such anthologies as *Horror at the Drive-In* (2001), *Edgar G. Ulmer: Detour on Poverty Row* (2008), and *The Films of Joseph H. Lewis* (2010). He is also the writer-director of documentary films and is on *The Horror Journal* editorial board.

Wieland Schulz-Keil has been active as a producer in the United States, France, Italy and Germany for 20 years. Among his better known productions are *Under the Volcano* (1983) and *The Dead* (1987), both directed by John Huston; *The King's Whore* (1990; Axel Corti); *The Innocent* (1993; John Schlesinger); and *Mesmer* (1994) and *The Children of the Silk Road* (2009; both Roger Spottiswoode). In recent years he arranged financing, or served as executive producer, for *Enemy at the Gates* (1999; Jean-Jacques Annaud); *The Score* (2001; Frank Oz); and *The Cat's Meow* (2002; Peter Bogdanovich).

Neil Sinyard is emeritus professor and head of film studies at the University of Hull. Among his many books are *Graham Greene: A Literary Life* (2003), *Fred Zinnemann*

(2003), *British Cinema of the 1950s* (co-edited with Ian MacKillop; 2003), *Jack Clayton* (2000) and *The Films of Nicolas Roeg* (1991). He is co-editor of the British Film Makers series for Manchester University Press, and editor of the film section in Pears Encyclopedia, and wrote BFI booklets for the DVD releases of *This Happy Breed* and *Room at the Top*.

Tony Tracy is associate director at the Huston School of Film and Digital Media, National University of Galway, Ireland, and directs the B.A. program in film studies. He writes about silent cinema, Irish cinema and Irish-American cinema. He is a frequent broadcaster on film for RTE, Ireland's national radio station, is on the board of the Fresh Film Festival for young filmmakers, and serves as senior education officer for the Film Institute of Ireland.

Richard Vela teaches in the English and theatre department of the University of North Carolina at Pembroke. A contributing editor to *Literature Film Quarterly*, his recent publications include *Shakespeare into Film* and articles in *Apocalyptic Shakespeare, The Encyclopedia of Orson Welles, The Encyclopedia of Stage Plays into Film, Pembroke Magazine, Postscript*, and *Film & Philosophy*. He has presented papers on Shakespeare, film adaptation, and film representations of Americans in Mexico.

Index

Academy Awards *see* Oscars
Ace in the Hole (1951) 74
Adam's Rib (1949) 22, 28, 30, 31, 32n4
The Adventures of Robinson Crusoe (1954) 75, 79–80
The African Queen (1951) 22–7, 68; character and environment, conflict between 58; characters 4; conversation with Wieland Schulz-Keil 201; creative period 47; external action as metaphor for internal conflict 76; Fenton Smith, Basil 12; finance 194; Huston, Anjelica 9; impossible love relationships 78; naked woman photo 20; politics 6; religion 79; romantic comedy tradition 27–32; theme 125; *White Hunter, Black Heart* 50, 52–3
L'Age d'Or (1930) 78
Agee, James 22
Aherne, Brian 59
Alarcon, Daniel Cooper 58
Alleney, Tamba 189
Allied Artists 35
Altman, Robert 197
American Film Institute (AFI) 15
American Legion 117–18, 121n15
American Mercury 200
American otherness 4, 5
American South 5, 82–93
And Starring Pancho Villa as Himself (2004) 70n10
Anderson, Ernest 12, 137, 139, 144, 145, 146, 192
Andrews, Anthony 67
Andrews, Geoff 2, 3, 6
animal imagery 79–81
Annie (1982) 25, 76, 199
Annis, Francesca 13
anti-heroes 44–5
Ardmore Studios 191, 193, 195, 197
Armstrong, Louis 13
Arthur, Jean 28
The Asphalt Jungle (1950) 3, 77, 120; animal imagery 80; creative period 47; gender 5; Monroe, Marilyn 98; politics 6; style 96; and *A Walk with Love and Death*, comparison between 161
Astor, Mary 5
auteurism 1–2
Avedon, Richard 13–14
Avout, Jacques, comte d' 167

Bacall, Lauren: HUAC 49, 115, 116; *Key Largo* 111; *To Have and Have Not* 113; *The Treasure of the Sierra Madre* 71n19
Bachmann, Gideon 126
Baechelor, Lea 159n4
Bagley, Desmond, *The Freedom Trap* 186
Bakhtin, Mikhail 174, 179, 183, 184
Banderas, Antonio 70n10
The Barbarian and the Geisha (1958) 26, 54, 78, 161
Barbie, Klaus 119
Barrymore, Lionel 111
Barthes, Roland 44
Basehart, Richard 128, 132
Bataille, George 161
Battle of Saint Petro (1945) 10
Beat the Devil (1953) 5, 26, 77, 194; themes 125, 143
Beaton, Cecil 101
Beatty, Ned 83, 85, 178
Bedazzled (1967) 174
Bedoya, Alfonso 61, 71n19, 71n20
Beery, Wallace 59
Bellamy, Ralph 29
Belle de Jour (1967) 77
Benayoun, Robert 123, 125, 161
Bennett, Bruce 61
Bergman, Ingmar 76
Berry, John 54
Bessie, Alvah 121n15
Bhabha, Homi 42
The Bible... in the Beginning (1966) 3, 79, 124, 135
The Big Lebowski (1998) 174
Bisset, Jacqueline 67
Black, Lesley 138
Blake, Robert 62
Blake, William 183
Blanke, Henry 70n12
Bloom, Harold 125
Blue, Monty 111
Boetticher, Budd 120n3
Bogart, Humphrey 76; *The African Queen* 25; *Beat the Devil* 194; HUAC 49, 115, 116, 118–19; *Key Largo* 111, 118, 119, 120; *The Man Who Would Be King* 35; *To Have and Have Not* 113; *The Treasure of the Sierra Madre* 25, 61, 70n14, 71n20, 80
Bolitho, Walter 35

219

Bond, Ward 53–4
Boorman, John 170
border-crossing films 58–9
Borman, Moritz 199, 200
Boulting, Ingrid 14, 15
Bovasso, Julie 16, 21n1
Boyum, Joy Gould 72n31
Bradbury, Ray 47, 55, 55n2, 123–4, 126–9, 131, 133–5
Brando, Marlon 73, 83
Brecht, Bertolt 55n3
Breen, Joseph 144
Brennan, Walter 176, 182
Brent, George 137, 138
Brialy, Jean-Claude 76
Bridges, Harry 114
Bridges, James 51
Brill, Lesley: *The African Queen* 23, 24; home, quests for 30; identities of characters 69–70n7; literary adaptations 124; *The Man Who Would Be King* 38, 39, 44, 46n6; *The Night of the Iguana* 63, 71n24; resilience of characters 25; romance 22; *A Walk with Love and Death* 161; water and fire, link between 27
Bringing Up Baby (1938) 30
Brion, Patrick 161
Brooks, Richard: *Crossfire* 121n13; *Key Largo* 111, 112, 113, 117, 119, 120
Brown, Norman O. 161
Bruce-Novoa, Juan 70n10
Buñuel, Luis 5, 73–4, 81–2; *The Adventures of Robinson Crusoe* 75, 79–80; *L'Age d'Or* 78; artistic formation 74–6; *Diary of a Chambermaid* 75; *The Discreet Charm of the Bourgeoisie* 75, 77, 77, 79; *El* 75, 77, 77, 79; *Evil Eden* 77; *The Exterminating Angel* 75; *Gran Casino* 71n19; *Nazarin* 73, 74, 75, 77, 79; *Los Olvidados* 74, 75, 77; personal themes and motifs 78–80; *Phantom of Liberty* 76, 77, 79; professional and artistic outlooks 76–8; *Under the Volcano* 199; *Viridiana* 77, 79, 80–1
Burke, Billie 139
Burnett, Carol 76
Burton, Richard 63, 74, 83, 84, 86
Bus Stop (1956) 100
Busch, Niven 124
Butch Cassidy and the Sundance Kid (1969) 44, 173, 182
Byrnes, C.J. 195

Cabrera-Infante, Guillermo 199
Cagney, James 115
Caine, Michael 33, 35, 37, 134
Canby, Vincent 34
Canetti, Elias 179
capitalism 6
Capone, Al 118
Capra, Frank 31
Captain from Castile (1941) 70n13
Cardenas, Lázaro 60
Carrière, Jean-Claude 199

Carroll, Lewis, *Alice in Wonderland* 174
Casablanca (1942) 114, 121n6
Casino Royal (1967) 186
Castries, Duc de 166
Cat Ballou (1965) 174
Cavell, Stanley 28, 29, 30, 31, 32n3, 32n4
Cazalis, Anne-Marie 167
Cervantes, Miguel de, *Don Quixote* 174
Champlin, Charles 34
Chaplin, Charles 54
Charles the Bad, King of Navarre 168–9
Chinatown (1974) 79, 143
Chowdhry, Prem 34
Chuma, Boy Mathias 52
Ciment, Michael 85
Clayton, Jack 11
Clift, Montgomery 5, 96–7
Coburn, Charles 138, 139, 140
Cockburn, Claude, *Beat the Devil* 194
Coen, Ethan 174
Coen, Joel 174
Cohen, Allen 161
Colley, George 195, 196
Collier, John 22
Columbia Pictures 35, 199
comedy, romantic 22, 24, 25, 27–32
Committee for the First Amendment (CFA) 6, 47, 49, 111, 115–20; *The Man Who Would Be King* 53
Communism 49–50, 54, 113–14, 115–18
Condon, Richard 15
Connery, Sean 33, 35, 37, 68, 134, 141
contact zones 70n8
continuity 205
Cooper, Gary 175, 176, 182
Copaleen, Myles nag 185
Corcoran, Vincent 190
Cornered (1945) 57
Cortés, Carlos E. 70n10
Cotten, Joseph 107
Council of Hollywood Guilds and Unions 115
Craigie, Ingrid 153
Crane, Stephen, *The Red Badge of Courage* 83, 91, 124, 127, 134, 150
Craven, Frank 136
Crosby, Bing 197
Crossfire (1947) 117
Crowther, Bosley 145
Cukor, George 28

Daisy Town (1971) 174
Dali, Salvador 82
Dassin, Jules 50, 54
Davenport, Doris 177
Davis, Bette 136, 137, 138, 139, 140–1, 142, 146
Day, Doris 28
Day Lewis, Daniel 2
Dayan, Assaf 160, 164, 170, 171n3
The Dead (1987) 1, 3, 7, 74, 123, 173; complexity of characters 25; conversation with Wieland Schulz-Keil 201–4, 205–6; gender

Index

5; human condition 3; Huston, Anjelica 5, 8, 9, 18–19, 98, 156, 158; Ireland 148–59, 186; Mexico 57; theme 125
Dee, Sandra 71n25
de Havilland, Olivia 25, 136, 138, 139, 144, 145
de Havilland Decision 138
Delany, Cathleen 149, 154
Delerue, Georges 171n3
Deleuze, Gilles 42, 105
Delevanti, Cyril 64, 92
DeMille, Cecil B. 50
Democratic Party 86, 115, 116, 117–18
de Mordha, Micheal 186
desert, *The Misfits* 95, 96, 104, 105–8
The Devil and Daniel Webster (1941) 10
Diary of a Chambermaid (1964) 75
Dienes, André de 104
Dies, Martin 115, 118
Directors Guild 50
The Discreet Charm of the Bourgeoisie (1972) 75, 77
Disney, Walt 57
Dmytryk, Edward 57, 117
Donahue, Troy 71n25
Donen, Stanley 174
Donnelly, Donal 18, 149, 203
Dourif, Brad 83
Down Argentine Way (1940) 70n15
dreams and dream sequences 75
dressage 56
Drew, Bernard 163
Drew-Smythe, Richard "Dicky" 33
Dreyfuss, Richard 17
Dubček, Alexander 163
Dunne, Irene 28
Dunne, Philip 48, 50, 111, 115, 116
Durgnat, Raymond 80

Eades, William 195
Eastwood, Clint 25, 50, 51, 52–3, 124
Ebert, Roger 34
Eco, Umberto 165–6
Eisenstein, Sergei 74
El (1952) 75, 77, 79
Eliot, T.S. 133
Elliot, Sam 174
Emmett, Daniel 88
empire films 34–5, 39; see also *The Man Who Would be King*
Engell, John 63, 70n7
Escape to Victory (1981) 5, 77
Estabrook, Howard 121n5, 121n9
European film industry 8
Evil Eden (1956) 77
Excalibur (1981) 170
The Exterminating Angel (1962) 75

Faithfull, Marianne 13
Farnsworth, Arthur 138
Fat City (1972) 1, 3; dreams 75; interview with Anjelica Huston 19; resilience of characters 25; style 96
Faye, Alice 70n15
FBI 120n1
Feld, Don 16–17
femininity, *The Misfits* 94, 95, 96–7, 98–102
Fenton Smith, Basil 12
Fernandez, Emilio 65, 71n19
Fifth Avenue Girl (1939) 28
Figueroa, Gabriel 75, 204
film noir 57
Fini, Leonora 11, 171n3
Finney, Albert 66
Fitzgerald, Michael 200
Flanagan, Fionnula 18
Force of Evil (1948) 114
Ford, Cecil 187, 190
Ford, Glenn 57
Ford, John: auteurial voice 2; *The Fugitive* 60, 70n13; McBride's biography 53–4; *The Quiet Man* 151–2
Forester, C.S., *The African Queen* 31, 32n1, 194
Forman, John 173
Foster, Stephen 89
The Four Feathers (1939) 35
Franco, General Francisco 112, 117, 121n15
Freemasonry 37, 38, 40
French, Brandon 128
The French Lieutenant's Woman (1981) 203
Freud: The Secret Passion (1962) 3, 10, 75, 159n7, 173
Freund, Karl 72n30
Froissart, Jean 167, 169
Frost, David 13
Frye, Northrop 22, 27, 174, 181–2
The Fugitive (1947) 60, 70n13

Gable, Clark: *The Man Who Would Be King* 35; *The Misfits* 5, 96, 101, 103
Gael Linn 194, 195
Gallo, Guy 66, 71n27, 200, 201
García Riera, Emilio 70n10
Gardner, Ava 70n14; *The Life and Times of Judge Roy Bean* 180; *The Night of the Iguana* 63, 71n21, 71n23, 83, 85, 92
Garfield, John 60
gender 5–6; *In This Our Life* 139; interview with Anjelica Huston 19; *The Misfits* 94, 95, 96, 97; romantic comedy tradition 27–8
Gerber, Richard 159n4
Get Carter (1971) 33
Gilda (1947) 57
Ginna, Robert Emmett, Jr. 61
Girl of the Rio (1932) 59
Glasgow, Ellen, *In This Our Life* 7, 136, 137, 140, 142, 144
Godard, Jean-Luc 174
Goldstein, Richard 164
Gomez, Thomas 114
Gone with the Wind (1939) 139, 144, 146
Gonzalez-Crussi, F. 66

Good Neighbor Policy 57, 60
Gordon, Ruth 54
Goscinny, René 174
Grable, Betty 70n15
Graebner, William 71n18
Gran Casino 71n19
Grant, Cary 29, 57
Greene, Graham, *The Power and the Glory* 71n16
Grimes, Stephen B. 171n3, 202–3, 204, 206n1
Grobel, Lawrence 54; *The African Queen* 25; Irish film industry 196; Mexico 57, 69n2; *The Night of the Iguana* 92; *A Walk with Love and Death* 163–4
Gunga Din (1939) 34, 35

Hackett, Mike 188–9
Hall, Grayson 64
Hamblett, Charles 55n2, 124
Hamlet (stage production, Tony Richardson) 13
Hammen, Scott 34, 161
Hammett, Dashiell, *The Maltese Falcon* 91
Harlan, Josiah 36
Harty, Kevin J. 165
Hathaway, Henry 70n13
Haughey, Charles J. 198n1
Hawks, Howard 29, 30, 82, 113
Hayden, Stirling 80, 161
Head, Edith 36
Heaven Knows, Mr. Allison (1957) 26, 75; HUAC 54; impossible love relationships 78; religion 79; theme 125
Heber, Reginald 43, 46n9
Hellinger, Matt 70n13
Hemingway, Ernest 25, 96; *The Killers* 96; *To Have and Have Not* 96
Henreid, Paul 116, 121n6
Hepburn, Audrey 28
Hepburn, Katharine: *Adam's Rib* 22, 28; *The African Queen* 22, 25, 28, 70n14; American Legion 121n15; *Bringing Up Baby* 30; *The Philadelphia Story* 27, 28; romantic comedy tradition 28
Heredero, Carlos Hernández 161
heroes 44–5
Hickey, Bill 16
Higham, Charles 138
Hill, Gladys 12, 35, 171n3
His Girl Friday (1940) 29, 30
Hitchcock, Alfred 2, 23, 57, 82
Holiday (1938) 28
Holiday in Mexico (1946) 70n15
Holifield, Chet 116, 117
Holland, Norman 125
Hollywood blacklist 47, 49–50, 53–4, 115–16, 119; *see also* Committee for the First Amendment; House UnAmerican Activities Committee
Holt, Tim 19, 61, 80
home, quests for 30–1

Hoover, J. Edgar 114, 120n1, 121n15
House UnAmerican Activities Committee (HUAC) 6, 7, 8, 47, 53–4, 114–20; *Key Largo* 111; *The Way We Were* 48, 49–50, 55; *White Hunter, Black Heart*
Hugenholtz, F.W.N. 168
Hughes, Howard 49
human condition 2–3
Hundred Years' War 160, 161
Hunter, Tab 183
Hussey, Olivia 164
Huston, Anjelica: *The Dead* 5, 8, 9, 18–19, 98, 156, 158; interview 8, 9–21; *Prizzi's Honor* 8, 9, 15–17; *A Walk with Love and Death* 7, 9, 11–12, 13, 14, 18, 160, 164, 170, 171n3
Huston, Danny 21, 66
Huston, Pablo 4
Huston, Tony: *The Dead* 157, 202; interview with Anjelica Huston 10, 11, 13, 18, 20
Huston, Walter: *In This Our Life* 138; interview with Anjelica Huston 10; *The Treasure of the Sierra Madre* 61, 80
"Huston Committee" 193–7, 198
"Huston Report" 185, 195–6

I Was a Communist for the FBI (1951) 114, 121n16
The Ice Pirates (1984) 15
In This Our Life (1942) 7, 60, 136–7, 146; African-American experience 143–6; family ties 137–41; personal responsibility 141–2; private gain and public commitment 142–3; resilience of characters 25
innocence 19
The Innocents (1961) 11
Insausti, Gabriel 26
Insignificance (1985) 101
International Alliance of Theatrical Stage Employees (IATSE) 113
Ireland 4, 7–8, 147–8, 185–7, 190–8; conversation with Wieland Schulz-Keil 202; *The Dead* 148–59; interview with Anjelica Huston 20; *Moby Dick* 147, 185, 186, 187–90, 191, 192
Irish Film Finance Corporation 191
Ishiguro, Kazuo 150
It Happened One Night (1934) 30, 32n3, 32n4
It's All True (1942) 57
Iversen, Gunnar 165, 166
Ives, Burl 187
Ivory, James 150

Jacquerie (1358) 161–2, 163, 165, 166–70, 171
Jaffe, Sam 77
Jaffrey, Saeed 33, 45n1, 46n10
Jaikumar, Priya 34
Jarre, Maurice 38
Jeakins, Dorothy 204
Johnson, Nunnally 53, 54
Johnston, Eric 121n18
Jones, Jennifer 5
Jones, Terry 174

Joyce, James 74; *The Dead* 7, 57, 74, 123, 149–51, 201–2; *Finnegans Wake* 174; *Ulysses* 3, 74, 147–8, 151, 174, 200
Juarez (1939) 56, 59–60, 68
Jurado, Katy 67

Kael, Pauline 45, 71n27, 75
Kalem Company 185
Kaminsky, Stuart: categorization of Huston's work 26; *The Man Who Would Be King* 46n7; *The Night of the Iguana* 64; *The Treasure of the Sierra Madre* 61; *A Walk with Love and Death* 161
Kanin, Garson 54
Kaplan, E.A. 137
Katz, Ephraim 53
Kaye, Danny 49
Kazan, Elia 9, 14–15
Keach, Stacey 25, 75, 178
Kean, Marie 203
Kelly, Gene 49
Kelly, Seamus 190
Kennedy, Burt 51, 120n3
Kerr, Deborah 52, 64, 85
Key Largo (1948) 6, 37, 111–15, 117–20
Kibre, Jeff 113
The Killers (1946) 96
King, Henry 70n13
King, Pee Wee 87
Kipling, Rudyard: Huston on 36–7, 40; *The Man Who Would Be King* 34–9, 41, 43–5, 46n3, 46n7, 123, 134, 173
Kiss of Death (1947) 70n13
Koch, Howard: HUAC 48, 49; *In This Our Life* 136, 137–8, 140, 141, 143, 144
Kohner, Paul 60, 70n12
Koningsberger, Hans, *A Walk with Love and Death* 7, 162–71
Koszak, Theodore 124
Kozloff, Sarah 35, 37, 41, 45
The Kremlin Letter (1970) 48
Kubrick, Stanley 10, 65
Kupfer, Joseph 31
Kurnitz, Harry 77

The Lady Eve (1941) 30
The Last Tycoon (1976) 9, 14–15
Laurents, Arthur 48, 49, 50, 53, 54, 55
Laurot, Edouard 127
Laverne and Shirley (television series) 15
Lawson, John Howard 115
Lawton, Harry 124–5, 161
Lazar, Swifty 17
Ledebur, Friedrich 189
Lennon, Peter 191
Leone, Sergio 181
Let There Be Light (1946) 10, 75, 122n21
Lettnhove, Kevyn de 168
Liedebur, Friedrich 132
The Life and Times of Judge Roy Bean (1972) 7, 161, 173–84

The Life of Emile Zola (1937) 69n1
The Life of Louis Pasteur (1936) 69n1
Lindley, Arthur 166
Lipovetsky, Gilles 31
The List of Adrian Messenger (1963) 10, 79, 186
literary adaptations 2–3, 6–7, 91, 123–6, 134, 149–50, 173; *see also specific adaptations*
Little Caesar (1931) 120n2
Litz, A. Walton 159n4
The Lives of a Bengal Lancer (1935) 34–5
Lloyd, Russ 12
Lolita (1962) 10, 65
Lollobrigida, Gina 5
Long, Robert E. 126, 127
Lopez, Ana 57
Lopez Tarzo, Ignacio 67
Lorre, Peter 66–7
Lorris, Robert de 167–8, 169
Losey, Joseph 8, 54, 199
Lovejoy, Frank 114
Lowry, Malcolm 56, 57, 69n5, 75
Luce, M. Siméon 167, 168
Lumière brothers 202
Lynch, Jack 192, 193, 196
Lynch, Paddy 19–20
Lyon, Sue 64, 65, 74, 83, 85

MacAvin, Josie 171n3
MacCannell, Dean 64
MacDonald, Philip, *The List of Adrian Messenger* 186
MacKenzie, Aeneas 59
The Mackintosh Man (1973) 3, 77, 147, 185, 186
MacLane, Barton 61
Madsen, Axel 63, 69n7, 71n19, 161
Maguire, Conor 195
Mailer, Norman 104, 110n11
The Maltese Falcon (1941) 60, 76, 78, 136, 173; gender 5; and *In This Our Life* 7; setting 106; theme 125; themes 141, 143
The Man Who Would Be King (1975) 3, 68, 123, 134, 173; adventure 26; character and environment, conflict between 58; characters 4; external action as metaphor for internal conflict 76; Foreman, John 15; gender 5; ideological adventure 33–46; setting 26, 36; themes 125, 141, 143
Marcel, Etienne 166, 168
March, Fredric 115
Marcus, Louis 191–2, 193, 194, 195
Marshall, Penny 15
masculinity 5–6; interview with Anjelica Huston 19; *The Man Who Would Be King* 37, 39–40, 42; *The Misfits* 97, 99–100, 104
Mason, James 77
Mason, Marsha 17
Mayersberg, Paul 78
McArthur, Colin 76, 78
McBride, Joseph 53–4
McCann, Donal 18, 19, 149, 156, 203

McCarty, John 161
McClory, Kevin 190
McClory, Sean 204
McCullers, Carson 83, 124
McDaniel, Hattie 139, 144, 145, 146
McDowall, Roddy 179, 182
Melville, Herman: conversation with Wieland Schulz-Keil 200; *Moby Dick* 123, 125, 126–8, 129–35, 187
Mencken, H.L. 200
Menippean satire 174, 181–4
Method acting 94, 109n1
Metty, Russell 106, 107
Metz, Walter 128
Mexico 4, 56–72; Buñuel 73, 75
Meyers, Jeffrey 36
militarism, *The Man Who Would Be King* 40
Milius, John, *The Life and Times of Judge Roy Bean* 175, 180–1, 182
Miller, Arthur, *The Misfits* 5, 94–100, 102, 103, 106–9, 109n6
Miranda, Carmen 70n15
The Misfits (1961) 3, 94–6; absences 96–8; animal imagery 79; character and environment, conflict between 58; complexity of characters 25; the double woman 98–103; dreams 75; gender 5–6; Jeakins, Dorothy 204; Menippean satire 182; resilience of characters 25; themes 125, 143; woman as lack 103–9
Mr. North (1988) 21
Mitchum, Robert 21
Moby Dick (1930, dir. Bacon) 128
Moby Dick (1956, dir. Huston) 6, 123, 124, 126–35; animal imagery 79; fictionalized accounts 55n2; HUAC 54; human condition 3; Huston, Anjelica 9; Ireland 147, 185, 186, 187–90, 191, 192; religion 79; theme 125; Welles, Orson 2
Moiselle, Nuala 203
Molinier, Auguste 167
Molinier, Émile 167
Monroe, Marilyn: *The Asphalt Jungle* 5, 98; Method acting 94, 109n1; *The Misfits* 5, 6, 94, 96, 98–105, 107–8, 204; romantic comedy tradition 28
Monty Python's The Meaning of Life (1983) 174
Moonstruck (1987) 16, 21n21
Moore, Thomas 46n9
Morandini, Morandino 161
Morgan, Dennis 137, 138
Morris, Oswald 33, 83
Motion Picture Alliance 54, 115, 118
Moulin, Jean 119
Moulin Rouge (1952) 10, 47, 124, 161
Mulvey, Laura 100
Muni, Paul 56, 60
The Murders in the Rue Morgue (1932) 91
Murphy, Audie 134
Murray, Mick 188, 190
music 205

The Naked City (1948) 70n13
Nancy Goes to Mexico (1950) 70n15
Naremore, James 61, 69n4, 71n19
national cinemas 76
National Front (NF) 33, 45–6n3
Nazarin (1958) 73, 77, 79
Neillands, Robin 166
Nerval, Gérard de 172n6
New Deal 115, 117, 120
Newhall, Richard A. 167
Newman, Paul: *Butch Cassidy and the Sundance Kid* 173; *The Life and Times of Judge Roy Bean* 173, 175, 180; *The Man Who Would Be King* 35, 44
Niagara (1953) 107–8
Nicholson, Jack 14, 15–16, 17
The Night in Rio (1941) 70n15
The Night of the Iguana (1964) 4, 5, 63–6, 68, 69, 124; American South 83–4, 85–6, 88–90, 91–3; animal imagery 79; complexity of characters 25; conversation with Wieland Schulz-Keil 200; Figueroa, Gabriel 75; horror and comedy 74; Mexico 56, 57; religion 79; theme 125
Nolan, William F. 60, 71n19, 123
North, Alex 87, 108, 205
North by Northwest (1959) 23
Notorious (1946) 57
Now, Voyager (1942) 141

obituaries 1
O'Connor, Flannery, *Wise Blood* 83, 91, 92, 123, 201
Office of the Coordinator for Inter-American Affairs 57
O'Herlihy, Dan 149
O'Kelly, Betty 10
Olimbrada, Colonel José 56
Los Olvidados (1950) 74, 77
O'Morain, Donal 194, 195
O'Neal, Patrick 48
Oscars: *The African Queen* 25; Bogart, Humphrey 25; Davis, Bette 141; Huston, Anjelica 9, 17; McDaniel, Hattie 144; Muni, Paul 69; *Prizzi's Honor* 9, 17
The Other Side of the Wind 2
Owens, Lewis 58, 70n9

Palmer, Barton R. 107
Paramount 14
Paris, Alexandre de 11
Parnell Thomas, J. 115, 116, 121n15
Pat & Mike (1952) 28
patriarchy 6
Paxton, John 121n13
The Pearl (1948) 71n19
Peck, Gregory 9, 128, 130, 133, 185, 190
Perkins, Anthony 182
Pettit, Arthur G. 71n20
Phantom of Liberty (1974) 76, 77, 79
The Philadelphia Story (1940) 27, 28

Pilipp, Frank 159*n*6
Pinal, Silvia 80
Plummer, Christopher 38, 134
Poe, Edgar Allan, *The Murders in the Rue Morgue* 91
Polanski, Roman 79
politics 6; Huston on his 48–9; *The Way We Were* 53; *White Hunter, Black Heart* 51
Polonsky, Abraham 114
post-production 205
post-romantic seduction 31
The Postman Always Rings Twice (1981) 15
Poulain, Claude 167
Powell, Dick 57
Powell, Jane 70*n*15
Pratley, Gerald 137, 161
Pratt, Mary Louise 70*n*8
Press, David P. 109*n*7
Principal, Victoria 176
The Private Lives of Elizabeth and Essex (1939) 138
Prizzi's Honor (1985) 1, 8, 9, 15–17
Production Code Administration 144
propaganda films 6
Purcell, Noel 190

The Quiet Man (1952) 151–2, 186
Quinn, Aileen 25
Quintana, Àngel 25

Rabal, Francisco 80
Rabelais, François, *Gargantua and Pantagruel* 174
Raftery, Anthony 187
Raiders of the Lost Ark (1981) 39
Rains, Claude 59
Randolph, John 16, 17
The Reckoning (1969) 33
The Red Badge of Courage (1951) 124, 126, 127, 134, 150; American South 83; creative period 47; gender 5; literary source material, faithfulness to 91; themes 141
Redford, Robert 48, 53
Reed, William 69*n*2
Rees, Ellen 165, 166
Reflections in a Golden Eye (1967) 73–4, 78, 124; American South 83; animal imagery 79; Menippean satire 182
rehearsal 18–19
Reisz, Karel 203
religion 5; *The African Queen* 26, 27, 79; Buñuel 78–9; conversation with Wieland Schulz-Keil 201; *Heaven Knows, Mr Allison* 79; *The Man Who Would Be King* 43; *Moby Dick* 79; *The Night of the Iguana* 63–4, 79; *The Treasure of the Sierra Madre* 61–2; *A Walk with Love and Death* 161, 162, 164, 170; *Wise Blood* 79
The Remains of the Day (1993) 150
"The Report of the Film Industry Committee" 185, 195–6

Republican Party 54, 115, 116
Rey, Fernando 77
Richardson, Tony 13
Rilke, Rainer Maria 27
Ritter, Thelma 101
River of No Return (1954) 107
Rivkin, Allen 117, 121*n*12, 121*n*13
Robertson, George Scott 46*n*3
Robeson, Paul 49
Robinson, Edward G. 111, 120*n*2
Rockefeller, Nelson 57
Roeg, Nicholas 101
Rogers, Ginger 28
Roland, Gilbert 59
romance and romantic comedy 22–4, 25, 27–32
Romeo and Juliet (1968) 12, 164
Roosevelt, Franklin D. 57, 86, 117
Roots of Heaven (1958) 54, 79
Rubin, Martin 42, 44, 124
Russell, Theresa 101
Ryan, Robert 121*n*13
Ryan's Daughter (1970) 186

Saludos Amigos (1942) 57
Santacroce, Mary Neil 85
Sarris, Andrew 2
Sartre, Jean-Paul 3
satire, Menippean 174, 181–4
Sbardelatti, John 53
Scafe, Ted 12
Scaife, Edward 171*n*3
Schultz-Keil, Weiland 18, 66, 71*n*27, 127; conversation with 8, 199–206
Scott, Adrian 121*n*13
Scott, Randolph 120*n*3
Screen Writers' Guild 121*n*12
Sea Beast (1926) 128
Second World War 6, 112, 115, 119
Seguin, Louis 161
Selepegno, Annie 16
Server, Lee 69*n*1, 70*n*14, 71*n*23
The Seven Year Itch (1955) 100, 109*n*8
Shakespeare, William 130, 131, 164
Shaw, Tommy 18, 203, 204
Shor, Dan 83, 85
Sievernich, Chris 202–3
Signoret, Simone 77
Silverstein, Elliot 174
Simon, John 14
Sinful Davey (1969) 11, 77, 186, 191, 192, 197
Singer, Irving 159*n*6
Slotkin, Richard 39, 44, 57–8
Sobchack, Vivian 128
Sokolsky, George 116
The Sopranos (television series) 16
The Sound of Fury (1950) 114
Spanish Civil War 112, 117
Spiegel, Sam 14, 194
Stanton, Harry Dean 83, 85
Stanwyck, Barbara 28

Starke, Roy 63
Steinbeck, John: *The Grapes of Wrath* 118; *The Pearl* 71*n*19
Stern, Milton 128–9
Sternberg, Josef von 78
Stewart, Redd 87
storyboards 20
Streisand, Barbra 48, 53
studio system 1, 194
Studlar, Gaylyn 40, 41, 45
Summers, Neil 182
surrealism 74, 82
Swift, Jonathan, *Gulliver's Travels* 174

Taft, William Howard 189
Taylor, Elizabeth 11
There Will Be Blood (2008) 2
third space 42–3
Thompson, David 124, 138, 144
Till the End of Time (1946) 117, 118
To Have and Have Not (1945) 96, 113
Topper (1937) 28
Tovar, Lupita 70*n*12
transitional spaces 42
Traven, B. 56, 60, 71*n*19
The Treasure of the Sierra Madre (1948) 3, 4, 56, 58, 60, 61–3, 66, 67, 69, 78, 173; animal imagery 81; Bogart, Humphrey 25; Buñuel on 73; creative period 47; denouement 25; external action as metaphor for internal conflict 76; gender 5; Huston, Anjelica 10, 19; Mexico 75; setting 26; spilled gold 43; themes 125, 143
Tres Caballeros (1945) 57
Trumbo, Dalton 11
Turner, Kathleen 17
Twentieth Century–Fox 11, 54
Tyler, Parker 77

Ullmann, Liv 165, 166
Under the Volcano (1984) 4, 66–8, 173; conversation with Wieland Schulz-Keil 199–201, 203, 204, 205; Figueroa, Gabriel 75; theme 125
Undset, Sigrid, *The Wreath* 165, 166
The Unforgiven (1960) 26
United States Constitution 6

Vanderwood, Paul J. 59, 60
Venette, Jean Fillon de 167, 169
Vestron Video 203
Veterans of the Abraham Lincoln Brigade 121*n*15
Vidor, Charles 57
Viertel, Peter: *The African Queen* 22; *The Man Who Would Be King* 35; *White Hunter, Black Heart* 48, 50–3, 55, 124
Viertel, Salka 55
Viridiana (1961) 77, 79, 80–1
Vitoux, Frédéric 174

Viva Villa! (1934) 59
Vogue 13–14
Voltaire, *Candide* 174

Waldorf-Astoria Statement 114, 121*n*18
A Walk with Love and Death (1969) 7, 26, 160–72, 195; Huston, Anjelica 7, 9, 11–12, 13, 14, 18, 160, 164, 170, 171*n*3
Walker, Alexander 33, 140, 142
Wallach, Eli 5, 97
Walt Disney 57
Ward, Skip 64
Warner, Harry 145
Warner, Jack 119, 138, 144
Warner Bros.: black actors 144; contract writing 1; HUAC 54; *In This Our Life* 136, 138, 144, 145, 146; *Juarez* 56, 60; radical employees 118; *The Treasure of the Sierra Madre* 70*n*12
Wasserman, Dale 163–4, 171*n*2
Watts, Jill 145, 146
The Way We Were (1973) 4, 48, 49, 50, 53, 55
We Were Strangers (1949) 96; creative period 47; historical context 161; politics 6; setting 26
Weekend (1967) 174
Weekend in Havana (1941) 70*n*15
Welles, Orson 2, 57, 129
The Westerner (1940) 173, 174–81, 182
Westerns 173–4, 176, 180; *see also The Life and Times of Judge Roy Bean*; *The Misfits*; *The Westerner*
Wexman, Virginia Wright 124
White, Walter 145
White Hunter, Black Heart (1990) 4, 50, 51–3, 55, 124
Whiting, Leonard 164
Wiene, Robert 72*n*30
Wilder, Billy 74
Wilkerson, W.R. 116
Williams, Tennessee, *The Night of the Iguana* 56, 57, 63, 71*n*26, 83, 91, 92, 123–4
Williamson, Nicol 13
Wise Blood (1979) 5, 73, 76, 123, 173; American South 83–8, 90–3; conversation with Wieland Schulz-Keil 201; human condition 3; religion 79
Woman of the Year (1942) 28
The Woman on Pier 13 (1949) 114, 121*n*16
World War II 6, 112, 115, 119
The Wreath 165
Wright, Amy 83, 85
writing 200
Wyler, William: Committee for the First Amendment 49, 111, 115, 118; *The Westerner* 7, 173, 175–81, 182

Zanuck, Darryl 194
Zeffirelli, Franco 12, 164
Zenith productions 203

www.ingramcontent.com/pod-product-compliance
Lightning Source LLC
Chambersburg PA
CBHW021353300426
44114CB00012B/1207